THE WAYS OF DESIRE

THE WAYS OF DESIRE

New Essays in Philosophical Psychology on the Concept of Wanting

Edited by
Joel Marks

Precedent Studies in Ethics and the Moral Sciences
Thomas E. Wren, *General Editor*
Precedent Publishing, Inc.
Chicago, Illinois

Precedent Publishing, Inc.
737 North LaSalle Street
Chicago, Illinois 60610
Copyright © 1986 by Precedent Publishing, Inc.
Printed in the United States of America
All Rights Reserved
Distributed by Transaction Books, New Brunswick (USA)
and Oxford (UK)

Library of Congress Cataloging in Publication Data

Main entry under title:
The ways of desire.

    (Precedent studies in ethics and the moral sciences)
    Bibliography: p.
    Includes index.
    1. Desire.   2. Desire—Moral and ethical aspects.   3. Act (Philos-
ophy)   4. Emotions.   I. Marks, Joel, 1949-   . II. Series
BF575.D4W39   1986   128'.3   86-15112

ISBN 0-913750-44-1
ISBN 0-913750-03-4 pbk

To Mary Coykendall, for her unstinting support

Contents

FOREWORD

The series within which the present volume appears relates philosophy, especially moral philosophy, to what John Stuart Mill called "the moral sciences." This term, which was later translated into German as *die Geisteswissenschaften*, refers to what are now called the social and behavioral sciences. Accordingly, the general subject matter of the Precedent Studies in Ethics and the Moral Sciences is the rich and problematic interspace between philosophical ethics and such empirical but person- and society-oriented disciplines as developmental psychology, sociology, and anthropology, to cite a few of the more salient "moral sciences."

The specific subject matter of this volume is what its editor has called "theory of desire," a term which refers to a domain of inquiry rather than to any particular set of answers. For all their diversity of content, every essay in this volume rests on the assumption that the concept of desire is central to some of the most important philosophical controversies of our time, which concern moral theory, the nature of mind, the philosophy of action, and other such issues. Moral philosophers have a special stake in the attempt to map out a logical and ontological geography of desire, for reasons that will be different, but equally vivid, for deontologists (for whom moral judgments create desires), utilitarians (for whom moral actions serve desires), virtue theorists (for whom moral traits embody desires), and so on.

The concept of desire is also central to many important but controversial issues in the social and behavioral sciences, although its importance there is frequently obscured by the practice in those disciplines of couching discussions of the conative dimension of human life in terms of constructs such as "motivation" or "drive." Since the utility of those relatively nonintentional, and often militantly mechanistic, constructs is itself a matter of much dispute, the present volume should be of use not only to philosophers but also to various sorts of *Geisteswissenschaftler*, at least those whose theorizing has a consciously philosophical dimension.

In short, this volume provides an agenda for research into the springs of human action. This agenda can be summed up by saying that philosophers and others interested in human action must account for the intentionality as well as the causal efficacy of desires and such cognate states as hopes and aversions. The contributors to this volume have begun to carry out this agenda, from various theoretical perspectives and with a selectivity of focus that is inevitable, given the great diversity of the "ways of desire." The collective result of their work will surely challenge many current assumptions about cognitive and affective states (beliefs and emotions), how these states are related to conative ones (desires), and how they all actually come together in the moral life.

Thomas E. Wren
General Editor

Preface

This volume began with a telephone call to Jerry Shaffer at the University of Connecticut. We had both already published the view that many important emotional phenomena can only be accounted for by reference to desire. Now we discovered that we were both pursuing the investigation of the concept of desire itself. I was intending to write an essay; Jerry was intending to teach a seminar. Jerry noted that no anthology existed which he could use as a text, so he suggested that I might put one together in conjunction with my research. The book was conceived.

A follow-up telephone conversation with Harvey Green at Tulane University added a crucial element to the project. Harvey had also published at an early date on the importance of desire in the theory of emotion. Now he pointed out that a number of other theorists working in various philosophical disciplines were turning their attention to desire and that, therefore, what was needed was a collection of *new* essays. The idea of a collection rather than an anthology presented me with the delightful prospect of sharing the labor of reflection with the leading thinkers on desire. But a project of such ambition requires more than a pleasant possibility. I give chief credit for its coming to fruition to Harvey, who has provided me with guidance and encouragement throughout the three years since that conversation. I believe that Harvey must be one of the true behind-the-scenes movers and shakers of the contemporary field of philosophy, not to mention his being the author of an ever-growing opus of original and articulate thought. I am proud and thankful to be one of those who have benefited from his tireless dedication.

The Philosophy Department of the University of Connecticut, my alma mater, has continued to nurture its academic offspring. While I feel I can find philosophical and friendly support from any member of that marvelous department, in the preparation of this volume I have taken particular advantage of the continuing interest shown by Joel Kupperman, Mitchell Silver (now at the University of Massachusetts, Boston), Steve McGrade, John Troyer, and Sam Wheeler.

I would like to thank David White and Florence Weinberg, at St. John Fisher College, for helpful criticisms of the original proposal, and Richard Feldman and Anna Harrison, at the University of Rochester, and Robert Audi, at the University of Nebraska, for special assistance at subsequent junctures. Louise Allen at the University of New Haven has cheerfully kept me abreast of recent developments. I am also grateful for research support provided by St. John Fisher College, the University of Rochester, and the University of New Haven.

Tom Wren of Loyola University of Chicago has proved a patient, responsive, and spirited overseer and sharer of editorial labors — a very good person to work with. My debt to him is boundless.

Finally, I want to express my appreciation to all of the essayists, who through a long haul have remained faithful to an idea and from whom I have learned so much about the concept of desire.

Joel Marks
New Haven, Connecticut
March, 1986

Introduction
On the Need for Theory of Desire

Joel Marks

This volume marks the coming into its own of a discipline in philosophy: theory of desire. Like the concept of motivation (its analogue in the field of psychology), desire is a tremendously important concept, as one can judge by the wide range of contexts in which it has appeared. Furthermore, issues about desire lie at the heart of major controversies in contemporary theory of action and emotion. Yet this breadth of attention has been matched by a shallowness of scrutiny given to the notion of desire itself. Indeed, the more recent philosophical discussions of the nature of mind and psychological attitudes show a relative neglect of desire, with belief serving as the paradigm of the intentional. But desire is intentional, and it is interestingly different from belief. Therefore the time is ripe for a volume devoted to the nature and function of desire.

This volume reverses the usual practice of giving only a passing mention of desire in the midst of discussions of ethics, action, emotion, the nature of mind, and so forth. Instead, the essays in this book present discussions whose primary focus is on desire, with secondary mention of its implications for ethics, action, emotion, mind, and so forth. Since an abstract has been included at the beginning of each essay, there is no need for summaries here. Instead I shall take this opportunity to review, first, some of the broader issues in which desire has figured and, then, various issues which arise within the confines of theory of desire itself. (At appropriate points references will be made to the other essays in this volume.) For the most part the latter issues are suggested by the former in that they are necessary for a resolution; nonetheless, they are distinctive as problems about desire. My intent, then, is to show the importance of desire in philosophy and to suggest some of the directions in which the philosophical study of desire may profitably proceed. In this way a domain for the theory of desire will be sketched out.[1]

One preliminary clarification: In the beginning is the word, "desire." Distinct phenomena go by this name. For instance, "desire" often connotes passion or intense wanting. Sometimes there is the suggestion of sexual wanting. But the focus of this book is desire in the broad sense of wanting simpliciter. Thus, "desires" and "wants" will for the most part be used indifferently as the generic conative term, much as one might speak of "judgments" and "beliefs" interchangeably while recognizing possible distinct usages. The variety of ways of wanting will certainly not be ignored, nor will the variety of what is wanted ("desire" can refer to what one wants as well as to the wanting of it). But the emphasis is on the psychological state which is their common thread. In this there is perplexity enough.

1. BROADER ISSUES

Theory of Action

Desire has seemed most at home in discussions of action. If you are *walking down the street*, it must be that you desire to buy some milk at the store, or that you desire to stay fit, or at the very least that you desire to go for a walk "for its own sake." At the level of what used to be called the "springs of action," desire commonly takes pride of place in analyses of motivation and intention; for example, any of the cited desires can function to help *motivate* you to go for a walk or help constitute the *intention* with which you go for a walk.

In the recent literature, however, this "standard view" has been questioned by a number of theorists (Nagel, 1970; Locke, 1974, 1982; Staude, 1979, 1982; Silver, 1980).[2] The criticism has focused on the notion (or notions) of desire implicit in the desire-based explanations of action. Does "desire" stand for anything more than "motivational state"? If not, then the explanations have no psychological import; they are mere analytic assertions. A reaffirmation of the significance of desire for action, therefore, requires development of theory of desire.

Other relevant sources are Alston (1967b), Anscombe (1976), Armstrong (1968, pp. 151-158), Audi (1973a, 1973b, 1979, 1980a, 1980b, 1982), Brand (1984), Brandt and Kim (1963), Davidson (1980), Davis (1984a), Fleming (1981), Foot (1978), Goldman (1970), Montmarquet (1982), Morton (1980), Myers (1964), O'Shaughnessy (1980), Pears (1975), Prichard (1945), Rachels (1969), Searle (1983), C. C. W. Taylor (1980), Charles Taylor (1964), Richard Taylor (1966), Wheeler (1982), and Wiggins (1978-79). In this volume, see the essays by Audi, Baier, Davis, Gordon, Green, Marks, Stampe, Staude, and Stocker.

Theory of Emotion

The dominant view in contemporary analyses of emotion[3] is a cognitivist one, in which the tendency has been to place belief—to the neglect of desire—at the very heart of the phenomenon (Solomon, 1976; Neu, 1977; Lyons, 1980). This trend had its beginnings in the move away from affective or feeling-based theories of emotion, toward theories which stress the intentionality or "directedness" of emotion (Kenny, 1963; Solomon, 1976). For example, if Mr. Smith loves Ms. Jones, then Smith's emotion is *directed toward* Jones; but any feelings which Smith may experience in this matter, such as a weakness in the knees, will have no such orientation toward Jones (so the argument goes). Somehow in the process "intentional" became assimilated to "cognitive," and the intentionality of desire was sidestepped or unrecognized.

Recently the proponents of desire have begun to rally (Green, 1979, in preparation; Davis, 1981b; Marks, 1982; Robinson, 1983; Shaffer, 1983). Their view is that the intentionality of desire is as full-blooded as that of belief, and so desire is equally adequate to help account for the intentionality of emotion. Furthermore, desire seems especially well-suited to help account for the affective, expressive, and motivational dimensions of emotion.

A problem, however, faces this conativist rebuttal, one which comes, interestingly, from the affective camp (Stocker, 1983b; Kraut, 1985). Is the appeal to desire in danger of working too well? If desire is so handy to explain affectivity as well as intentionality, perhaps that is because "desire" in this context picks out nothing other than "feeling." (And perhaps feelings can carry their own intentionality after all.) In other words, desire-based analyses of emotion run the risk of question begging or triviality. They may be as empty of significant psychological content as the appeals made in action theory to desire qua motivation have seemed to be. Therefore, as with theory of action, any attempt to vindicate desire will have to involve further elucidation of the concept.

If we may now suppose, for the sake of further discussion, that beliefs and desires together constitute emotions, interesting questions arise as to the particulars of these constructions. For example, it seems nonproblematic enough to parse a state of happiness into desiring that p plus believing that p; you are happy because of your wanting it to be a sunny day and your seeing that it is one. (It would not be sufficient simply to have a satisfied desire; to win the lottery which you desire to win will not make you happy if you do not believe you have won it.)[4] But what of the case when you are mistaken in the belief that you desire that p: will you then be happy if you believe that *p*? Resolution of issues like this one awaits additional investigation of the concept of desire itself; for example, does it even make sense to suppose that desire is the sort of thing which can admit of mistaken belief?

In this volume, see the essays by Baier, Green, Marks, and Taylor.

Person Theory

A great deal of recent work on the nature of the person has stressed the notion of higher-order desires (the locus classicus is Frankfurt, 1971). These are desires which take other intentional states as their intentional object; for example, a person may *desire* to *believe* in God, or *desire* to cease to *desire* to smoke. Matters of the will — its freedom, its weakness — are especially susceptible to this sort of analysis: for example, to take a drink "of one's own free will" is not simply to drink because one desires to do so, but to drink because one desires that one's desire to drink be effective. If willing does turn out to be a function of desire in this way, then volition assumes a less schizoid appearance; there will no longer be the need to postulate two utterly distinct principles of action — will and desire — in order to account for more and less voluntary behaviors, respectively.

Other relevant sources are Alston (1977), Grandy and Darwall (1979), Jeffrey (1974), Neely (1974), Penelhum (1979), Schiffer (1976), Watson (1982), Wren (1982), and Zimmerman (1981). And in this volume, see the essays by Baier, Gordon, Green, and Staude.

Philosophy of Mind

Intentionality is considered by many theorists to be the hallmark of the mental. And among these, a prevalent view has been that desire and belief are the basic intentional states, to which all others — emotions, intentions, and so forth — can be reduced. However, with the rise of cognitive psychology in recent years, these concepts of what is somewhat deprecatingly called "folk psychology" (Stich, 1983) have come under sustained attack. It is anybody's guess what notions will survive or emerge from this conceptual shakedown.

One thing is clear: the enterprise is a philosophical one as well as an empirical one. Metaphysics, as is now well understood, is a matter of word as much as object. A decision to detach "unicorn" from horsiness saves the unicorn from extinction. And, thus, what we *say* about desire — the theory which develops — will be decisive for the very *existence* of desire.[5]

Other relevant sources are Armstrong (1968), Churchland (1984), Davidson (1980), Dennett (1978), Saunders (1983), Searle (1983), Stalnaker (1984), and Woodfield (1982). See also Baier's essay in this volume.

Value Theory and Ethics

A correlation between objects of value and objects of desire has often been remarked; as Hobbes (1972 [1651], pt. 1, chap. 6) put it, "whatsoever is the object of any man's appetite or desire, that is it which he for his part calls *good.*" But the fit is as notoriously imperfect as it is tempting. Desire is regarded as contingent, relative, and unstable, and so appears to be an unsuitable foundation for enduring ethical values. Furthermore, the very stubbornness of certain cravings puts desire in a bad light; for example, shall alcohol be considered a *good* for a person simply because his or her desire for it *persists?*

Closely linked with the view of desire as the ground of value is the theory of ethical egoism. The basic premise of this theory is that the only thing which can possibly have value is one's own welfare, since the ground of value, desire, is in its nature egoistic. The premise is conceptual, not merely an empirical claim about the trend of human striving (indeed, it ignores the apparently strong evidence that nonegoistic concern is widespread). Instead, ethical egoism reasons that, since desire is always a *tending toward satisfaction*, the object of all desire must be one's own well-being.[6]

However, the above argument has been found wanting by many philosophers (classic statements are Butler, 1897 [1726]; Broad, 1952). It appears to conflate the conditions of desire satisfaction with desire satisfaction itself.[7] For example, if Smith desires that Jones be happy, then indeed, ceteris paribus, Smith will also be happy if he believes that Jones is happy; but this certainly does not imply that what Smith really desired all along was that *he himself be happy* (i.e., that his desire be satisfied). For one thing, a vicious regress would ensue; Smith's desire that *he be happy* would also turn out to be a desire, not that he be happy simpliciter, but that *his desire* (that he be happy) *be satisfied*, and so on ad infinitum.[8]

Far from demonstrating the truth of conceptual egoism, this line of reasoning suggests that *anything whatsoever* can be the object of a desire. The egoism-altruism dichotomy does not come close to exhausting the possibilities. For example, a person can have a purely "aesthetic" desire for a certain kind of experience and be indifferent to its effect on his or her own well-being as well as that of anyone else. However, this expansion of its original claim hardly bodes well for a desire-based *ethics*. Hence the question arises: In winning the battle against conceptual egoism, has the conativist view of value lost the war? Furthermore, there is still the *empirical* claim for human egoism to contend with; perhaps human beings, though conceptually capable of desiring selflessly, never or hardly ever do so.

Various theoretical attempts have been made to weed out undesirable desires in some principled way or to pass desires through a refining process. The characterization of desire is central to any such effort, for the kind of thing desire is and the way desire operates will determine the outcome in these cases. One well-known attempt of this kind is that of Brandt (1979), who imports into the philosophical literature Lewin's technical synonym for desire, "valence," a construct whose meaning is given in terms of laws of scientific psychology. Brandt then develops a notion of "rational desire" on which to base ethical value: rational desire is desire which survives a certain process of exposure to beliefs under the conditions of "cognitive psychotherapy." A rather different example of the attempt to differentiate desires is provided by Blum (1980), who presents a sustained defense of the vitality and reliability of altruistic desires in particular.

Desire has been conceived not only as the source or ground of values but also as a component of certain valued states. For example, on the account of emotions sketched above, desire would be an essential ingredient of happiness (construed as a feeling); ceteris paribus, a person would be happy whenever one of his or her desires was believed to be satisfied (cf. Davis, 1981b). On this view, value inheres not (or at least not only) in desired objects but also in satisfied desires per se. That is, there is intrinsic value in having one's desire satisfied, regardless of what it is a desire for.[9] Or, going one step further, there may be certain desires, whether satisfied or not, in which value inheres, for example the desire for wisdom.

At this point Oriental ethics becomes especially relevant, since one finds there certain conceptions of ideal, "desireless" states that stand at the opposite extreme from the desire-based views of value outlined above. Nevertheless, an understanding of desire is also a central concern of these ethics. For example, the "Third Noble Truth" of Buddhism is that the key to contentment is the elimination of all desire (for the content of contentment, so to speak, is the absence of desire). This evidently is supposed to follow from the "Second Noble Truth," that desire is the source of all suffering.

On the face of it the inference seems fallacious. For the premise to be plausible, it would apparently have to mean that *frustrated* desire is the source of all suffering, from which it would hardly follow that a desireless state is a desirable state, for the possibility of *satisfied* desire would also have been eliminated in the process (Danto, 1972). (This is the Throwing the Baby Out with the Bath Water Objection.) But a proper evaluation of the argument depends on a careful examination of the ways — conceptual and empirical — of desire.[10] For example, a Buddhist may first point out the conceptual distinction between satisfied desire and extinguished or absent desire and then make the empirical claim that the former is intrinsically uncomfortable relative to the latter or less likely to be preferred.[11]

A further objection to the Buddhist ethical project would then be that a state of desirelessness might *feel* good, but would be ethically bankrupt on practical and moral grounds (Danto, 1972). This objection is based on the claim, central to the desire-based views of action and emotion described above, that acting and caring are impossible in the absence of all desire.[12]

This would also be an objection to the related Oriental ideal of desireless *behavior*, which is associated with Taoism as well as with karma yoga in Hinduism (cf. Fleming, 1981). These seem to be deontological ethics; value resides not so much in the intended goal of one's activity as in the very manner of one's activity (what matters is *how* one serves the tea rather than that the tea be served). But all such behavior is simply impossible on the account of action sketched earlier.

Of course such criticism carries over to certain distinctively Occidental ethics, such as Kantianism. Here, it can be argued, the emphasis is on the quality of one's volition (as opposed to the resulting behavior, not to mention the consequences of that behavior), and the quality increases to the degree that one's volition involves will and reason *rather than* desire. But this view is incompatible with a desire-based theory of action: high-quality volition in this vein will be simply idle in the absence of any further account of how the so-called rational will can be motivationally efficacious apart from its linkage with desires.

Thus, much of moment in the theory of value rests on how one conceives desire.

Other relevant sources are Adams (1980), Bond (1983), Bricker (1980), Conee (1984), Foot (1978), Gosling (1969), Greenspan (1980), Marks (1983), Nagel (1970), Perry (1926), Schiffer (1976), Selby-Bigge (1897), Silver (1980), Staude (1979), and Williams (1981). And in this volume, see the essays by Baier, Davis, de Sousa, Gordon, and Staude.

Decision Theory

On any instrumental view of right action, establishing a ground of values is still a step short of knowing how to behave or knowing what is appropriately desired *as a means* to achieving desired (or desirable) ends. Decision theory tries to fill this breach. Typically, it seeks a way to *quantify* a *rational* connection between means and ends.

A central project, accordingly, has been the development of a calculus for desire. The work of Frank Ramsey (1931) was pioneering in this regard, but assessment of its implications and significance remains a matter of controversy. For example, Troyer (1981) notes that one consequence of Ramsey's work (not to mention the work of numerous economists) is the preference for speaking of "preferences" rather than "desires," and this, he argues, has resulted in a kind of reification of "utility" and a misguided emphasis upon its maximization. Weirich (1984), on the other hand, defends "interpersonal utility in the classical vein, viz., unvarnished interpersonal intensities of desire." Similarly, Davis holds (with certain qualifications) that desire is cardinally measurable (cf. 1981b, p. 112). Once again, resolution of such issues will presumably go hand in hand with clarification of the concept of desire.

Other relevant sources are Bentham (1983 [1817]), Elster (1982), Hare (1981), Jeffrey (1965), Page (1968), Schick (1982), and Wheeler (1982).

2. THEORY OF DESIRE

Problems of Desire

All of the issues discussed above have this feature in common: their resolution depends upon a better understanding of the ways of desire. So let us now turn our theoretical gaze upon the phenomenon of desire itself.[13]

One area which begs for clarification is the causal functioning of desire. For instance, what is desire such that it is subject to so wide an assortment of causes? Desire appears to be sensitive to the intentional influence of other desires and beliefs. Desire is also evidently responsive to nonintentional influences such as biological homeostasis, heredity, conditioning, surgery, drugs, warm baths, and cold showers. Desire also, of course, functions as a cause as well as an effect; but exactly how does it go about its own causal work? According to one influential tradition, only an event, such as the *onset* of a desire, can be a cause (Staude, 1982). But suppose that the onset of a belief engages some *standing* desire (which is a state and not an event), as presumably occurs when the sight of a bear elicits avoidance behavior; does not the standing desire (in this case, the desire *to live*) cause the resultant behavior as surely as does the onset of the belief?[14]

A related question concerns the proper way to understand the distinction between dispositional desires and occurrent desires. In the example above, does *the desire to live*, which normally lies latent within us, give rise to a *second* desire, say, *the desire to run away*? Or is *the desire to run away* simply *the desire to live* made operative? Or is *the desire to live* merely a manner of speaking, meaning only that we are disposed to want to do certain things, such as run away, under certain circumstances?

It may seem that these questions are more appropriately explored as part of a general theory of causality rather than within the theory of desire. However, one main point of the present volume is that the latter investigation can be an important source of data for investigations such as the former. As with the broader issues discussed in the first part of this introduction, we should probably anticipate the opening of a two-way street between problems in other domains and in the theory of desire.

Some other questions about desire are as follows. (1) How are intrinsic desires (desires for things "for their own sake") related to extrinsic desires (desires for things which are means to other desired ends)? (2) What is the paradigm case of a satisfied desire: when the objective conditions obtain, when they are believed to obtain, or both together? (3) What are the connections and differences between the satisfaction of a desire and the elimination or cessation of a desire, and how is each of these related to the mere absence of a desire? (4) How is strength of desire to be understood? This last question is especially problematic. Armstrong (1968, p. 153) mentions two quite distinct criteria: intensity and pervasiveness of influence, to which I would add a third: persistence or resistance to change. And why is it that different sorts of desires whose *satisfaction* may be experienced with equal intensity may yet be experienced utterly differently when *frustrated*?

Yet another problem area is the "end" of desire; *what does a person want*? On the face of it anything seems capable of being a "material" end of desire; for example, one can want world peace or to touch somebody's knee. Are there any "formal" constraints? Many theorists maintain that desires can only be for *future* states of affairs (Descartes, 1977 [1649], pt. 2, art. 86). Classically, it has also been held that at the very least only something which the desirer *believes good* can be desired (Stocker, 1979, demurs on this point). And can one desire only something which one believes *possible*? Another common claim is that desires always take propositional "contents" rather than (or in addition to) nonpropositional "objects"; for example, "to want a house" is elliptical for "to want to own a house" which is elliptical for "to want that one owns a house" (Jeffrey, 1965, pp. 48f; Searle, 1983, pp. 17, 30).

Other relevant sources are Alston (1967b), Audi (1973a), Brandt (1979), Brandt and Kim (1963), Chisholm (1981), Daveney (1961), Davidson (1980), Davis (1984b), Dennett (1978), de Sousa (1974), Hare (1971), Hempel (1965, sec. 10), Hume (1978 [1739]), Locke (1982), Morton (1980), Neu (1977), Prichard (1940), Schiffer (1976), Smythe (1972), and Staude (1979). And in this volume, see the essays by Audi, Baier, de Sousa, Gordon, Marks, Staude, and Stocker.

The Nature of Desire

The most basic question one can ask about desire is: What is it?[15]
There have been several attempts in the modern literature to provide
an analysis of desire, or at least to initiate one (Brandt & Kim, 1963;
Alston, 1967b; Goldman, 1970, chap. 4; Audi, 1973a). However, all
such analyses are rendered problematic by the recent claims of many
theorists that more than one sense of "desire" is current in philosophical usage (Nagel, 1970; Locke, 1974, 1982; Staude, 1979, 1982; Silver,
1980; Davis, 1984b).[16] The question now is: Which of those senses
have the above-mentioned theorists taken as the object of their various analyses? Furthermore, is any one of these senses to be considered desire proper?

At this point we must confront the possibility that the only feature
shared by the various "broader issues" inventoried above is their concern about A Something Named Desire. Many important claims have
been made in the name of desire, but it may be that theorists (not to
mention lay folk) have been talking about completely different phenomena. Perhaps this very book is about the use of a word and not
about a unified "thing" at all.

In other words, a critic of the present project might say: "Who cares
about establishing the boundary lines for a new discipline (viz., the
theory of desire)? Suppose philosophers have all along been discussing
at least two distinct phenomena which go by the same name. Why
insist that the laurels go to just one of them? Do we refuse the word
'bank' to savings institutions just because there were rivers first? As
long as people know from the context what is being referred to, there
is no reason to appropriate a word for just one use and deny it the other
accustomed uses; a fortiori there is no justification to direct theoretical energies into the study of only one of the word's designata."

My response to this sort of objection is twofold. First, there is no
doubt much confusion abroad concerning the language of desire, and
to untangle it is hardly a trivial task. Here as elsewhere, the history of
philosophy is rife with ambiguities and equivocations. Given the
complexity of language and the breadth of philosophical concerns, it
is easy enough for misapprehensions to arise. If indeed the word
"desire" is homonymic and theorists in disparate philosophical disciplines are not aware of this (and they do not give much evidence of
being so),[17] then there is great value in pointing this out. Perhaps,
then, the first task of theory of desire is a verbal one.[18]

Second, once the "merely verbal" confusions are dispelled,[19] it may
well be the case, as I believe, that there remains a single, significant,
psychological phenomenon appropriately named "desire." If so, then
it is this—desire proper—which, ultimately, constitutes the subject

matter of the theory of desire.

Note that verbal issues do not vanish at this juncture. First of all, it may be that none of the established uses of "desire" will correspond precisely to the final notion of what I have just called desire proper, for the relationship between them may not prove to be simply homonymic after all (and so will not be merely a matter of selecting one favored use and suppressing the rest). The theorist may need to construct a new concept out of parts taken from this and that old concept, with perhaps a dose of the wholly new added from some modern discipline like neurophysiology or psychiatry.

But, further, it is a commonplace of contemporary analytic philosophy that word and object are part and parcel of a truly metaphysical investigation, having a curious interdependency. Throughout my discussion I have left it open as to whether I refer to the *concept* of desire or the *phenomenon* of desire. On a subject of this nature, conceptual and empirical work cannot be neatly separated. For example, there is no point embarking upon an exclusively *empirical* study of the ways of desire, as if one could simply go out and count instances of desire the way one can count televisions per household: how would you know when you've got one? Similarly, there is little hope of carrying out a purely *conceptual* study of the ways of desire, as if one could determine a priori the behavior of desire the way one can determine the marital status of bachelors. One must look and think and look and think again. What one wants is neither analytic truth nor synthetic truth, but plain truth.

In this volume, see the essays by Audi, Baier, and Davis.

Types of Desire

Even if we were to agree upon one legitimate sense of desire, there would remain *types* of desire having intrinsic interest or important applications in other theoretical areas. Examples of desire types which have been singled out in the literature are sexual desire (Shaffer, 1978), self-regarding desire (Broad, 1952), unconscious desire (Smythe, 1972), competitive desire (Cooper, 1984), higher-order desire (as already noted), desire to do something (I call this "practical desire"), and desire which takes as its end pleasure or believed pleasure (this is desire proper, according to Staude, 1979). A special case is aversion. Bentham (1983 [1817]) and Duncker (1940) offer fascinating surveys of the variety of wants.

In this volume, see the essays by de Sousa, Gordon, Green, and Taylor.

Desire and Belief

Why is a desire not a belief? A special task for an adequate theory of
desire will be to distinguish the two. It may strike the reader as odd
that this distinction poses a problem: are not desire and belief as
different as night and day? On the one hand, it seems obvious that a
hallmark of desire is that it moves us to act. Belief, on the other hand,
can pass judgment and even bring us to a conviction, but would leave
us with impotent sentimentality, at best, were it not for the power of
desire to turn belief to account (cf. Hume, 1978 [1739], bk. 2, sec. 3;
1975 [1751], app. 1).

However, a little thought belies this neat dichotomy. A desire without a belief seems to be as powerless to move us to action as a belief
without a desire. It is true (speaking with the usual ceteris paribus
qualification) that you will not donate to Oxfam even if you believe
millions of people are starving, if you have no desire to help relieve
suffering in the world, but neither will you give if you are very sensitive to human suffering but happen to be ignorant that people are
starving.

Where, then, lies the difference between desire and belief? Is the
difference "brute," like that between red and green, or can it be further
characterized in some way? If it can be further characterized, will the
difference be simple and intuitive (as the linkage between desire and
action is sometimes thought to be), or must we resort to complex
theoretical construct analyses? The form that a theory of desire
should take is one of the questions for theory of desire (Brandt & Kim,
1963; Alston, 1967b; Audi, 1973a; Staude, 1979).

The following points of difference have been claimed for desire and
belief. (1) Desire is "directed at" good, belief is "directed at" truth (cf.
de Sousa, 1974). (2) Desire must be for a future state of affairs, while
belief may range over the past, present, and future.[20] (3) Many if not
all desires imply beliefs (e.g., your desire to run away from the dog
implies the belief that there is a dog present),[21] but the presence of a
belief never implies the presence of a desire (e.g., your belief that there
is a dog present does not imply that you desire to run away from the
dog) (cf. Barnes, 1977). (4) Desires are especially prone to indetermin-
acy of content, as exhibited in the various ways a person can go wrong
when submitting his or her wishes to a jinni (Ronald de Sousa has
referred to this as the Monkey's Paw Problem, from the story by W. W.
Jacobs).[22] (5) Desires have world-to-mind "direction of fit," beliefs are
mind-to-world (Searle, 1983; Green, in preparation; cf. Woodfield,
1982).

Also to consider is the possible metaphysical significance of our
differing linguistic tendencies with respect to desire and belief. Thus,

we say that one believes that something *is* the case but that one desires that something *be* the case. Another way to put this point is to ask whether *your desire that it be a nice day* has the same "content" as *your belief that it is a nice day*.

On the other hand, points of similarity are if anything even more intriguing, since belief and desire are curiously correlative (cf. Wheeler, 1982; Stalnaker, 1984). For example, the likelihood of an action seems to be a function of both strength of desire and strength of belief. You will run away from (or react in whatever way to) a fierce-looking dog if you have the slightest suspicion of imminent attack provided you have an intense desire to avoid being bitten; you will also run away if you have a moderate desire to avoid injury but are absolutely certain of an attack. Also suggestive is the apparent constraint that belief-desire interactions must be *rational* (cf. Dennett, 1978; Moore, 1975). For example, it would seem to be impossible that a person should desire to eat ice cream because he desired to be thin and believed ice cream is fattening, period. Why is this so?[23]

One reply to this question is provided by the following argument (with a Spinozan flavor) to the effect that belief and desire are two sides of a single coin. (1) Suppose you desire not to be bitten by a dog which you believe is about to attack you. (2) Then you discover that the dog is really playful and not dangerous. (3) Lo and behold, both your belief *and* your desire are extinguished in one swoop, for it is impossible for you to desire anything about *the dog which you believe is about to attack you* if you do not believe that any dog is about to attack you. (4) Now, no *causal* influence has been exercised upon your desire by your change of belief; the desire blinks out by conceptual necessity. (5) But two distinct psychological states must interact causally if they interact at all. Therefore, (6) your belief and your desire were not distinct states after all. Analogously to the physicists' distinction between space, time, and spacetime, perhaps we can speak of belief, desire, and beliefdesire.

Some theorists go so far as to identify desire as a species of belief, if only implicitly. Desires are taken to be desirability judgments; for example, to *want* to have a certain experience *just is* to *believe* that the experience will be pleasurable. Conversely, a Cartesian tradition holds that a belief partly consists in an act of will: "For by the understanding alone I [neither assert nor deny anything, but] apprehend the ideas of things as to which I can form a judgment" (Descartes, 1977a [1642], *Fourth Meditation*).

The affinity between desire and belief has long been sensed; however, it has seldom been the subject of scrutiny in its own right. Furthermore, in much of the recent philosophical discussion about mind (for reasons which are perhaps revealing in themselves; cf.

Woodfield, 1982; Keller & Grontkowski, 1983), desire has been treated as the silent partner of belief. When they are not simply mute on the subject, philosophers of mind and other theorists have made their cases mostly in terms of belief and then simply extended their arguments "mutatis mutandis" to desire. The intent of the present volume is to cast doubt on that strategy.

See the essays herein by de Sousa and Stampe.

A final word about this volume. As a survey of the summaries placed at the beginning of each essay will reveal, it is not intended to provide a single theory of desire. Neither is it meant to tell you everything you always wanted to know about wanting. Rather, it highlights a problem area. Indeed, when so many thinkers are brought together around a common theme, their points of difference should be evident, perhaps strikingly so. But it is precisely by demonstrating the need for a great deal of theoretical housekeeping that a new discipline can be given a firm foundation. If, therefore, this volume serves to stimulate further thinking on desire, it will have served its purpose.

NOTES

1. In what follows I shall refer to this domain as "the theory of desire" in the same general way that we speak of "the philosophy of mind," " the philosophy of science," etc. — i.e., without any suggestion of there being only one theory that constitutes the domain in question.

2. Complete citations for all sources referred to in this book appear in the consolidated bibliography at the end.

3. In the theory of emotion, the term "emotion" is usually understood to encompass the "calm passions" as well as the agitated ones. Thus, under this rubric comes the whole range of psychological or intentional attitudes which, on one interpretation, go by the name of "feelings."

4. On the other hand, suppose some dreadful bodily pain suddenly ceases. Need you *believe* that the pain ceased in order to be happy or relieved, or is the cessation itself sufficient, i.e., the objective satisfaction of your desire that the pain cease? (Cf. Marks, 1983, p. 71.)

5. One thing which makes such an enterprise distinctively philosophical, I submit, is humanistic sensitivity to the actual use — historical, literary, etc. — of the word in question; definition by fiat will not do.

6. Another inference sometimes drawn is that of ethical hedonism.

7. Not to mention desire satisfaction with psychological satisfaction; the Buddha for one would deny that getting what one wants is equivalent to contentment.

8. A paradigm case of desiring that one's desire(s) be satisfied would be the attitude of a participant in an assertiveness training course, who has the generalized wish that more of his or her desires could be realized, whatever they may be. However, this is obviously not a requirement on desiring per se.

9. At least insofar as happiness is a good thing.

10. One researcher notes, "Perhaps in the future someone will attempt to clarify the concept of 'desire.' This would be an interesting philosophical project and an obvious contribution to Buddhist studies" (Alt, 1980, p. 58).

11. It is also possible that "desire" is being used distinctively in the Buddhist context; for example, it may refer just to intense egoistic wanting.

12. The notorious "Paradox of Desire" also arises at this point in the argument (Herman, 1979, 1980; Alt, 1980; Visvader, 1980). Buddhism enjoins us to *desire* the elimination of our desire; the end of desire should be the end of desire, so to speak.

13. Actually, a number of questions about desire itself inevitably arose in the preceding discussions. Also, many of the issues to be discussed in the present section will be treated more fully in the essays which follow.

14. To the objection that the standing desire should not be cited as the cause because it can be assumed as a background condition, I reply that there are any number of cases where an *unusual* standing desire — for example, the desire to eat tacks — will play a necessary explanatory role.

15. Aside from: "Does it exist?" But these two questions go hand in hand; cf. the discussion above under "Philosophy of Mind."

16. More precisely: different senses of "desire" have been recognized all along, but only certain theorists have considered this to be a *problem.*

17. Aside from those who have suggested there is a problem, of course.

18. This would certainly be an extreme case of homonymy, though, for it would involve at least a pair of words, viz., "desire" and "want," not to mention both verbs and nouns.

19. Cf. my "preliminary clarification" at the beginning of this essay.

20. But is not a wish a desire, and cannot one wish that things *had been* different or *were* different *now?*

21. But suppose you desire simply that some sensation continue (cf. n. 4).

22. As G. B. Shaw has observed (in *Man and Superman*, act 4), there are two great disappointments in life: not getting what you want, and getting it.

23. Decision theory, conceived as a normative discipline, presumes that practical reasoning can be fallacious. The present example seems to deny that.

Intending, Intentional Action, and Desire

Robert Audi

Abstract. This paper presents an account of intending, explains how intending so conceived is related to intentional action, and connects both with desire, which is construed as a kind of wanting. Intrinsic and extrinsic wants are distinguished, but without positing two senses of "want." It is argued that intending entails wanting, and that the concept of wanting is implicit in that of intentional action. The issue of whether intending, too, must figure in intentional action is also explored. The paper questions this view and provides alternative explanations of some of the data that support it. In examining all these issues, the paper shows how the position it defends, which takes wanting rather than intending as the most basic motivational notion in commonsense psychology, can approach a number of major questions in action theory.

The subject of intending is of major interest in itself, but it is also widely felt to be pivotal for understanding many other topics in the philosophy of mind. Among these are intentional action, motivation, practical reasoning, rational conduct, and the explanation of action. There has been much debate about whether intending is irreducibly distinct, and in particular about whether it is in some sense composed of desires and beliefs. There is also controversy regarding what beliefs, if any, the subject must have about the realization of the intention. And there are widely differing views about the place of intending in practical reasoning. In a previous paper (Audi, 1973b), I have developed an account of intending which represents it as largely a complex of certain wants and beliefs. That paper makes extensive use of the notion of wanting, construed broadly enough to include desiring, and it will serve as a good point of departure here. In discussing some of the issues raised by the account, we can explore the relation of intending to a number of philosophically important notions. Those that will be my special concern are wanting, believing, intentional action, and practical reasoning.

1. A SKETCH OF INTENDING

There are several forms of intending. For instance, there is intending to A (where A-ing is an action or activity); intending to bring about a state of affairs *by* A-ing; and intending that something be the case. For our purposes, it will be sufficient to consider just *simple intentions*, intentions to A. These might be plausibly characterized as follows:

> A person, S, intends, at time t, to A, if and only if, at t, (1) S believes that he will (or that he probably will) A; (2) S wants, and has not temporarily forgotten that he wants, to A; and (3) either S has no equally strong or stronger incompatible want (or set of wants whose combined strength is at least as great), or, if S does have such a want or set of wants, he has temporarily forgotten that he wants the object(s) in question, or does not believe he wants the object(s).[1]

The relevant incompatibility is psychological, in the sense that two wants, say for x and for y, are incompatible provided S *believes* x and y cannot jointly occur. The core, but only the core, of the idea is simply this: one intends to do something, say, to decline a drink, when one wants to do it more than one wants to do anything one believes is incompatible with doing so, and one believes at least that one probably will do it. If one has a stronger incompatible want, such as to drink some gin (and has not, say, temporarily forgotten that one also wants to decline), then while one may be very strongly motivated to decline, and may even sincerely say one intends to decline, one does not intend to. Similarly, if one believes only that there is a small chance of one's successfully declining, one may hope, but not intend, to decline.

This account was put forward with various reservations and qualifications. For instance, one possible revision suggested by the original discussion of difficult cases is a condition to the effect that S *not* believe either that he will not A intentionally or that he will A only as a result of compulsion.[2] These and other beliefs are at least abnormal for a person who intends to A, but it is not clear that an account of intending should explicitly rule them out: for one thing, an intention to A simpliciter (which is the sort under discussion) is surely different from an intention to do so in a particular *way*, and it is capable of being accompanied by quite a variety of beliefs about how one will A. If we do not build these into the content of the intention to A simpliciter, it is doubtful that their absence should be built into it either: the content slot of a simple intention does not appear to contain places for anything but the act, and to add specifications of its manner, even if they are negative, is apparently to describe a different intention. Granted, the absence of certain beliefs, such as the belief that one will be compelled to A, *could* be a condition on having an intention, without being part of its content. But we should not expect this: the suggested condition might be a plausible requirement on *rational* intention, but it is difficult to see why the absence of such beliefs should be a condition for intending itself.

It may also be thought that (as the literature on intending sometimes suggests) where S intends to A, S's belief that he will A must be noninferential. The terms "noninductive" and, at least in the case of H. P. Grice, "not dependent on evidence" are also sometimes used here, but they seem narrower (1971, p. 266). This view is surely too strong. For one thing, even if, at the time the intention is formed, the relevant belief is noninferential, it could come to be based on evidence (and in that sense be inferential). After forming the intention to A, for instance to convince Tom to forgive Joe, S might discover obstacles to his A-ing, conclude that his chance of doing so is slim, and as a result come only to hope, rather than intend, to A, and to intend to try to do so. But he then might acquire evidence that he will succeed in A-ing; he might now once again intend to A, this time with his belief that he will do so being inferentially based on his evidence that his efforts to accomplish it will succeed.

This case naturally suggests that the noninferentiality thesis should be applied only to the time of formation of intentions. And it surely is true that very commonly, and perhaps typically, when S intends to A, his belief that he will A is both noninferential and in some complicated way grounded in his motivational constitution together with his total outlook on the relevant aspects of his future, especially the options he takes to be open to him. But imagine that S is aware of the difficulties of convincing Tom to forgive Joe, *before* he decides to convince him to do this and, in so deciding, forms the intention to convince Tom. Surely the formation of the intention does not suddenly obliterate the evidential basis of S's belief that he will A, even if it *adds* a kind of support to that belief beyond S's evidence that he will succeed in overcoming the obstacles to A-ing. Perhaps a decision process that issues in intending to A is itself normally sufficient for formation of the belief that one will A, but that is consistent with the belief's *also* being inferential. The evidence beliefs, as well as other factors entering into the decision process, might both be necessary for, and partly sustain, the relevant belief. It appears, then, that while there *is*, at least typically, a noninferential grounding relation between what produces intending and what produces the belief constituent in it, it is a mistake to think that the belief must be noninferential, either initially or throughout the time S holds it.

These points about the relation between intending and believing leave much to be explored, and there are other difficulties which the suggested account of intending must face. It is not my purpose here to defend its details. My special concern is to explore the relation between intending and wanting, and to indicate what a correct understanding of this relation shows about intentional action and practical reasoning. I begin with some points which strongly suggest that despite certain appearances intending does entail wanting.

This issue has long divided philosophers, and there may be no way to settle it in a short space, if indeed it can be settled. But it is useful to note some of the considerations that support the entailment thesis. Here are three. First, notice the breadth of "What do you want?" asked of someone whose intention, purpose, aim, project, or whatever, is not clear. Even if Ann is offering a passerby a pamphlet only out of a sense of obligation and with real revulsion at stopping him with her outthrust hand, she cannot properly answer this question with "I don't want anything. I simply have to (or intend to) offer you this pamphlet." To rebut the suggestion that there is something (relevant) that she wants, she would have to say something like "Excuse me, I took you for someone else," where the implication is that her stopping *him* was not intentional. Second, consider how one can reply to accusations. Suppose one is accused of intending (or meaning) to slight Smith. One can rebut this by saying, "Why on earth would I want to do that?" If we took it that one could intend without wanting, we could not plausibly regard the suggestion that we do not want to do the thing in question as implying that we do not intend to. It could be replied that we take only prima facie reprehensible intentions to imply wanting; but this move seems ad hoc, and in any case a rhetorical "Why would I want to do that?" can be used to imply the absence of any intention. Third, recall Anscombe's point that the primitive sign of wanting something is trying to get it. If, as seems uncontroversial, intending to *A* entails being disposed to try to overcome obstacles to one's *A*-ing, and hence also being disposed to try to *A* should one encounter an obstacle to *A*-ing, then there is good reason to think that intending also entails wanting. It could be held that the wanting to *A* arises only *when* the obstacle is encountered. But surely that applies just to wanting *to overcome the obstacle,* for instance to wanting to get a dog out of one's path as one walks along, not to wanting to offer the pamphlet to Smith.[3] One is in some sense trying to offer it when the question what one wants arises.

2. INTENDING, WANTING, AND DESIRING

Why has it seemed to many philosophers that intending does not entail wanting? One point is that we often use "want" to refer to an *intrinsic want,* which is a want for something simply for its own sake, i.e., roughly, a want such that either one has no belief to the effect that realizing it would bring about something further (particularly something to which it is a means), or, if one does have such a belief, one does not want the thing in question even in part on the *basis* of that belief. For instance, people often say "Do you really want to do that?" intending to ask whether one is looking forward to it for its own sake. Moreover, some people do not distinguish wants from *desires* conceived as either intrinsic wants or, even more often, as in some way passional, in the broad sense that they are either appetitive—say, having sensual objects—or emotional, say, having as their object the welfare of a loved one. In appetitive cases, furthermore, the desires may be *felt*, and people are sometimes said to be overcome by such desires. Here, to be sure, the term "want" does not serve well; but the association of wants with desires remains strong, and one source of resistance to conceiving intending as entailing wanting is the quite justified sense that it does not entail desiring. But I do not claim that it does, nor that it entails intrinsic wanting of any sort.

At this point one may wonder whether there is not more than one sense of "want," so that at best intending entails wanting in just one, perhaps special, sense. There may be no clear-cut way to distinguish between different senses of "want" and different kinds of wants; in any case, I see no conclusive reason to think that we need to countenance different senses. Intrinsic and extrinsic wants can be conceived as wants for which the subject has different sorts of grounds: in the former case, the object is wanted for something taken to be intrinsic to it, as where one wants to do something just for the pleasure of doing it; in the latter case, the object is wanted for its believed contribution to something S does not take to be intrinsic but, say, to be an effect of realizing the object. Since something can be wanted for both sorts of reasons at once, a single want can be partly intrinsic and partly extrinsic. Moreover, I believe that a single account applies to both sorts of wants.[4] This account also applies to at least many desires, and by strengthening the conditions of the account it can apparently serve to explicate desires in general.

Whether a univocal account of wanting applies not only to intrinsic and extrinsic wants, but also to what Wayne Davis calls appetitive desires, is not obvious. He points out that we can have a desire to eat, yet "not want to eat because we are on a diet" (Davis, 1984a, p. 45). This is true. But could it be that we extrinsically want not to eat, in order to avoid calories, say, yet intrinsically want to? I think so; yet if we imagine our subject overcome by a desire for tortes it is not natural to say that he was overcome by his wanting them. This point lends some support to Davis's view. But perhaps it is not wrong to speak so, and we can, with less strain, say that he wanted tortes so badly that he couldn't resist them. Suppose, however, that the noun "want" will not do precisely the work of the noun "desire," for instance that the former cannot, without at least linguistic strain, be substituted for the latter in all contexts. We may not infer that the concept of wanting, which figures in our talk of felt wants as well as in more common want-locutions, cannot (with suitable qualifications) do all the work of the concept of desire. Nor may we infer that desires are not a proper subset of wants. In any case, if some desires are not naturally called wants, that may indirectly confirm, and certainly does not disconfirm, the thesis that intending entails wanting. For we can then make explicit that intending is not being held to entail (though some intentions may embody) any desires there may be that are not naturally called wants, and it is the association of wants with the sorts of desires most likely to fit this description that is responsible for much of the resistance to the view that intending entails wanting.

In addition to the sorts of objections so far discussed, there are systematic reasons for denying that intending entails wanting, or at least (apart from unusual cases such as temporary forgetting) having a want *on balance*, i.e., a want stronger than any incompatible want or combined set of such wants. Hugh McCann, for instance, has argued that, whereas one can have, and know one has, strong conflicting desires, say, to go to Europe for July and to go to the Rockies for that month, it is hard "even to imagine someone having conflicting intentions and knowing about it. . . . To have conflicting intentions, then, is in normal circumstances to be in a state that is irrational. . . . The same, however, is not true of desires, no matter what their strength" (McCann, forthcoming, pp. 6-7). Alfred Mele, on the other hand, has maintained that a person can reach a decision, such as to cut his hand in order to become someone's "blood brother," and hence form an intention to do so, "on the basis of his *evaluation* of his reasons for and against cutting his hand, and his evaluation of these reasons need not be in line with their *motivational force*" (Mele, forthcoming, pp. 5-6). Thus, while S might intend to cut his hand, he might be more motivated to avoid cutting it than to cut it. This motivational fact might be evidenced by his being simply horrified as he brings the knife against it. Hence, even if intending entails some motivation, it does not entail wanting on balance. Both of these objections are plausible and illuminating. Let me take them up in turn.

Most of what McCann says seems correct and significant. But his focus is on the *absolute* strength of the relevant wants, whereas my account concerns relative strengths: a want on balance is one not equaled or outweighed in strength by an incompatible want or set of incompatible wants; it need not itself be strong. One reason this is an important point is that intentions themselves can vary in what we might call their strength ("firmness" is the usual term for this). Even more important for our purposes is the point that once we focus on wants on balance we find that we may say the *same* sorts of things about them as McCann points out regarding intentions. If, for instance, one wants *x*, and also wants *y*, on balance, yet does not realize that they cannot be jointly satisfied, one is somehow in error, since one is disposed to act in order to realize each *as if* doing so would not deprive one of the other. Since one wants the other on balance, it may well be something whose importance to one is at least sufficient to give one pause; one's oblivious disposition to ignore it, then, might be criticizably irrational. On the other hand, if one believes that *x* and *y* are not jointly realizable, one cannot want both on balance; and just as "to adjudicate between conflicting intentions is to abandon one of them,"[5] to adjudicate between two wants vying for predominance (i.e., roughly, vying to become a want on balance) is to abandon one of them *as* a want on balance. One of them, the one against which S decides, is no longer (if it ever was) his want on balance.

Mele's point that one's evaluation of one's reasons need not parallel their motivational strength is correct and important. But he does not show that his subject, in positively evaluating his reasons for cutting his hand (in order to become someone's blood brother), really *decides* to cut his hand. The boy *agrees* to cut his hand; but this does not entail intending to, even if the agreement is sincere. He may even *resolve* to cut it; but this does not entail intending either. Resolution (of one kind, at least) is, roughly, making up one's *mind*; intending is, roughly, a disposition of the *will*. As weakness of will shows, the latter does not follow from the former.

Still another possibility in Mele's interesting case is that the boy decides *that he should cut his hand.* In fact, this is a natural locution to use where what he is evaluating is his *reasons*, and, often, where evaluation is the source of a decision. But deciding *that*, like resolving, does not entail intending. To be sure, the boy might sincerely say that he has decided *to* cut it, since otherwise it may be plain that he does not intend to, or, in any event, the situation demands more than the evaluation expressed by his cognitive decision *that*. In any case, what he naturally says in such a case need not be taken at face value. Suppose, however, that he does decide *to* cut it. Must we assume, as philosophers usually do, that deciding entails intending? I am disinclined to deny this entailment, nor does an account of Mele's example consistent with my view require it. But the assumption is surely less than self-evident. I believe, then, that if we observe all the distinctions available to us, cases of disparity between evaluation and motivation do not refute the view that intending entails wanting on balance.

A quite different consideration thought to show that intending cannot be understood along the lines I have suggested concerns *inten-*

tion transmission. Myles Brand maintains that "If a person intends to do something, say *B*, and if he realizes that *A*-ing is the means to *B*-ing, then he intends to *A*. . . . But it could happen that a person desire to *B* and realize that *A*-ing is the means to *B*-ing and not desire to *A*" (Brand, 1984, p. 126). It is not clear that, given the understanding of wanting suggested above, Brand's second point holds for wants, at least where other things are equal; and as we shall soon see, his first claim holds only with a similar qualification. Concerning that claim, suppose that you intend to buy a certain book which you discover on the shelf, and you then realize that (since this requires cash) the means for doing so is giving the clerk your last twenty dollars. It certainly does not follow that you now intend to do the latter. For one thing, you may at the same time recall that you need the cash to get home. It could be replied that you formed, and immediately abandoned, the intention to give the clerk the cash; but surely you might have *already* been well aware of your needing it to get home. Reflection on this and similar cases will show that it is a difficult question under what conditions a person who intends to do something, and then comes to believe that something else is the means (or a necessary condition) for doing it, will intend to do the latter. Change of mind eliminating the original intention is only one case; weakness of will is another. In any event, to return to the relation between intending and wanting, surely quite parallel points hold for wanting on balance. The parallels are indeed strong enough to *confirm* rather than disconfirm the thesis that intending entails wanting.

It is appropriate to stress here that the notion of wanting on balance is by no means unproblematic. For one thing, it is not easy to spell out what it is for one want to be stronger than a second one. For another, there are practical problems in determining which of two incompatible wants is stronger even if the relevant concepts are clear. The following will illustrate both points. We should not say unqualifiedly that if S wants *x* more than *y* and believes he cannot realize both, then he wants one of them more if and only if he would prefer to realize that one. This is generally true, but the notion of preference needs explication and may in fact be analyzable only by appeal to wanting or a similarly complex notion. We also may not say that he wants *x* more if and only if he acts in order to realize it; for so acting indicates a stronger want only on certain assumptions about his beliefs. Nor can we rely fully on his sincere affirmations about which want is stronger; these are surely fallible, though not to be lightly dismissed. Far more could be said about intrapersonal comparison of want strengths, but my purposes here require just two points. First, there is more than one indicator we may appeal to; for instance, there is verbal affirmation as well as selection in situations of forced choice. Second, given the complexity of intending with respect to both variations in strength and interactions with other propositional attitudes, it should not be a surprise that any motivational notion suitable for explicating it presents the sorts of difficulties just sketched.

It should be stressed that if there is, as some philosophers have argued, a sense in which intending to A commits one to A-ing,[6] then wanting on balance can at least do justice to the motivational aspect of that commitment. For what we want, on balance, to do, we are *motivationally committed* to doing: if nothing interferes, we will do it; and, if we also believe at least that we probably will do it (as where we intend to) then if we do not do it we tend to feel that we have (say) failed to get what we want, or to carry out our plan, or to complete our attempt. The more *firm* the intention—roughly, the greater its resistance to being abandoned or forgotten by S—the greater the motivational commitment, other things equal. Firmness is in part a matter of the strength of the want constituent in the intending; but any want on balance tends to provide some motivational commitment, however weak it is compared to that generated by wants that are absolutely stronger. This sense of "commitment" is, to be sure, rather weak; but if one considers how wide the range of our intentions is, it will be apparent that a significantly stronger sense would not do. An important case here is that of akratic intention. Since what one intends to do is against one's better judgment, one may not be *normatively committed* at all; and should one fail, one might have no good grounds for self-criticism because of the failure, but instead, excellent reason to be glad one did not act against one's better judgment.

Having suggested that the conception of intending as, typically, entailing a want on balance helps us understand some basic properties of intentions, I want to close this section by indicating how the belief component of my account of intending is similarly useful. My comments here will range over four aspects of intending: its connections with planning; its relation to our beliefs about the rationality of agents; its role as a basis for assessments of persons; and our confidence with respect to our intentions.

It has been noted that intentions play a major part in our *planning*.[7] Now suppose that the concept of intending is not such that intending to A entails believing at least that one probably will A. We would then probably tend less than we in fact do to plan on the assumption that we *will* do what we intend. For unless it just happened that intending to A implied, without entailing, believing at least that one probably will A, we would probably be quite aware of cases of the former without the latter; and we would quite likely be more inclined to think of our intending without conceiving ourselves as doing the intended thing. Moreover, if we did not generally believe that we would do what we intend, we would not be as rational in basing our plans in part on what we intend. To be sure, none of this shows that intending *entails* the sort of belief I have indicated. But if the entailment does hold, it helps us account for the role of intending in our planning; and that role is of major importance in giving an account of intending.

Now consider how this entailment bears on the rationality of agents. Suppose it is an entailment figuring in the way I have suggested in the *concept* of intending, and that we presuppose it in drawing inferences on the basis of applying that concept. This helps to account for our *beliefs* to the effect that it is rational to plan in part on the basis of our intentions; for we quite naturally believe one should plan in the light of what one believes one will do: otherwise one plan, or intention, might defeat another, or interfere with realizing it.

My third point concerns our assessments of persons. In assessing one another we are very much concerned with intentions. It is important to be a person of good intentions; one can be criticizable for harboring malicious intentions; and various sorts of errors are not counted against one's character if one's intentions in so acting are acceptable. Now if intending entails the kind of belief my account indicates, these points are easy to understand, and certainly more comprehensible than on the view that intending is compatible with believing one will probably fail. For one thing, our character tends to be more revealed in what we believe we will do than in what we merely believe we may do. Particularly if what we believe we will do is something we intend to do, we are disposed to *identify* with it. More important, if one believes one will or that one probably will *A*, then, if *A*-ing is wrong, one can be expected to try to change one's course, and, if *A*-ing is right, to be disposed to exert some effort not to be deterred.

My fourth point here concerns the fact that with respect to some intentions we have more *confidence* than in regard to others. We could speak of *confident intentions* here, but that is misleading because it may invite conflation of the firmness of an intention and our confidence with respect to the intention. The latter is mainly determined by those of our beliefs determining how likely we take (or are disposed to take) our *A*-ing to be; the former is mainly determined by how *rooted* the intention is. These variables tend to be connected, but either can be strong while the other is weak. Now the belief constituent which I attribute to intending helps us to understand our confidence with respect to our intentions. For instance, if we come to believe that doing something we have been intending is less likely, we are less confident with respect to the intention; and if we come to see it as unlikely, we tend to talk of hoping rather than intending to do it.

Other things equal, the stronger the belief that one will *A*, the more confidence we have regarding the intention; and when confidence is reversed, intending gives way to hoping or, if S comes to believe *A*-ing impossible, to mere wishing. Since, in either case, we cease to intend, the belief condition also helps to clarify the firmness of intentions: other things equal, the more readily we are subject to ceasing to believe at least that we will probably *A*, the less firm our intention.

If intending may be conceived along the lines I have indicated, then it should be well worth exploring how, conceived as embodying wanting, it is connected with intentional action. This is the main business of the next section.

3. INTENDING, WANTING, AND INTENTIONAL ACTION

A number of philosophers have conceived intending as fundamental in all action. Perhaps the clearest and most characteristic expression of this conception is the view—which I shall call *the intention thesis*—that every action has some description under which it is intended.[8] If one does not wish to speak of actions under descriptions and prefers to individuate actions in terms of act properties, one could express the same basic idea by saying that every action is either intended or performed *by* (or in) performing one that is intended. The intention thesis gives great importance to intending; for if it is true, we should be able to understand action in general, whether intentional or not, as (roughly) behavior suitably generated by intending.

It is doubtful, however, that the intention thesis is true. Take an example. Jane may know that she has little chance of being heard by Sue, who is half a mile away; Jane might then only hope, but not intend, to call Sue to the phone. Perhaps she does intend to do something like this: to call out in Sue's direction. Yet that is by no means self-evident. Granted she does not call out in that direction unintentionally; but must she have formed an intention with the specific content just mentioned? Since her calling out, given the intention to summon someone to the phone, is automatic, need she form a specific intention to call out? This is at least not obvious. But suppose we grant that for every (nonmental) action there is some such generative bodily movement toward which S forms some motivational attitude. Must the attitude be intending? Let us explore this.

Suppose that Sally has hurt her arm and very much doubts that she can move it. She has, however, kept still and does not know what she can do with it. The doctor asks, "Can you move your arm?" and to her surprise she does so fairly easily. Here it seems that she did not intend, but only hoped, to move her arm. She *wanted* to, surely, as she also wanted to cooperate with the doctor. But the appropriate sort of beliefs for intending are missing. One could object that she at least intended to *try* to move her arm. But suppose that she simply moves it in the normal way immediately on the doctor's request. What has she done, or formed an intention to do, that is plausibly called trying? And if there is such an action, why must she have formed an intention (or even a want) to perform it, in order to have moved her arm intentionally?

If we reject the intention thesis, however, how are we to explain why intentional actions are so called? Here it is helpful to think of paradigms of intentional action: above all, bodily actions under our direct control. A great many of these *are* intended. That may be all the explanation we need; for supposing that "intending" is, linguistically, the more basic term, it is to be expected that extensions of it stem from paradigm cases. Moreover, if my account of intending is correct, then for those intentional actions that are not intended the problem is cognitive and not motivational: if the agent had the right belief, he would intend. Thus, these intentional actions can be viewed as deviating only in one respect, and only by degree, from the case of intentional actions that are intended.

We can see, then, both why intending is very important and why, nevertheless, there can be actions not intended under any description. However, the same data do not show that wanting is not fundamental to intentional action. Jane did want to move her arm, and it may be plausibly argued that every action *is*, under some description, such that the agent wanted to perform it. Perhaps the most direct way to support this view is by arguing for what I shall call *the intentionality thesis:* the claim that every action is, under some description, intentional, even if not intended. This may be thought to entail or be entailed by the intention thesis, but neither implication holds. For one thing, as our paralysis case apparently shows, one may intentionally *A* without having intended to *A*, or even having intended to try to *A* or to do anything in order to *A*. Moreover, since one may intend to do something which one then does unintentionally, even if every action has a description under which it is intended it would not follow from that alone that all actions are intentional under some description. But are they? It is not clear that there is anything properly called action that cannot be given at least one description under which it is intentional. To see this, let us consider apparent counterexamples to the intentionality thesis.

When we are sitting, we move our feet. Should we suppose that either this is not action or it is intentional, for instance done in order to get more comfortable, or to stay comfortable? And suppose Joe bites his fingernails. Is he acting intentionally even when he does this unknowingly? One might say that either this is nervous behavior of an automatic sort that does not qualify as action, or he does it intentionally, say, to relieve nervousness. I have some sympathy with this reaction, though on balance I suspect that it is simply not clear whether the sorts of behavior we are considering are or are not action. But suppose we do endorse the suggested interpretation of such examples, and thus maintain the intentionality thesis. This still leaves *wanting* in a central position in relation to action. For if every action has a description under which it is intentional, then even if it is not intended, it surely has a description under which S wants to perform it: if not the same one(s) under which it is intentional, then at least a description linking it to a further end, say, "cooperating with the doctor," "bringing Sue to the phone," or "illuminating the room."

Suppose, on the other hand, we conclude that the data simply cannot be fitted to the intentionality thesis, that, for example, when we move our feet under the table or make certain gestures, we are acting, but nonintentionally and hence not in order to realize any want. We might then consider the intentionality thesis to admit of a class of exceptions, yet still maintain a related view, *the motivation thesis:* roughly, the claim that every action has a description under which S wants to perform it. To accommodate such cases as moving one's feet under the table, we might note that if there is resistance, say, a cardboard box, S will tend to *try* to move his feet, and his doing this would imply his wanting to move his feet.

Granted, S's wanting to move his feet under the table could arise only as he perceives an obstacle; but it is not clear that it must arise thus. If it need not, however, then perhaps we have as good reason to call the actions intentional as to say that S wants to perform them. There is, however, one possible difference. Since the sorts of actions we are considering are basic for S, in the sense that S can normally perform them at will and without doing anything in order to perform them, we might suppose that no belief (such as a belief that by moving certain muscles one will move one's feet) need figure in their generation; and this *might* warrant concluding that while they are motivated in virtue of at least one want, say, to move one's feet, they are not intentional. It could be that bodily needs simply produce a want to move one's feet and that one does so in direct response to so wanting. If we say this, however, must we also say that even when one quite consciously does something basically, such as whistle, wholly for its own sake, the action is, though motivated, not intentional? I think not; for consciousness of what one is doing seems to be an important element in action; indeed, its absence is at least the main thing that makes the apparent exceptions to the intentionality thesis prima facie counterexamples.

Perhaps, then, wanting could be fundamental to action even if the intentionality thesis is false. I am not prepared to deny that thesis, however, since it may be quite plausibly defended along the lines I have suggested. My point here is simply that even *if* that thesis turns out to be mistaken, wanting may still be fundamental to action in the way suggested by the motivation thesis. I believe, however, that the motivation thesis, too, may be mistaken. But if it is, I suspect that the reason is that the kinds of behavior we have been considering are just barely actions at all, but appear to be clear cases of actions because of at least two important properties: they are *natural movements*; and they *behaviorally match* actions we commonly perform, such as moving our feet *in order to* get more comfortable. In any case, we have seen no good reason not to conceive wanting, rather than intending, as a (and perhaps the) motivational concept fundamental to the notion of action.

4. JUDGING AND WANTING: INTERNALISM VERSUS EXTERNALISM

It has been argued above that even when, out of a sense of obligation, one intends to do something, one at least extrinsically wants to do it. This should not be taken to imply that an action cannot be properly *explained* by citing the agent's sense of obligation, or that the sense of obligation *reduces* to a kind of wanting, say, a desire, to do what one takes to be obligatory. Surely the sense of obligation has *cognitive* roots, whatever motivational roots it may also have, though there is much controversy about whether the former are chiefly (propositional) beliefs and thus true or false, or, instead, attitudes, or indeed something more nearly emotive than attitudes need be. This section will attempt to clarify the relation of wanting to judgment, particularly moral judgment, and thereby to the sense of moral obligation.

A good place to begin is with *internalism*. This view has been variously characterized, and to simplify matters I shall work with a moderate version. According to this version, if S judges that on balance he ought to *A*, then he has some motivation to *A*, and normally motivation strong enough so that, if he intentionally *A*'s on the basis of that judgment, his doing so can be adequately explained by attributing the action to the judgment. The "ought" here need not be moral, though moral obligation is what most internalists have had in mind. The name, in fact, is generally meant to suggest the idea that some degree of motivation is internal to (the sense of) moral obligation. What is essential to internalism, however, is that the "ought" represent whatever point of view is most important for S at the time, whether it be moral or prudential or some overall kind representing a combination of diverse prima facie obligations, such as the point of view of one's overall interests. Plato apparently held a similar, though perhaps stronger, internalist doctrine, at least for judgments representing *knowledge* (which he took to imply virtue). Kant also seems to have held a form of internalism, at least insofar as he thought of desire as different from wanting when he spoke of the possibility of acting out of — in a sense implying explainability in terms of — duty as contrasted with desire. And many other philosophers have been internalists of a kind, including Hare and Davidson.[9]

It might seem that the position outlined in this paper is inconsistent with internalism. But I doubt that it is. Internalists do not usually make clear what they take motivation to be. Suppose that, as some internalist texts suggest, the basic internalist idea is simply that someone who judges that on balance he ought to *A* has a tendency to *A*, and is such that, if he *A*'s on the basis of that judgment, then appeal to the judgment is sufficient to explain why he *A*-ed. Let us assume that S so judges and then acts on the basis of so judging in a way that permits explaining the action by appeal to the judgment. All of that is surely consistent with his wanting to *A* and indeed with his *A*-ing because (i) he wants something, for instance to fulfill his obligation to Smith, and (ii) he believes his *A*-ing to be necessary for doing that.

Granted, internalists have characteristically denied that there generally need be moral wants of this sort involved in acting on a judgment of one's obligation. But I believe that this is mainly because they are thinking of wants as desires, or at least as intrinsic or in some way self-interested. They are perhaps above all denying psychological egoism. This point is often overlooked, and its importance is seldom noticed. It helps to explain, for instance, why moral and not aesthetic judgments are the sorts of normative judgments internalists use in arguing against the ubiquity of wanting in our motivation. But if wanting is understood as I have suggested, then internalism as just described is consistent with the sort of pervasive motivational role which this paper attributes to wanting.

Indeed, the conception of wanting I have suggested may well be capable of *explaining* internalism. For perhaps we are at least normally so structured that our judging that we ought *on balance* to *A* produces appropriate wants in us whose strength in motivating us to *A* is sufficient to enable the judgment that generates it to serve the internalist's explanatory purposes. This would not imply that we actually *A*; for even motivation sufficient to explain our *A*-ing if we should *A* can be outweighed by stronger incompatible wants. Now it may be objected that if wanting *is* implied by such judgments, the notion is surely trivial, in the sense that to say S wants to *A* is to say nothing more than that he is motivated or inclined to *A*. I grant that the sort of want implied here need not be a *desire*, nor even intrinsic. It is true, then, that in affirming the implication one is saying less than one might – and far less than the psychological egoist would. But I cannot see any good reason to conclude that the attribution of wanting here is trivial. The relevant wants can have all the properties of wanting, broadly conceived, in virtue of which a nontrivial account of the concept is available: the connection with actions, via beliefs; the tendency to influence discourse, fantasy, and feelings; and other properties. [10]

This discussion presupposes that the internalist thesis stated above is contingent. If it is taken to be necessary, then it seems mistaken. As I have argued elsewhere (Audi, 1979), there is very good reason to think that the criteria for holding the appropriate judgment can be satisfied without S's having the motivation required by the internalist thesis in question. It is not contingent, I grant, that if S judges (with some minimal degree of rationality) that on balance he ought to *A*, then he has some *reason to A*; but the notion of a reason operative here is surely normative rather than motivational. These kinds of reasons often go together in a way that encourages their assimilation, yet they are surely quite different. One might of course retreat to a weaker motivational internalism on which the relevant overall judgments entail only *some* motivation to act accordingly. But is it really true that one cannot be sufficiently abnormal to judge that one ought on balance to *A*, yet lack motivation to act accordingly? Such dissociation between cognition and motivation would bespeak impaired agency, but it is not obviously impossible. If it should be impossible, doubtless the reasons for that, such as that judging is intrinsically a practical attitude, would imply that wanting is embodied in (or constitutes) the motivation carried by the ought-judgment.

If this last point seems to imply that motivation is just being assumed to be equivalent to wanting, one might recall the examples of Section 1. In such contexts as "What do you want?" asked of someone whose purpose or concern or project (or the like) is unclear, it appears that "want" simply does have that breadth and applies to any motivation one might appeal to in answering. (It would not apply to just anything one might *mention* in answering; for that would include mere facts, as where a friend, rummaging for an old newspaper on one's desk as he leaves one's office, says that it is about to start raining.) I have been assuming that "want" has this motivational breadth; I have not assumed that nothing else *can* incline one to act, or explain why one has acted when one has (intentionally) done so. It surely appears, however, that the factors we take to be motivating in this sense are such that they are either a kind of wanting or may be plausibly conceived as playing their motivating role by virtue of producing, or bearing some other appropriate relation to, one or more wants.

5. WANTING AS THE BASIC MOTIVATIONAL NOTION

So far, I have maintained that the notion of wanting is fundamental in the concept of action. My main reason for saying this has been roughly that actions must have a certain intimate connection with wanting (this is often, though not necessarily, through intending). Is there any other motivational notion which is fundamental in this way? I shall not try to show by a general argument that there is not, but it is instructive to consider some representative candidates for such a role. The prime candidate is surely intending, which has now been explored in some detail. Let us consider a few others.

It has already been suggested that hoping implies wanting, and it seems unlikely that there need be any other motivational element in it: if S A's in the hope of realizing x, he surely does so because he wants to realize x, and there need be no further motivational element involved. It is important to note here that a hope may develop into an intention as one becomes optimistic about success: if I hope to please Jones (by A-ing) and come to believe that I definitely will please her, I now intend to please her. No change in motivation need occur; and if wanting is the motivational component in hoping, it is also the motivational component in the resultant intention. Since just about any kind of intention could conceivably arise in this way, the fact that this transition is possible by mere change of belief confirms that wanting is a constituent in intending. That hoping is, in addition, apparently explicable in terms of suitable wants and beliefs also confirms the importance of both wanting and believing as major building blocks in the philosophy of mind.

Consider some other motivational notions, say, aims, goals, and purposes. That these entail wanting can be plausibly argued on the basis of the sorts of points made above. Might they still involve some distinct motivational elements? The likeliest candidate would be moral or other evaluative motivation, say, a moral purpose; and we have noted how moral motivation can be associated with appropriate wants without being tainted by desire or self-interest. Still, one may wonder why we have so many motivational terms if there is only one fundamental motivational notion. The beginning of an answer is that wants are so complex and so variable in kind, strength, and content, that we gain much in expressive power by using terms which restrict the sort of want in question. Note, too, that while I am suggesting that wanting is the motivational notion embodied in the concepts of aim, goal, and purpose, I am not suggesting that no *non*motivational notions are implied. Perhaps a purpose entails the presence of certain beliefs, or an aim a bit of forethought.

Another case we should consider is that of a plan. On Goldman's view, it appears that plans *are* composed basically of wants and beliefs (Goldman, 1970, pp. 56-63). This is quite plausible, particularly if intending, which is arguably a constituent in planning, is explicable in terms of wanting and believing.[11] Might there be a distinct motivational element in plans or other "pro attitudes"? But if "pro attitude" is not a technical term to cover wants, intentions, aims, and the like — the sorts of items we have been discussing — then I doubt that it will lead us to any motivational concept not analyzable in terms of wanting. For one thing, attitudes, as we ordinarily understand them, seem to be analyzable in terms of wanting, believing, and affective elements whose motivational components appear to be one or another kind of want.[12] An attitude of resentment, for instance, may certainly motivate; but there is no good reason to think it does so other than by virtue of a want, perhaps one which may also be called a desire. For example, S may want (or have a desire) to punish the person in question.

Other examples could be considered, and there are undoubtedly objections that must be met before we should conclude that wanting is the basic motivational notion. But enough has been said to indicate along what lines further support for that view may be found. Here I would only add that I am of course not denying that other propositional attitudes can be *cited* in answering questions such as "What motivated S to A?," most notably beliefs. But so can such facts as that it is about to rain. Indeed, beliefs play an essential guiding role in action and are as important as wants for understanding intentional action. It is to be expected, then, that they should be citable in answering questions about motivation: not only are they crucial themselves; they also indicate, given a suitable context, *what* want is the motivating element. If one thinks it is arbitrary not to consider beliefs (and other cognitive attitudes) as motivators, I would not argue the point. My thesis could then be put as the view that wants are the basic noncognitive motivational elements.

6. WANTS AS ELEMENTS IN PRACTICAL
REASONING

Practical reasoning is often thought to be important in motivating and producing intentional action, and some philosophers have held or implied the strong view that all intentional actions arise from practical reasoning.[13] Whether or not the strong view is correct, practical reasoning is certainly important in the genesis of action, and we would do well to consider how wanting may figure in such reasoning.

From Aristotle onward, paradigms of practical reasoning have been cases of reasonings that are undertaken in order to determine what to do and are composed essentially of a major premise expressing a want for something, a minor premise expressing a belief about how one might get it, and a conclusion favoring the action specified in the latter premise. There has been diversity in the conception of all three elements, however, particularly the conclusion. I cannot here discuss practical reasoning at length (and have provided a detailed account of it in Audi, 1982); but it is possible to indicate quite briefly how wanting may be understood in relation to the major premise.

To begin with a negative point, certainly neither the term "want" nor any translation of it need occur in a linguistic expression of the major premise. S may, in affirming that premise, express an intention of his or a goal or aim, or indeed an obligation, for instance that he must keep his promise to Smith. But if we are to understand how practical reasoning motivates, and provides a basis for explaining, action, we surely have grounds for conceiving the major premise as expressing a want of some sort. Given how many concepts have wanting as a constituent, however, this is not unduly restrictive. Indeed, no motivational concept need figure explicitly in S's thinking; he may, for instance, say to himself: "It's raining cats and dogs; I can stay dry by taking a long route under the eaves; so I'll just take the time to do that." But clearly we conceive this as practical reasoning only if we think of the major premise as expressing, in the context, S's wanting to avoid getting rained on. For if the premise does not express any such want, why should S's concluding as he does motivate his taking the long route? And if he does take it, how would the practical reasoning provide a basis for explaining his doing so?

The point that, in the relevant context, the major premise expresses a want suggests the importance of the notion of a want on balance. Suppose S does not want on balance to avoid getting rained on, because he wants more to save the time he would lose by staying dry. We would then *not* expect him to walk along the eaves; and if he did, his saying that he did so in order to avoid getting rained on would not normally explain his action: we would indeed doubt that it could be true, given that he wanted more to save the time, and believed that required taking a shorter route. We would have to consider his reasoning to be, say, *exploratory*; he is not, at the time, motivationally committed to realizing the goal expressed in his major premise, viz., avoiding getting rained on, but is figuring out (perhaps wistfully) how he could do so. What we might expect here is further reasoning to figure out how to save time while getting minimally wet.

This sort of case corresponds to *one* kind of weakness of will, except that in that case S is presumably not doing exploratory reasoning, and likely does not believe that the goal expressed in his major premise is outweighed by a stronger incompatible want. Suppose that S had reasoned from his goal (to be on time), and from his belief that he must race across the quadrangle in the rain to meet that goal, to the conclusion that he must race across. Now imagine that as he looks at the pouring rain he shudders and ashamedly goes under the eaves. Here one want prevails over another, over the one aligned with judgment. It is not that the judgment has no motivational force; its force is simply derivative from the want it produces, which, though it may be very strong, is outweighed by an incompatible one.

Thus, a moderate internalist of the sort described above can countenance weakness of will if it is conceived as involving a conflict of wants in which the want aligned with one's judgment is outweighed. My view opposes only a strong internalism of a kind requiring that one's best judgment entails preponderant motivation and hence that intentional action cannot go against such judgment. Such internalism seems mistaken (as argued in Audi, 1979). Moreover, whatever internalist principles we use, if we do not construe them as deriving their action-explaining power from wanting, we cannot give as simple an account of the explanation of action, since we must countenance at least two ultimately different kinds of motivation. Notice that the motivational unification I propose does not preclude our recognizing that judgments, including moral judgments, may produce, and yield an explanation of, certain wants, such as wanting to keep a promise. Thus, cognitive and even moral elements can have explanatory power on the view taken here. It is only their power to explain actions independently of wanting which is being denied.

The concept of wanting, then, is immensely important in the philosophy of mind. It is indispensable in understanding intending. Neither the nature of intentional actions nor the logic of commonsense explanations of such actions can be adequately explicated without appeal to the concept of wanting. The relation between judgment and action can be best understood in the light of an adequate account of wanting; and when this relation is understood in that light, we can preserve the insights of the most plausible forms of internalism. Other motivational concepts, including hopes, plans, purposes, aims, and of course desires, seem explicable in terms of various kinds and combinations of wants, taken together with appropriate beliefs. Practical reasoning and weakness of will can be clarified by appeal to the notion of wanting, and seem to be largely inexplicable without at least tacitly invoking it. And by conceiving the concept of wanting as the most basic motivational notion, and drawing the appropriate connections with believing, we can develop a unified theory of the nature and explanation of human action.[14]

NOTES

1. Audi (1973b), p. 395. I have altered the variables in this formulation. In some ways "competing" is preferable to "incompatible"; but I use the latter here because incompatible wants *need* not compete, as where one of them is temporarily forgotten and S proceeds to *A* as if he were losing nothing he wants in doing so.

2. Audi (1973b), p. 399. For discussion of some of the issues here, see Audi (1980b), pp. 235-238. For supporting discussion of the breadth of wanting, see Davis (1984a).

3. We must individuate wants finely; wanting to overcome an obstacle to *A*-ing is not wanting to *A*, though it may naturally lead to *expressing* the latter want.

4. I have developed such an account in Audi (1973a), and answered some significant objections to it in Audi (1980b).

5. McCann (forthcoming), p. 6. I assume that one *can* have intentions one believes are not jointly satisfiable, though I doubt this happens except where one belief is temporarily forgotten. If one cannot, the intentions are even more like wants on balance; and that the latter are constituents in intentions can explain *why* one cannot, since, apart from temporary forgetting, intending implies wanting on balance.

6. For discussion of the kind of commitment implicit in intending (and a view of the matter quite different from mine), see Robins (1984).

7. See Bratman (forthcoming), and Brand (1984), esp. chaps. 1 and 8.

8. See Donagan (1981-82). In answering the question "In virtue of what is a piece of behavior or a mental process in an agent an action?" he says: "In virtue of being caused by that agent's intending a proposition which the occurrence of that piece of behavior or mental process makes true, provided that it depends on what the agent intends whether that proposition be made true or not" (p. 44).

9. See Hare (1963), esp. pp. 82-83, and Davidson (1970, 1980). Davidson says that "someone who says honestly 'It is desirable that I stop smoking' has some pro attitude toward his stopping smoking. He feels some inclination to do it; in fact he will do it if nothing stands in the way, he knows how, and he has no contrary values or desires" (Davidson, 1980, p. 86). For different versions of internalism, see Frankena (1958), esp. pp. 41, 58-59, and Darwall (1983), pp. 124-129. The most relevant internalist views are critically assessed in Audi (1979). For some assessment of Davidson's internalism (as well as points about wanting that are relevant to this paper), see Thalberg (1986).

10. For a variety of reasons to hold this, see Audi (1973a).

11. To be sure, if by "plan" we mean the content of the relevant attitude and not the psychological attitude S has in *having* a plan, then plans may be embodied in the content of (sufficiently complex) intendings. But at least normally the having of a plan entails the having of at least one intention.

12. For an account of attitudes which supports this view, see Audi (1972).

13. Davidson (1970) seems to hold this. For critical assessment of the view and relevant references, see Audi (1982).

14. This paper has benefited from comments by Robert M. Gordon, Hugh J. McCann, and Alfred R. Mele, and from discussions during the Institute on Human Action which I directed at the University of Nebraska in the summer of 1984.

For as to have no Desire is to be dead,
so to have weak Passions is Dulnesse.

—Thomas Hobbes

The Ambiguous Limits of Desire

Annette C. Baier

Abstract. Hobbes, Descartes, and Hume all see desire as essentially concerned with what the desirer does not yet "have," while love can be directed at what the lover "has." Their views are examined to see what might be plausibly claimed about the relations between desires and emotions or passions such as love. The views of these philosophers are invoked to resist any attempts to make desire, along with belief, *the* central psychical phenomena, or to reduce passions to them. The paper tries to put desire in its place.

My concern in this paper will be the connection between desire and passion, the extinction of desire and the dullness of a life lacking strong passions, as this has been understood by some of our philosophical predecessors. I turn to them, to Hobbes, Descartes, Hume, not merely for the intrinsic interest of what they have to say about desire and about human passions, but also for the contrast their treatment of these topics provides to some contemporary approaches which tend to reduce other passions to desire, and to see the main importance of the passions to be their role in motivating intentional action. But desires and other passions are important not just for their role in producing and explaining actions, but also because the particular form and order they take help to constitute the personality and the character a person has, and, along with beliefs, intentions, pleasures, pains, actions, and reactions, they are the very stuff of a person's life-history. We cite them to explain not merely our intentional actions, but our involuntary reactions, our self-deceits, psychosomatic illnesses, and intermittent glows of well-being. To understand a particular passion we have to consider it in its typical relation to other passions, to pleasures and pains, to expressive reactions as well as to intentional actions, and to thought processes both guided and free — to arguments, dreams, and fantasies, to self-deceptive thoughts, and to displays of strength or weakness of the will, to psychosomatic distress, and to *joie de vivre.*

In our complex mental geography, desire does have a particularly close relation to active goal-directed states like trying, intending, willing, and to other desire-related influences on the will such as preferring, wishing, longing, wanting, itching, and to close relatives of intending such as tending, inclining, and finding oneself drawn toward something. But it is also closely linked to reactive states, to pleasure, pain, enjoyment, discontent, gratitude, and anger. Its close relation to intention and action and to passionate reaction should not, however, be mistaken for a relation of reducibility, of them to it or it to them. Contemporary philosophers have not, as far as I am aware, shown any inclination to reduce desire to some other mental state or states, but they have sometimes over-assimilated other passions to desire. Hobbes says, "Nor can a man any more live whose desires are at an end than he whose Senses and Imaginations are at a stand" (*Leviathan* [11]).[1] As empiricists have tried to derive all thought from the material of sense and its reassembly in imagination, so some have taken desire to play a parallel role in generating other passions out of its own frustration, satisfaction, or delayed gratification. But why should we think that all pleasure must be heralded by desire for it or followed by desire for more of it? Is it our ability to remember and anticipate which is thought to ensure that all response to a perceived good will take the form of desire, as belief or grasping is our response to a perceived truth? But desiring is much more like seeking for a good than like finding it, and so is more like raising questions or entertaining hypotheses than it is like finding true answers or confirming hypotheses. And as some truths are realized or brought home to us without prior search for them, so some joy comes untouched by the sticky fingers of prior desire.

The concepts of believing and desiring have been recent philosophers' favorites, among mental states, in part because it has been thought that both of these always figure in the explanation of human action, and action is thought to be where the philosophical action is, or should be. Desires, along with beliefs about how to satisfy them, or, alternatively, beliefs about how it is best to act, along with the desire to act that way, seem natural partners as co-parents of intentional action. That beliefs, implicit or explicit, are involved in the causal ancestry of our actions seems undeniable, and equally undeniable is it that some other more dynamic element is involved — some *conatus*, will, inclination, or desire. I shall look at the views of Hobbes, Descartes, Hume, and others concerning the relation of desires to other apparently dynamic determinants of action such as love and despair, and concerning their relation to less energizing, more reactive passions such as joy and sadness.

One question about the scope of desire and its objects is a very old one, raised by Plato in *Symposium*, *Phaedrus*, and *Philebus* — can one desire that with which one is already united? Of course one can intend to remain united to something or someone one finds good, but is that intention desire-caused? And is the pleasure of being so united the pleasure of desire satisfaction? In *Philebus* Plato's Socrates distinguishes between those "mixed" pleasures, satisfactions of desires in which the pain of not having and the anticipation of having are mixed, and "pure" pleasures not heralded by the combined discomfort and excitement of unsatisfied desires, in which there is always a "mixture of bitter and sweet." Instances he gives of "pure" pleasures include those of hearing, presumably out of the blue, a single clear, smooth, beautiful note — say, a birdsong. The intentional listening to such a song, for as long as it lasts, will involve pleasure but not necessarily desire. Nor, even when one hopes for a repetition of such pleasures, and arranges one's life to make that likely — say, by taking one's vacations in forest areas or near bird sanctuaries — does that mean that one will be in a state of unsatisfied desire until one is vouchsafed the next birdsong. One can take steps to make certain sorts of pleasure come one's way without being in a state of desire for those pleasures. The eager anticipation with which an audience awaits the first notes of a musical performance is not properly called desire to hear, if desiring implies impatient discontent with the way things are. For to be about to hear good musicians play a great quartet is a blessed state to be in, not one of impatience for delayed consummatory ecstasies. When we are confident that joy is in store for us, as much as when we are surprised by joy, talk of desire seems out of place. The Goethean impulse to say "Stay, sweet moment, stay . . ." is not one expressive of unsatisfied desire, but rather of appreciation. What one feels as the final notes of a sensitively played Beethoven quartet sound out is not discontent that it was not longer, nor wish for its instant repetition, but simply "Amen" — or "so let it be, until the next performance." The futile wish, if there is one, is to remain within the finite period of music-redeemed time that is ending, not to prolong that time.

I am aligning myself with Descartes and Hume, against Plato, Spinoza, and maybe Hobbes, in saying that one can enjoy what one has not desired and what one may not ever desire. To these philosophers I now turn. There are, of course, translation difficulties which arise, and it is possible that there is no one cross-cultural and cross-language concept of "desire" about whose centrality as a mental phenomenon philosophers have disagreed. Is Spinoza's *conatus* more like Descartes's *volunté* than like his *désir*? Is Hobbes's and Hume's *will*, the last appetite in deliberation, the transition to new action, the same concept as that *voluntas* and *volunté* which Descartes finds so pervasive, at work whenever we assent to $2 + 2 = 4$ as much as whenever we decide how to act, or endorse a value judgment? How can we tell a substantive disagreement from a terminological difference? In the end, we may not be able to. We may just have to grasp the proposed network of concepts a thinker offers us, see what sort of contrasts and emphases it enables us to make, compare that with alternatives, and judge which seems to enable us to say more interesting true things about our mental life. First I will look at Hobbes's treatment of desire and other passions.

For Hobbes, as later for Hume, desires and other lively passions are the masters which all our thought serves. "For the thoughts, are to the Desires as Scouts and Spies, to range abroad, and find the way to the Things Desired: all Stedinesse of the mind's motion and all quicknesse of the same, proceeding from thence" (*Leviathan* [8]). Desire is for Hobbes the very life force of the mind. What of love, and the other passions whose weakness amounts not to death but maybe to a fate worse than death, namely, dullness? "That which men Desire they are also sayd to Love: and to Hate those things for which they have Aversion. So that Desire, and Love, are the same thing; save that by Desire, we always signify the Absence of the Object; by Love, most commonly the Presence of the same" (*Leviathan* [6]). Is desire the same thing as love? How can it be if desire conceptually requires the absence of its object while love conceptually allows or prefers the presence of what is loved? Hobbes seems to need a more generic notion, something like that of a "pro-attitude," to signify what is common between desire for what one does not yet have, or have present, and love of what one has, and has present. But that recent coinage is warranted only if there is indeed some one attitude of mind, or component of one, which is common to desiring what one has not yet got and to appreciating what is securely in one's possession. Is there? There may indeed be the commitment to some judgment of the form "This appears good," which the desirer and the lover each make of what each desires or loves. But if our interest is in affective and motivational states, this common element may not mean very much. To desire or long for what one has not yet got feels different from exulting in what one has, and what these feelings lead one to do may also be very different — desire leads to striving to get, while usually love leads to less frantic purposive activities, ones aimed at conservation, growth, perpetuation, full expression. The only common element seems a negative one — the absence of what Hobbes calls a "fromward" motion, away from the object of the mental attitude.

Hobbes's most basic concept is that of "endeavor," or the small beginnings of voluntary motion, which may be toward or away from the cause of that motion. Desire and love are "toward," aversion and hatred "fromward," while what he calls "contempt" is indifference. (See *Leviathan* [6].) Desire taken in its strict sense for Hobbes, then, is endeavor toward an absent cause of that endeavor. If the absence in question is, as it usually is, due to the futurity (and possible uncertainty) of the desired event, then Hobbes is faced with the problem of how an absent and future thing or event can cause any motion in the present—he seems stuck, as much as any teleologist, with the particularly intractable form that the problem of action at a distance takes when the distance in question is distance in the future. Hobbes can get over this problem by letting the thought or imagining of the future event stand in as cause of the endeavor, and letting that thought have some unproblematic cause, such as revived memory of experienced things or events of that sort, along with predictions made by one's more calculative thoughts once they have spied out one's likely future. At any rate I put aside the action at a distance problems which might arise if we took seriously both Hobbes's claim that desire is for the absent, and his claim that it is for that which itself causes the desire. I shall stick with the question of what the relation is between desiring what is absent or unpossessed, and loving what is present and possessed.

Poets of Hobbes's century delighted in the near paradox of the temporal distance between desire and its satisfaction. "Desire attain'd is not desire, but is the cinders of the fire," wrote Sir Walter Raleigh, and John Wilmot, Earl of Rochester, exploits the "absence" of past and future into a glorification of present enjoyment:

1
All my past Life is mine no more,
The flying hours are gone:
Like transitory Dreams giv'n o're,
Whose Images are kept in store,
By Memory alone.

2
The Time that is to come is not,
How can it then be mine?
The present Moment's all my Lot,
And that, as fast as it is got,
Phyllis, is only thine.

3
Then talk not of Inconstancy,
False Hearts, and broken Vows;
If I, by Miracle, can be
This live-long minute true to thee,
'Tis all that Heaven allows.

"Love and Life: A Song"

The present moment is not the primary intentional object of current desire, any more than it is of current memory, or of currently made vows, but it can be indirectly included in all of these—one can remember the forebodings one had about this current occasion, one can now vow never to forget it, and one can desire that keeping that vow not prove too difficult. The present moment can be a proper object of intention, and of pleasure or pain, although neither of them is restricted to it—one's intentions often are to complete what one has already begun, so they span past, present, and future, and what pains one may be the remembered past or the predicted future wounds, not only those being inflicted in the present. If we see desire as, like intention, anchored in the present yet transcending it, then we can dissent from Raleigh's conclusion. Desire attained can be the glowing and possibly rekindling embers, not just the cinders, of the fire, and the lineaments of satisfied desire need not be a death mask. Even if there are some sorts of desire, for some sorts of person, that really are killed by being satisfied,[2] even when no false expectation was involved, there is no conceptual necessity that desire not overlap in time with satisfaction of its own identical ancestor desires. The killing of desire by its own satisfaction should be seen as a pathological, not a normal, phenomenon. Is Hobbesian desire killed by its own satisfaction?

Hobbesian desire is necessarily for what is absent from one, or at least from one's current possessive grasp. What would satisfy the desire is the becoming present, grasped by one, of that currently absent good. Satisfaction of desire replaces "absence of the object" with its presence, and so, presumably, terminates that desire, which will have as its successor love of what *was* desired and is now possessed, or a new desire for some other good (possibly for more of what one has just got), or both. The "felicity" at which we aim, Hobbes says, is a matter of the "continuall progresse" of desire from one object to another, "the attaining of the former being still but the way to the latter" (*Leviathan* [11]). Does this claim imply that the only reason we *wanted* the former object was because it was the way to the latter? Or is it merely that in fact the attaining of one desire is immediately followed by a new desire for something else (or some further quantity of the good we have just got)?

Hobbes's words do not make clear whether the intentional object of our desire is "power after power," or whether each felt desire has a limited object, but one which, once got, propagates a new similar successor desire. If the former were the case, then there would be no cases of satisfied Hobbesian desire, but Hobbes does want to speak of our experience of "attainment," so presumably what he means is that we set ourselves a succession of individually attainable goals and are kept "alive" by our sometimes satisfiable desires, each of which generates a new not-yet-satisfied successor desire. Most of us will realize that the satisfaction of one desire is but the way to a new unsatisfied desire, but this knowledge need not transform our desires into necessarily unsatisfiable desires for an endless succession of objects as such. Hobbesian desire is not necessarily directed on "power after power," as its intentional object, but can be directed first on one attainable power, then transferred to another. Were it directed on endless power, then it would be a hopeless desire, and known as such to a minimally intelligent person, so accompanied by despair or at least by resignation to the futility of keeping such a desire alive (and of being kept alive by such a desire).

Hobbes does not portray us as resigned to the frustration of our impossible desires, nor as prone to that *ennui* or nausea which can come from the satisfaction of our "lower" and more easily attainable desires. Such power as a Hobbesian person attains need not, it seems, turn to ashes once possessed, but can continue to be valued. Love of attained power can coexist with desire for more or different sorts of power. Is it the fact that Hobbes emphasizes power, not pleasure, as the good we have in view in most of our endeavors, which explains why he is not as preoccupied as his poet contemporaries with the perversity of some desire, its death by its own satisfaction? Are the "higher" desires, those more removed from their hedonic base, robuster, more satisfaction-tolerant, than their "lower" relatives? Those who have set their hearts on power rather than sensory pleasure have, sometimes, in the end sickened of it, but their nausea was longer in coming than that of the typical sensualist.

Hobbes's desire-enlivened man knows no pure contented rest, even when he appreciates rather than is sickened by the goods he has so far attained. His appreciation of what he has got will always be made piquant by not-yet-satisfied desire for more or for other goods. The instability of the Hobbesian desirer stems neither from the impossible intentional object of his desire nor from his failure to appreciate desired goods once they are possessed, but rather from the regeneration of his desires from their ancestors' satisfaction. Hobbes's vagabond contemporary Richard Flecknoe is quoted by Rose Macauley as uncertain whether his insatiate desire for world travel was due to the fact that "the more one sees of it the less he is satisfied, or that it satisfies so much that one has still a desire of seeing more"[3]. One explanation of the insatiability of a desire is the intensity of the experienced enjoyment of its evanescent but memorable partial satisfaction. So, perhaps, with the Hobbesian's power. It may be such a heady intoxicant that it constantly regenerates itself, or at least regenerates itself as long as the power-desirer's "liver" can take this mode of enlivenment. His liver may hold out longer than the sensualist's "stomach" for his more immediate satisfactions. Some goods are such that we spit them out after the tasting, some are, after a slightly longer ingestion, vomited out, while the higher pleasures such as power and virtue irritate only more remote and slower-reacting parts of us, so take longer to stimulate rejection mechanisms. The periodicity of desire and postsatisfaction aversion seems different with different levels of goods, and it seems to be a mark of the higher goods that it takes us longer to sicken of them. Once sickened, however, it may be harder than with the lower goods to revive the desire for them. Or are there spiritual equivalents of peacocks' feathers, to empty the soul ready for the revival of higher desires? At any rate Hobbes is not the person to tell us about them, nor even to envisage a possible role for them. Fear and insecurity are tonic enough to protect the Hobbesian soul from *ennui* or apathy—it needs no artificial stimulants nor appetite revivers.

Hobbes's treatment of human desire is instructive because it alerts us to the necessary reference to the (possibly quite close) *future* involved in desire, to the fairly wide scope of desire compatible with that restriction. Desire is for future improvement of our situation. This reference to future goods, or strictly to a better future, can become reflexive. Desire can be for the satisfaction of future desires. Desire is for a change from the present state to a better state, and its reference to the present in relation to the future becomes reflexive when what we desire is power, assurance that the way of future desire satisfaction is cleared of obstacles. The future-orientation of desire and the possible reflexive versions of desire arising out of that, are made plain by Hobbes's account of our desires. His account also raises in an instructive fashion the question of what states of mind can coexist with the satisfaction of desire, and what the relation is of desire to love. Hobbes's thesis (with which, as we shall shortly see, Descartes is in agreement) that desire implies the absence of its object and is therefore forward-looking, looking toward its future presence, while love, since it typically has or has had its object present, can enjoy the present or be gratified with the past, is not a thesis which we would be led to accept by reading contemporary discussions.

What Thomas Nagel (1979, chap. 4) has said about desire and what Harry Frankfurt (1982) and I myself (Baier, 1982) have said about caring and loving suggest, indeed, the opposite—that it is desire which is shortsighted and preoccupied with the present, while love is always future envisaging, and takes a longer view. Is it that desire is concerned with the immediate or near future, to the time of its own satisfaction, while love looks further, both before and after the immediate future? Or is it that love is not, like desire, satisfaction-oriented, and so the question "Satisfied or frustrated?" does not so automatically arise? We speak of happy and unhappy loves, and, with some sorts of nonerotic love, the characterization "frustrated" or "unsatisfied" scarcely makes sense. What would count as frustrated parental love, or as frustrated love of a friend? Particular love-based desires to do particular sorts of good to the loved child or friend, or to have their company, can of course be satisfied or unsatisfied, but the love itself seems to admit of different sorts of success and failure.

More light on this may come from looking at what Descartes says, since he makes love the central psychic phenomenon in the life of the heart. For desire, a less central phenomenon, he sees restrictions similar to those Hobbes discerned. "It is evident that [desire] ever regards the future" [57].[4] Hence "we desire to acquire a good which we do not yet have, or avoid an evil which we judge may occur; but also when we only anticipate the conservation of a good or absence of an evil, which is as far as this passion may extend..." [57]. The more pervasive and more basic phenomena for Descartes are love and hatred, not desire and aversion. Desire and aversion (which is treated as desire with a negative object) are the forms love and hatred take when we consider our *future* relation to the loved or hated thing or person, and cannot be involved at all as long as our attention is restricted to our present or past state. Of course this essentially future-oriented character of Cartesian desire may not, any more than did Hobbesian desire, involve a very great actual restriction if our concerns always do tend to include the future as well as the present, and if the future is usually uncertain.

Desire, for Descartes, is one of six primitive passions—wonder, love, hatred, desire, joy, and sadness. Desire is officially defined as "an agitation of the soul caused by the spirits which dispose it to wish for the future things which it represents as agreeable" [86]. What should be noted here is that both "wishing" and "the agreeable" are involved in this definition, as desiring is not in theirs. The agreeable or delightful is that which we find to give us one of the other six primitive passions, namely, joy. "Joy is an agreeable emotion of the soul in which consists the enjoyment that the soul possesses in the good which the impressions of the brain represent to it as its own" [91]. That is the "passion" of joy, and there is also a more active sort of joy "that is purely intellectual and which comes to the soul by the action of the soul alone." Possession of knowledge or of the exercised capacity for clear and distinct perception will give the Cartesian soul this active joy in a present good.

At the successful end of the *Third Meditation*, when the Natural Light had revealed its source to him, Descartes spoke eloquently of this "greatest satisfaction of which we are capable in this life," and paused in order to "consider, and admire, and adore, the beauty of this light so resplendent." No desire contaminated this enjoyment—no worries about possible darkness in the future. Total confidence that the light would remain as long as he remained seems to block any "wish" that it remain—if one is certain of continued possession of a good, one does not waste one's mental energies in "desiring" that one keep it. Only the uncertain can be the object of Cartesian desire. Of course in most respects the future is uncertain, so there is plenty of room for desire in future-concerned souls, but the Cartesian meditator achieved in the *Third Meditation* what is claimed to be his highest certainty, that "from the fact alone that this idea [of a God, a complete and independent being] is found in me, or that I who possess this idea exist, I conclude so certainly that God exists, and that my existence depends entirely on Him in every moment of my life—that I do not think the human mind is capable of knowing anything with more evidence and certitude" (*Fourth Meditation*, par. 1). The God who "concurs" with the Cartesian soul in its willing assent to, and love of, the objects it distinctly grasps gives it an assurance that seems to banish the anxious agitation of desire.

Some religious thinkers have spoken of the relation between the human soul and God as "desire" for a not-yet-completed union. Descartes, with his unorthodox version of God and of the human soul, seems to see the "enjoyment of God" as completed here and now, not ahead in an afterlife. As love between mortal or fickle persons tends to degenerate into desire when accompanied by the ability to think about the future and worry about the lack of assurance of love's continuation, so desire when directed upon an eternal being will be transformed into love once there is certainty that one is united with that being. Love can coexist with its own consummation without having to shift its focus into the future in order to do so. It need not be ahead of itself, as desire must be, but can enjoy the present, or be backward looking, or look at long stretches of time which span past, present, and future. When it does include thought of the future, that may lead to desire for assurance of continuation, but may also bring trust in the faithfulness of the loved one, and resignation to or acceptance of the mortality of human lovers, so that there will be little room for unsatisfied desires. Those of course are theoretical possibilities for human love—actual cases are usually less calm and confident, more disturbed by uncertainties, discontents, impatience, jealousies, and various frustrations, and love can be wholly unreciprocated. The usual human phenomenon is either desire without love, or love subject to occasional agitations from unsatisfied desires for a whole range of love-related things, from assurance of returned love to various particular expressions of love, or for these at times when they are not forthcoming. But in theory love could be unaccompanied by any unsatisfied desires, and so by any desires at all, if desire must, to be desire, begin by being unsatisfied. Only unhappy loves will be accompanied by at some time unsatisfied desires.

Love, according to Descartes, is the will to unite oneself with agreeable objects, "so that we imagine a whole of which we conceive ourselves as only constituting one part" [80]. The will that love involves is distinguished from desire: "By the word will I do not here intend to talk of desire, which is a passion apart, and one which relates to the future, but of the consent by which we consider ourselves from this time forward as united with what we love" [80]. Will or consent can be free, as it is when guided only by purely mental judgments of what is good, or less free, when what induces the will's consent is the "animal spirits" in the brain and pineal gland. Love is a passion of the soul when the mind is passive, acted on by the body, but it is an action of the soul when its consent to union with the object of love is induced by its own clear and distinct judgment or estimation.

The relation between Cartesian will *(volunté)* and Cartesian desire *(désir)* is not made easy to grasp in the Haldane and Ross translation, since they sometimes translate *volunté* as "desire." Hence they have Descartes saying in the first part of *The Passions of the Soul* [18], headed "Of the Will," that our *desires* are actions of the soul, where the same word *"volunté"* is used as in the title, there correctly translated as "will." Their apparent uneasiness with the plural "willings" led them to translate *"voluntés"* as "desires," which makes Descartes come out as wildly inconsistent, first claiming that desires are *actions* of the soul, then later, in the second part, defining desire as one special case of a *passion*. This unfortunate translation encourages that vacillation between a wide and a narrow sense of desire which has bedeviled the philosophical discussion of the topic. But whoever is guilty of that vacillation, Descartes is not. He is quite clear that willing or consenting is one thing, the prick of desire quite another. One can consent to some desires, or refuse them, since will can be directed on any other mental state, but desire is more restricted in its objects. One might have the meta-desire that one later consent to the satisfaction of some desire, but normally will is not involved in the objects of desire, as desire can and, for Descartes, should become the object of the will's ruling. Descartes does typically use *"désir"* for those willings which are directed on future goods, but he does not use it more widely than that. In these cases something, the felt desire, is a passion of the soul, if it involves the body, while the consent to the attempt to satisfy it is an action of the will. Hence desires in his strictest sense "dispose" the soul to willings, and so sometimes he broadens his usage to let it cover those willings which are positive responses to desires in the strict sense. But he does not broaden it to include *present*-directed willings.

Cartesian desires are always future-oriented, and disturb the soul and the body in ways Descartes describes at some length. Desire, he says, agitates the heart more violently than other passions, including love, and the subsequent increased flow of animal spirits to the brain and from there throughout the body "render[s] all the senses more acute, and all parts of the body more mobile" [101]. The agitation or restlessness of the person consumed with desire is quite different from the "gay and peaceful" concomitants of joy [104], and also from the concomitants of love: "I notice in love that when it occurs alone, that is when it is unaccompanied by any strong joy, desire, or sadness, the beating of the pulse is equal and much fuller and stronger than is usually the case, that we feel a gentle heat in the breast, and that the digestion of food is accompanied very quickly in the stomach. In this way the passion is very useful to health" [97]. Since Descartes believes that the point of all the passions is "their fortifying and perpetualizing in the soul thoughts which it is good it should preserve" [74], the gay, peaceful mental effects of joy, or the calm of steady love, are more "healthful" and "fortifying" to the soul than restless desire for ever new and uncertain futures.

The concept of desire we get from Descartes is of an agitating passion directed on possession of an insecure future good, or on insecure continued possession of a good we already possess. It involves a willing or wishing about how our future should be. It admits of some variety, since the goods we want to come to possess or continue to possess are various, and there are various modes of union with them that count as possession. There is curiosity, the desire for not-yet-possessed knowledge; there is the desire for glory, and for vengeance. Then there is a whole varied class of desires springing from delight in something which we can perceive by the senses before we "possess" it, and different modes of possession are aimed at for different such delightful things. "The beauty of flowers incites us only to look at them, and that of fruits to eat them. But the principal [delight] is that which proceeds from the perfections which we imagine in a person [who] we think may become another self; for with the difference of sex which nature has placed in men, as in the animals without reason, it has also placed certain impressions in the brain which bring it to pass that at a certain age, and in a certain time, they consider themselves defective, and as though they were but half of a whole, of which an individual of the other sex should be the other half" [90].

By addressing the question of what sort of *relation* between the desirer and the desired would satisfy the desire, Descartes in effect provides us with a way out of the puzzles which seemed to arise with

Hobbes's attempt to have the intentional object of love both a present cause of the passion, and an absent or future event. We do not have to choose between saying that what is desired is something or someone, possibly present with one, and saying that what one desires is a not-yet-actual event of somehow coming to "possess" that thing or person. The intentional object of desire must include reference to both the desire-inciting existent cause and the not-yet-actual fulfillment of the desire for possession.

Despite his somewhat sardonic quoted statement about sexual desire, where he seems to endorse Plato's theory in the *Symposium* of gender as the outcome of a splitting into two of an originally androgynous whole person, Descartes is in fact treating sexual desire, as so construed, as a model for the love of which desire as such is a special case, a case of unfulfilled and future-obsessed love. Or perhaps we could say that sexual desire, of all the forms of desire Descartes describes, approximates most closely to love as he defined it. It is unconsummated love, but at least its intentional object is that completeness by union which Descartes makes the *telos* of love, in which, whether it take the form of affection, friendship, or devotion, we always "consider ourselves as joined or united to the thing loved" [83].

Descartes indeed has implicitly a good explanation of the tendency of religious persons to describe their religious devotion to a divine person in sexual imagery. Both the love which is religious devotion and sexual desire concern a union of oneself with another, and although the former involves the soul's union and the soul's joy in union, not anything bodily, still "as soon as our understanding perceives that we possess some good thing, even although this good may be so different from all that pertains to body that it is not in the least capable of being imagined, imagination does not fail immediately to make some impression in the brain from which proceeds the movement of the spirits which excites the passion of joy" [91]. The soul's union evokes not just active intellectual joy, but the body-involving *passion* of joy, and even the Cartesian imagination cannot resist incarnating the cause of this joy in some bodily image. Sexual union is the natural symbol, or "typic" (as Kant called such incarnations when they involved a process in time), of the soul's union with God. Or, if you prefer, the concept of the soul's union with God is the spiritual shadow of sexual union with a loved person, "another self," especially when "we are always ready to abandon the lesser portion of the whole into which we both enter, in order to preserve the other portion," and see ourself as the lesser portion, so that "the thing loved is so much preferred to the self, that we do not fear death in order to preserve it" [83].

Love, not desire, is the passion which, for Descartes, is involved in all other passions, primitive or complex, since love is the time-neutral response to what is perceived as good, and so is source both of desire (when the good is future and uncertain) and of joy, when it is possessed in the present, and of that nostalgia Descartes called "regret," when it is past and gone. Desire is the outcome of impatience at delay in the satisfaction of love, or of dislocation of love from the present good on to a future good. Desire occurs when the lover and the loved are out of temporal phase; it is a premature response of the soul to a good it perceives as about to be actual.

To understand Cartesian desire, we must see it both as a temporally dislocated love, and as a special case of willing or consenting. It is consent to future possession of a perceived good. The basic concept is willing or consenting, and desire is the form it takes when what is consented to is future to the act of consent, and is a perceived good. Intention is the form consent takes to a good already within our grasp, and to a good willingly possessed both in the past and the present our response is "an internal satisfaction which is the sweetest of all the passions" [63], while, if our possession of it is not sustained from past to present, we feel "regret."

When we turn from Descartes to Spinoza, we find a sort of desire playing a more prominent role in the account of our mental life, indeed virtually taking over the part of Cartesian will. Desire is "appetite of which we are conscious" (*Ethics*, pt. 3, prop. 9n).[5] Since self-preservatory *conatus*, usually translated "appetite," is the dynamic essence of any finite thing, Spinoza can say, at the end of Part Three of the *Ethics:* "Desire is a man's very essence, insofar as it is determined by some specific state it is in, to act in some way" (Definition One). However, before imperialists for desire enlist Spinoza on their side, they should be aware of what Jonathan Bennett (1984, p. 222) calls the "dizzyingly abstract" character of this definition. Essence, and in particular the essence of mere "modes" such as we are, as well as determinism by previous states, and action, are all difficult notions to grasp in Spinoza, so the exact import of this definition of desire is not self-evident. I do not propose to try to translate it into more ordinary concepts, but simply note his recommendation that we try to convert all our "affects" or passive states into active ones, by achieving an unreciprocated desire-free "love of God," or union with the active universe, which would enable us to treat its inevitable activities as our own, so that we would not then be in the position of passive unwilling sufferers of what happens. Desire is central to his account of human bondage, but love without desire is what figures in his recipe for human freedom.

Hume, to whom I turn now, agrees with Descartes in making reference to the future necessary to desire, but he differs from him as regards the relation of desire to will. Where for Descartes a sort of will or consenting can be directed at past, present, or, as in desire, future, for Hume, as for Hobbes, will plays a much more restricted role, indeed it is as restricted to the present as desire is to the future. "The will has an influence only on present actions"[6]. Will's influence, of course, may be more restricted than its range of intentional object, but that, too, Hume restricts to the present and nearest future. "By the will I mean nothing but the internal impression we feel and are conscious of when we knowingly give rise to any new motion of our body, or new perception of our mind" (p. 399). Given his requirement of temporal continuity in a cause, this new motion or perception must be contiguous to or overlapping with the impression of willing. Will, being merely a consciousness of our own currently effective motives, has no great role to play in Hume's philosophy of mind. Hume here, as elsewhere, follows Spinoza. Whereas for Descartes free assent is the fundamental mental capacity, for Hume assent is always determined by felt motive or "impressed" sensory evidence, its apparent freedom in some cases being no more than one's consciousness of internal causes (of one's own passion and concurring beliefs) without any current consciousness of their external determinants. The best we can achieve in intention is more reflective assent — adding the input of careful consideration, and the testing of passions by turning them on themselves, to the decision-determining causal chains. But just how reflective we are or try to be will itself be the outcome of a causal story, one taking us eventually outside the assenter to the influences that shaped her or his habits of thought and feeling, that determined the strength or weakness of mind which is there to be displayed. So it is not surprising that Hume has no more reason to find willing ubiquitous in our mental life than he or Descartes has to find desire ubiquitous.

Desire gets almost as short a shrift with Hume as will. The influencing motives of the will for him are passions, not necessarily themselves desires, nor involving desires. Desire is the main topic of only one of the thirty-four sections of Book Two, entitled "On the Passions." It may be that I *"desire* any fruit as of an excellent relish" (my italics) when I act or am persuaded to refrain from acting (p. 417), but it may also be that I "prefer" the least uneasiness to an Indian or person wholly unknown to me to averting my total ruin (p. 416). Or my action may be expressive, and expressive of pride rather than of any desire. Pride, Hume says, is a "pure emotion in the soul unattended with any desire and not immediately exciting us to action" (p. 367). Pride is not, typically, any sort of a motive. When pride does "mediately" excite us to, say, display what we are proud of, welcoming that admiration by others which Hume thinks we need to sustain our pride, such proud display would be misdescribed as due to our *desire* or even our wish that others admire us. It is not as overtly purposive as actions directed by desire. Hume classifies desire as a "direct" passion, love and pride as "indirect" ones. They have "in a manner two objects" (the person, and what it is about them that inspires pride or love) but do not have an "end" in the way desire and will do.

Love, Hume thinks, usually does lead on to a desire for the well-being of the loved one, but this benevolent desire is separable from the passion of love. Pride, he says, has no such contingent but fairly regular follow-up in the way of a companion desire. It is a "pure emotion in the soul," but this is not to deny that some reactions and actions *express* pride. One of the good things about Hume's philosophy of mind is that he does not reduce expressive action to purposive action. Even when a passion like love does lead to purposive, benevolent actions, these are surely not the only actions which evidence the love. The more directly love-expressive actions, such as embracing, touching, and seeking the company of the loved one, or, when that is not possible, singing his praises and repeating his name, are not necessarily aimed to *please* the loved one, and may be done even when they are known to displease. They are clearly different from those benevolent actions designed to advance the good of the loved one which love may, less directly, inspire. As Hume puts it (p. 363), it has pleased nature to let benevolence normally accompany love, but the connection is not as close as that "original" relation there is between pride and letting one's thoughts dwell on oneself, or between love and letting one's thoughts, words, eyes, and hands turn toward the one loved. Such turning may or may not benefit the loved one, but is the direct expression of love. When some such mode of expression is blocked, then we have a sort of analogue to the frustration of desire.

But love can suffer not merely the enforced dumbness of lack of expression, but a variety of equally serious ills — lack of reciprocation, the harmfulness of the love to the one loved or to the lover, the loss by death of the loved one, and the ensuing grief, the failure of love to diversify itself enough to avoid self-stultifying boredom, its failure to perpetuate some memorial of itself, some "young one against old age" (Plato, *Symposium*, 207D), and so on. Failure of expression (including that "nonconsummation" possible for some, but only some, loves) is no more the occupational disease, so to say, of love than are any of these other ills. But frustration is the occupational disease of desire. It dominates the pathology of desire in a way that no one ill dominates that of love. Of course desires can go wrong in other ways than by going unsatisfied. The desired may, once got, prove a disappointment, and even when it does not disappoint one, may sicken or even kill one. There are noxious and non-self-perpetuating desires as there are noxious and infertile loves, and some desires, in particular sexual desires, may seem to derive their norms from those of the love which may accompany them, so that non-reciprocation and non-self-renewal may seem as pathological for the desire as for the love. But these are vexed normative questions into which I do not wish to enter. My point, which I take to be a conceptual point, is that to desire something is to want that desire to be satisfied, but not necessarily to want the desired to reciprocate the desire (this makes no sense for most desires), nor to want the desire to recur. But to love someone is necessarily to will that love to continue and to hope for return love. To love other persons is to want to be with those persons, and to want them to want that. Descartes's talk of "unification" as the telos of love may be a touch too metaphysical, but if we rephrase it as wanting to be in some way in touch or in contact with them, then we can accept it as a truth. Some of the forms of touching or contact will be, for some forms of love, erotic, and then the erotic desires properly accompanying such love will carry a derivative will to mutuality and continuation. But not all erotic desires arise in the context of love, and if such desires can seem to be well satisfied without such mutuality or expected regeneration, then whatever moral faults they may be seen to have, they seem, *qua* desires, perfectly successful. But nonmutual love is a failure as love—it may escape moral condemnation but it fails, just as short-lived love or frustrated desire does, to live up to its own intrinsic demands.

Hume, in his section on "the amorous passion," that form of love which includes sexual desire, sees it as combining a relatively calm, favorable evaluation of the character of the loved person with a more violent "appetite for generation" (p. 394), where these two different passions are mediated by finding *beauty* in the loved person. The will to unite oneself with a loved person, in such cases, will be a will to be close to, in the presence of, such physical beauty, as well as to have an otherwise agreeable companion. The evaluation of the loved one need not always be calm and critical—on the contrary, Hume says (p. 420), the perceived faults and blemishes enliven the lover's passion, enhancing what they contrast with—they serve as beauty spots. The desire intrinsic to the amorous passion, as Hume analyzes it, is not the desire to do good to the loved one, but to be with that one, and together to "generate."

Hume is famous for his thesis that it takes a passion (usually along with a belief about how and when it can be satisfied) to produce an action. This thesis is not, and does not imply, that it takes a desire to produce an action. When the passion from which the action springs is the amorous passion, desire may be involved, as it will also be with most of what Hume calls the direct passions, but there are other desire-free passions which may be cited to explain actions. The action of voicing moral disapproval, as much as the actions of boasting or bringing the conversation around to talk of one's beloved, arises from and expresses a passion without thereby being necessarily desire-directed. When one condemns an action, one need not think or desire that the condemnation will influence anyone, nor even desire that others be aware of one's moral judgment. One may just spontaneously blurt out "How disgraceful!" Of course if one desires that others *not* know one's feelings one will watch one's words, but the norm is for moral judgments to get expression.

Hume sees the passion which distinguishes moral beings such as we are from nonmoral sentient beings such as the other animals we know to be a "sentiment" of approval and disapproval, not a special motive, desire, or goal. The specifically moral feeling, which "excites" us to express moral judgments, is not a desire or any sort of goal-directed motive, but a reactive sentiment, issuing in expressive rather than goal-directed actions. Does our approval or disapproval make any other difference to what we do, and is it intended to make such a difference? Hume says very little about this. He of course supposes that we like being approved of, dislike being disapproved of, but this does not mean that we can or do change our behavior to avoid disapproval, nor that the disapprover is motivated by a desire to put a stop to what he disapproves of. We may have a desire for approval, and sometimes act so as to successfully satisfy it, but Hume does not seem to see that desire, or any other, as the peculiarly moral passion,[7] that which distinguishes us from nonmoral animals. The peculiarly moral passions are approval and disapproval themselves, that is to say pleasure and displeasure taken *in* other human pleasures and passions, be they motivating desires or other reactive passions such as pride. We certainly do not find in Hume any move to reduce other passions to desire, and in particular no move to reduce the peculiarly moral passion to any species of desire.

For Hume, then, desire is the passion we feel when, to the thought of a future pleasure, we respond positively and purposively, and thus have a tendency to act now in such a way as to tend to make that pleasure occur in our own future. To present pleasure our primary response is joy, not desire. To pleasure-giving persons our primary response is love (or pride, if that person is oneself), not desire. Love usually is "attended with" a variety of desires, both purely benevolent ones and desires for the company, presence, and favor of, or for news from and about, the loved person, but love itself is not these attendants. Other passions, such as ambition and curiosity, are officially analyzed by Hume as "love" of fame and of truth, not as desire for them, but he clearly intended these to cover desires for (yet more, or continued) fame, and for more or retained truths, and indeed he includes his wry discussion of "the love of truth" in the third part of Book Two of the *Treatise*, devoted to the "direct" passions, not in the earlier parts where the "indirect" passions of pride and love proper (that is, love of persons) were discussed. So he is willing to let the concept of desire range as widely as is compatible with its teleological or future-oriented essence. He accepts that limiting feature of desire as uncontroversial, and there he is following Hobbes and Descartes, and was to be followed by Kant.

I shall merely allude to Kant, whose treatment of desire confirms my general claim that many of our philosophical predecessors did not see desire as the central mental phenomenon which some contemporary philosophers want to make it. Kant defines the faculty of desire (*das Begehrungsvermögen*) as the capacity to make mental representations or ideas the cause of what they represent. First desire, then, if all goes well, later its fulfillment. So in the *Critique of Practical Reason* and in the *Introduction to the Critique of Judgment*, he can associate desire with reason, since both involve a separation of end or conclusion from starting point or premise, both are anticipatory or forward-looking, mediated, and teleological mental processes. Where understanding and pleasure are nondiscursive and nonteleological responses to fact or good, reasoning and desiring are mediated, drawn-out, discursive, and teleological phenomena, ones which transcend what is given in present intuition. Thus Kant can see reason as naturally suited to be legislative over desire, and so "practical," whereas in the theoretical realm it is merely regulative, and the understanding has authority.

The moral I think we should draw from this selective look at earlier treatments of desire is that we should be cautious in our claims about the centrality of desire. If we do wish to redefine it so that it covers any sort of "pro attitude" to a good, seen as past, present, or future, punctal or continuous, then we should ask what other terms we will use to mark the differences in temporal restriction and direction which most earlier philosophers marked with the aid of a narrower usage of "desire." Or, if we think these distinctions unimportant, we should be prepared to say why. We should also be clear whether, if we do claim that desire is mentally ubiquitous, that is put forward as a conceptual truth or as an observed contingent fact about us; and if the latter, exactly what contingent fact. For Hobbes it was the contingent fact that we cannot stop worrying about the future. If some of us do manage to live for the moment, at least occasionally, or direct our souls' passions on eternal objects, or live in the past, or if we purge our souls of all restless striving, as Eastern sages urge us to do, then will we or won't we have thereby falsified the claims of those who see desire as the life of mind, present whenever anything matters to a person, whenever we do, think, or suffer anything for the sake of, or in response to, some good?

The uncritical assumption made by some contemporary philosophers that there is desire whenever there is any intentional action, so that whatever we do — be it clean our teeth from habit, or kill ourselves in despair, or contentedly keep doing what we were doing — some "desire" to do tl at is automatically postulated, will be properly challenged by reading Hume, Descartes, or even Hobbes. Desires do indeed enliven our lives, but other passions, too, can brighten them. Desires do motivate, but not all motives are desires, nor need a mental state operate as a motive to play an important mental role. Reactions, their causes and their voluntary or involuntary expression, as well as actions and their causes, and beliefs and their causes, help constitute our mental life. Jerome Shaffer (1983) has recently argued that "emotions," including love, are dispensable and better dispensed-with mental phenomena. Like many other contemporary philosophers, he treats desire as obviously essential to our mental life, as if agreeing with Hobbes that without desires we are dead. What Shaffer seems to mean is that some cause of action, in addition to belief, must be present, if we are keeping going. But why call that "desire," and contrast it with emotion? It seems to me that either we should introduce some quite neutral theoretical term, like Hobbes's "endeavor" and Spinoza's "conatus," to serve as the theoretically postulated, always present, dynamic goal-directed force in a living thing, whether or not there is any consciousness of it, and whether or not thought and reflection make any impact on its direction, while reserving the term "desire" for consciousness of this forward-reaching restless life force (in which case it becomes an equally theory-laden concept, perhaps never actually exemplified), or we should, like Descartes and Hume, treat desire as *one* sort of phenomenologically discoverable passion, in which case it will be often exemplified, but will be by no means *essential* either to our psychical life or to the causation of our actions. It is no sillier to advocate the cleansing of restless desire from our souls than to advocate, as Shaffer pretends to do, the ridding of our souls of the perturbation of emotion. Normal people have desires, since they are sensibly concerned with their uncertain futures, and they also have other passions, since not all their hearts' passionate energy is reserved for the uncertain future. We can, surely, afford to be pluralists not imperialists in the philosophy of mind, granting an important role to desire without having thereby to banish all its equally vital passion-relatives. Nothing is gained, and much is lost, by trying to treat desire as both *the* dynamic force in human lives and the primary "affect."

I myself prefer to leave inherited terms with their more precise senses, to conserve rather than destroy the distinctions which have seemed to our predecessors worth making. I can see no good reason to think that there is any truth in any reductive program in the philosophy of mind. I have no more inclination to follow Descartes and reduce desire to love than to follow Hobbes and reduce love to desire. Nor would I want to reduce desire to anticipated pleasure any more than pleasure to fulfilled desire. It seems to me clear that mental phenomena like motivation, intention, and seeing good reasons are not reducible to wanting and believing, any more than the reverse reduction is possible. The sort of approach Descartes and Hume adopted, of looking to see what the full variety is in our extended family of psychical states, and what complex relations hold there, is the best one to adopt. Desire is a philosophically interesting phenomenon, however frequent or infrequent, avoidable or unavoidable it is, and however central or peripheral it is to other mental states. Like love, belief, fear, anger, and other of its fellow mental states, it admits of degrees of reflexivity, and like them, too, it can be more or less well informed. Its intentional objects, like theirs, have not yet received from philosophers an analysis that does justice to their actual variety and complexity.[8]

Desire is of most interest as a psychical phenomenon when it, with its variant of intentionality, is seen in relation to all its mental relatives with their variants, to pleasure, to satisfaction, to love, to beliefs about the good and how to get and sustain it, to discontent, to hopes and fears for the future, to confidence and to lack of confidence, to a sense of ability and to ignorance of the extent of one's ability; to depression, grief, despair, homesickness, nostalgia; to longing, craving, lusting, itching, wanting, preferring, and intending. Desire is what it is, and not these other things, and they are what they are, and not desires. It will be understood best, philosophically, when it is seen in clear relation to all of its many relatives among the actions, passions, and the mixed active/passive states of our complicated, variegated, self-complicating and self-diversifying souls.

NOTES

1. All quotations from Hobbes's *Leviathian* are from C. B. MacPherson's edition (Hobbes, 1972 [1651]), with the chapter numbers given in brackets. The epigraph at the beginning of this essay is taken from chapter eight.)

2. Ronald de Sousa, in his essay in this volume, investigates what sorts of desire, for what sorts of person, are of this suicidal nature. He calls

them "consummatory" desires, but it is possible that there are some consummations which are not followed by *tristitia* or by nausea, so the label may be misleading.

3. *They Went to Portugal* (Harmondsworth: Penguin Books, 1985), p. 78 (originally published: London: Cape, 1946).

4. All Descartes quotations are from the Haldane and Ross edition of *The Philosophical Works* (Descartes, 1977a [1642], 1977b [1649]). Unless otherwise indicated, the specific reference is to *Passions of the Soul*, with the article number shown in square brackets.

5. All Spinoza quotations are from Gutmann's translation of the *Ethics* (Spinoza, 1949 [1677]).

6. All Hume references are to the Selby-Bigge and Nidditch edition of *A Treatise on Human Nature* (Hume, 1978 [1739]). The present citation is from p. 516 of that edition.

7. By "moral passion" I mean not morally approved passion, but the passion which does the approving. Any passion might secure moral approval, so count as "moral" in the sense of "morally approved," but only one passion, requiring a special point of view, counts as what Hume calls "the moral sentiment," which pronounces judgment on the other passions and on the actions they lead to.

8. My selective dipping into the history of the philosophy of the passions, in this paper, has pointed up one feature of the intentional objects of desire which any more systematic account would need to bring out — namely, that the proper object of desire is not an event or state of affairs as such, nor a thing or person as such, but a thing or person in some future close relation to the desirer. Descartes surveyed the range of such intimate relations appropriate to various sorts of desired things. Hume speaks of desiring a fruit "as of an excellent relish" and ceasing to desire it when someone corrects his mistake about how it would taste (p. 417). This reference to the sort of pleasure expected if the desire were satisfied in the manner appropriate to it, within the phrase expressing what is desired, without collapsing the desired *into* that pleasure or that satisfying union, seems to be what we need, and the "as" or *qua* locution seems a good way to express the ontological complexity of the desired. The intentional objects of believing, and of intending, have equally complex but different internal structures. We see this if we consider what would happen to Hume's desire if he were corrected not merely by someone who told him of the bitter taste of the fruit he was about to take, but also told him that although it tasted bad he could extract from it a rare and precious fluid. Then one might still take it, and want to take it, but one's desire now would be a different one, not the same desire with different support. The desire seems individuated by its object with its "quality," as Hume (p. 279) calls what we might prefer to call its "desirability characteristic," the fruit with its promise of a particular mode of pleasurable possession. The support for a belief — *why* it is believed — may, by contrast, be replaced without that entailing the belief's replacement. One can go on believing what one used to believe, but now for quite different reasons. Can one go on intending the same action, when one has replaced a mistaken reason to do "it" with another reason? The *point* of what one is doing will have changed, but the point or end in view

seems not quite as integral to the individuation of intentions as to desires. There seems to be plenty work still remaining to be done before we see clearly how desiring fruit as of an excellent relish relates to liking apricots *for* their texture as well as for their taste, to intending to pick an apricot *to* eat it, and to believing that, if you tell me it will taste bitter, it will, *because* you are a trustworthy expert on these matters. The relation of the "reason why" to what it is a reason for seems different and of differing degrees of intimacy in all these cases. To understand the intentionality of any one of these mental states would be to see that state in relation to the others, to see why for some, such as beliefs, that-clauses are what naturally follows the verb ("I believe that he knows what he is talking about"), in others, strings of infinitives ("I intend to pick it to eat it"), in others, nouns with *qua* modifiers ("I admire her as a dancer"). Then there is Hume's now somewhat archaic modifier, "He desired that fruit as of an excellent relish." These different locutions seem to be needed to express the different degrees to which perceived reasons for mental attitudes, as it were, invade and individuate the attitudes themselves, and their intentional objects.

The Two Senses of Desire

Wayne A. Davis

Abstract. "Desire" is ambiguous, expressing two logically though not causally independent propositional attitudes, called "volitive" and "appetitive" desire. While both tend to generate action, to spread from ends to means, and to yield pleasure when satisfied, there are major differences: appetitive desire influences volitive desire, not vice versa; volitive desire is a better index of action, appetitive desire of pleasure; and only volitive desires are based on reasons, influenced by value judgments, or entailed by intentions.

It has often been said that "desire" is ambiguous. I do not believe the case for this has been made thoroughly enough, however. The claim typically occurs in the course of defending controversial philosophical theses, such as that intention entails desire, where it tends to seem ad hoc. There is need, therefore, for a thorough and single-minded exploration of the ambiguity. I believe the results will be more profound than might be suspected.

1. VOLITIVE DESIRE

In one sense, "desire" is synonymous with *want, wish,* and *would like,* and appears as a *transitive verb* with complements such as the following (VP stands for a verb phrase, NP for a noun phrase):

(1) S desires to VP.
(2) S desires NP.

I refer to desire in this sense as *volitive desire.* There are some grammatical differences among the synonyms. For example, "I would like to have gotten up earlier" is fine, but not "I want to have gotten up earlier."[1] And whereas "would like" does not take any sort of that-clause, "desire" takes an open subjunctive ("I desire that you should come"), "wish" a counterfactual ("I wish that you would come").

There are also some mild differences of connotation. "Desire" tends to suggest formality, while "wish" and "would like" suggest politeness. "Wish" suggests that the desire is not strong enough to produce action or emotion.[2] Several associations are responsible for this connotation. First, "wishing" is ambiguous. In a very different sense, it means *making a wish*, as in "Before he blew out the candles, Bobby wished for a bicycle." Unlike desiring, making a wish is an action, a superstitious one. It is a notoriously ineffective means to our ends. Second, a person wishes *that* he *would* do something only if he is certain he won't. With a counterfactual clause, "wish" expresses disbelief as well as desire. With an infinitive clause, "wish" has no such cognitive implication, however. And finally, we have the phrases *mere wish* and *idle wish*, and the term *velleity* (from the Latin *velle*, to wish), which do denote insufficiently strong desires. Weakness is definitely not part of the *denotation* of "wish," however. "I wish to live" and "I wish to beat my opponent" are true, even though my desires to live and win are plenty strong.

"Want" is ambiguous. In form (2) it can mean *lack* as well as *desire*. "Would like" means *desire* in sentences like "Jack would like to listen to a quartet." But "would like" also has the predictable meaning of *potential liking*, as in "Jack would like listening to a quartet." "Jack would like a quartet" is simply ambiguous.

A large number of concepts imply volitive desire without being equivalent to it. Three are wishing (that), hoping, and being happy. If someone *hopes* that he will win, or *is happy* that he will, or *wishes* that he would win, then he desires to win. Being happy, hoping, and wishing differ in their *cognitive* implications, which respectively are certainty, uncertainty, and countercertainty. If someone is happy that he will win, then he is certain that he will; if he hopes to win, then he is uncertain whether he will; and if he wishes that he would win, then he is certain that he will not win. Since certainty, uncertainty, and countercertainty exhaustively cover the belief dimension, the disjunction of being happy, hoping, and wishing is cognitively neutral and nearly equivalent to desiring.[3] "Happy" in this context has the exact synonym *glad*, and numerous near synonyms such as *pleased*, *elated*, *relieved*, and *proud*. Hoping can be divided into *optimism* and *pessimism*; the former implies belief, the latter disbelief. Wishing that something would occur is equivalent to *having no hope* that it will.

2. APPETITIVE DESIRE

In its second sense, "desire" has the near synonyms *appetite, hungering, craving, yearning, longing,* and *urge,* and appears as a *noun:*

(3) S has a desire to VP.
(4) S has a desire for NP.

I refer to desire in this sense as *appetitive desire.* "Urge" is restricted to context (3). "Appetite" is restricted to (4), but with "appetite" NP may be the gerund VP-ing. "Yearning," "longing," and "hungering" also occur as intransitive verbs, with no change of sense. "I have a yearning to play tennis" and "I yearn to play tennis" only differ grammatically. The article *a* can be replaced by *the* or *some* without change of sense.

In its narrowest sense, to have an appetite is to have a desire specifically for food. More generally, an appetite is a desire to consume things like food and water or to engage in activities like eating, drinking, and sex. *Hunger* is a familiar condition in which we have an appetite for food. Its unpleasant symptoms include stomach pangs and physical weakness. Hunger is typically caused by the lack of food, and eliminated by the consumption of food. Hunger makes eating especially enjoyable. *Thirst* is a similar condition in which we have a desire for water. Its unpleasant symptoms include parch sensations in the mouth and throat. Thirst is caused by lack of water, and causes drinking to be particularly enjoyable.

It cannot be said, however, that hunger *is* the desire or appetite for food. After consuming three-quarters of a delicious meal, I may still have an appetite — a desire to eat — even though I am no longer hungry. Furthermore, hunger typically *explains* a desire for food. But there are other possible explanations ("the food looks delicious"), and explanation is irreflexive. Finally, a being without the concept of food (such as a newborn baby) could perfectly well be hungry yet could not seriously be said to have a desire specifically for food. For similar reasons, thirst must be differentiated from the desire for water. Let us refer to hunger, thirst, and similar states as *physical drives.* Some people have physical drives for alcohol, caffeine, nicotine, and morphine, and everyone has physical drives for urinating, defecating, sleeping, and sex. Note that desires and appetites far outstrip physical drives. People often have a desire for music, for example, but no one to my knowledge has ever had a physical drive for music. And there is no physical drive corresponding specifically to the appetite for peanuts.

Many appetitive desires are not appetites, such as the desire to be wise, or to fulfill our obligations, and the desire for the semester to be over, or for lots of children. To be an appetite, the object of desire must be an activity or something we can be said to consume. So "desire" and "appetite" are near but not exact synonyms. "Hunger" and "thirst," in their generalized common sense, mean any *strong* appetitive desire. We may hunger for the semester to be over and thirst for news. "Yearning" and "longing" denote *unsatisfied, intense, persistent, and future-oriented* appetitive desires. I may still have a desire to play tennis after I have begun to play, but I can no longer be said to have a yearning to play. I have a desire for breakfast, but the desire is not strong enough to count as a yearning. And while a sudden urge may last no more than a second, a yearning must persist for minutes or hours, roughly, and a longing for days or months. Finally, while a regretful investor may have a desire to have invested in IBM thirty years ago, he cannot be said to yearn or long to have done so. Urges, appetites, and hungerings must also be future-oriented.

Objects of appetitive desire are *appealing.* Eating is appealing when, and only when, we have a desire to eat. Since I yearn to play tennis, the activity appeals to me a great deal. To say that a Corvette is not appealing is to say that you have no desire for a Corvette. In the sense we are interested in, to say that eating, or lobster, is appealing is to say that *the prospect of* eating, or lobster, is appealing. And to say that lobster, or a Corvette, is appealing is to say that the prospect of *having* lobster, or a Corvette, is appealing. The statement that something appeals to a person is ambiguous, however. "Lobster appeals to me" can mean either that I *have a desire for* lobster or that I *like* lobster. "The theory of evolution appeals to me" could only mean that I like the theory, while "Buying a house soon appeals to me" could only mean that I have a desire to buy one soon. The two senses are quite independent. Someone who likes lobster may not have a desire for any because he is already stuffed. And someone who has never had lobster before, and so neither likes nor dislikes it, could nevertheless have a desire for lobster because it looks so good.

Objects of appetitive desire are *viewed with pleasure.*[4] We view with pleasure the prospect of eating when we have a desire to eat. When I yearn to play tennis, I view playing with great pleasure. The expression "view with pleasure" is an *idiom.* It is not related, semantically, to "participate with pleasure" or even "watch with pleasure." Nor is it related to "play with vigor" or "watch with interest." To do something with pleasure is to enjoy doing it: the action gives you pleasure. To view something with pleasure, however, is not to enjoy viewing it: there is no such action as viewing prospects. "I viewed the prospect of eating" is incomplete and meaningless.

The fact that objects of desire are viewed with pleasure does not seem to entail any relation at all between desire and pleasure.[5] Viewing something with pleasure does not entail believing that it will or would give you pleasure. John may view with pleasure the prospect of having an elaborate and dignified funeral for his wife and himself without expecting to enjoy his wife's or his own funeral. Bob may view with pleasure the prospect of having a hot-fudge sundae (he has a craving for one) even though he knows that a dental problem would prevent him from enjoying it. Viewing something with pleasure does not entail *looking forward* to it. As such examples show, "Objects of desire are viewed with pleasure" does not mean that all desires are for pleasure nor that all desires are motivated by pleasure: it is not a form of hedonism.[6] Viewing something with pleasure cannot even be analyzed as enjoying the thought of it. Thinking about his wife's funeral, be it ever so dignified, may make John very sad. Thinking about sundaes may give Bob fits of frustration. Finally, viewing the prospect of VP-ing with pleasure does not mean being pleased by the fact that you will or might VP. Bob is also on a strict diet. Since he prides himself in being strong-willed, he would not be pleased by the fact that he even might have a hot-fudge sundae.[7] All we can say about "S views the prospect of VP-ing with pleasure," I conclude, is that it means S has a desire to VP.

3. SIMILARITIES AND DIFFERENCES

The two senses of "desire" are logically independent. There are cases of *volitive desire without appetitive desire.* I often want a hammer, in order to drive a nail. I am then glad that I have a hammer, or else wish that I had one. I never have an appetite for a hammer, though, and never hunger or yearn for one, though I probably would if I were a collector of hammers. I have not had an urge to use a hammer since I was a kid. A hammer is neither appealing nor unappealing. I desire a hammer, but do not have a desire for a hammer. We often want to eat, for social or nutritional reasons, when we are not at all hungry, and when we view the prospect of eating without pleasure. We desire to eat, but do not have a desire to eat. Imagine, finally, that James Bond has been captured. Having been informed that he is to be executed, Bond is asked whether he wishes to face a firing squad or be fed to the sharks. We would not be surprised to hear "I desire to be shot rather than eaten." In contrast, "I have a desire to be shot rather than eaten" would be most startling.[8]

There are also cases of *appetitive desire without volitive desire.* A woman who is extremely hungry may not want any food because she is on a diet. If the servant asked, "Madam, do you desire to eat?" she would have to answer "No." But if her husband asked, "Don't you have any desire to eat?" she could not give the same answer. Eating appeals to her, but not enough to make her want to engage in the activity. She has a desire to eat, but does not desire to eat. When I sit in my office on a beautifully sunny day, I yearn to play tennis. I long to be outside, and have an urge to cancel class. I view the prospect with great pleasure. But if a fellow tennis player came to the door and asked, "Do you want to play?" I would have to say, "No, thanks, I have to teach." I have a desire to play, but for the reason given I do not desire to play.

Failing to recognize the difference between *desiring* and *having a desire* can have some paradoxical consequences. For example, the following principle seems self-evident: *The desire to do A and the desire not to do A are mutually exclusive.* So are the desire to do A and the desire to avoid or refrain from doing A. Desiring not to do something entails not desiring to do it, and is equivalent to being averse to doing it. Suppose we ask someone whether he wants to play tennis or golf at noon today. He might answer, "I desire to do both." Such a response would be perfectly intelligible, even if we would be prompted to snap, "You obviously can't do both, so choose." In contrast, suppose we simply ask whether he wants to play tennis or not. The answer, "I desire both to play and not to play" would not even make sense. We would be prompted only to ask "What do you mean?" The reply that he meant exactly what he said would be dumbfounding. He might explain, however, that what he meant was that he has reasons for wanting to play and equally good reasons for wanting to refrain, which, if we were unamused, might lead us to ask why he just didn't say so in the first place rather than feign paradox. But now observe that the hungry lady on a diet has a desire to eat while desiring not to eat. This too will seem paradoxical unless the ambiguity of "desire" is recognized. We would have to give up the above principle,[9] or redescribe the case in some way, but neither is easy to do.

Another law holding for both volitive and appetitive desires is this: *The desire to do E together with the belief that doing M is a means of doing E tends to generate the desire to do M.* This principle of desire generation is a relative of the familiar Kantian slogan "To will the end is to will the means." The principle is of course only a *tendency* law: there are numerous cases in which desires for ends fail to generate desires for means. What is of interest to us, however, is that *the class of exceptions to the rule is different for appetitive and volitive desires.* Here are two typical examples. John desires to listen to music, and has a desire to do so. He believes that attending a New York Philharmonic concert is a means of listening to music. As a result, John has a desire to attend the concert. But he does not want to, since it costs too much. Bob has a desire to fulfill his obligations, and wants to. He believes that teaching today is a means of fulfilling his obligations. As a result, he wants to teach today. But he has no desire to do so, since for him teaching is a chore. Fulfilling his obligations appeals to Bob, but teaching doesn't, even though teaching is one of his obligations. He undoubtedly wishes that it weren't an obligation.

A distinction is often drawn between *intrinsic and extrinsic desires*.[10] A desire is extrinsic if its object is desired as a means to something else that is desired, intrinsic if the object is desired as an end in itself. The desire to flip a light switch is typically extrinsic, since people desire to flip a light switch as a means to turn on the light. The desire to be happy is typically intrinsic, since people desire to be happy for its own sake, not as a means to anything else. As defined, a desire may be both intrinsic and extrinsic. The desire to eat may be based partly, but not completely, on other desires such as the desire to gain nourishment. Since appetitive and volitive desires are *both* governed by the above principle of desire generation, *the intrinsic-extrinsic distinction cuts across the appetitive-volitive distinction*. John's desire to listen to music may be intrinsic, but his desire to listen to the radio is extrinsic, since his desire to listen to the radio is based on the belief that listening to the radio is a means of listening to music. This holds whether we are referring to John's appetitive desire to listen to the radio, or his volitive desire.

Volitive desires are often directed upon appetitive desires. It is well known that an appetite makes eating more enjoyable, so people often want to have an appetite when they are going to eat. They increase their appetite first by "starving" it and then by whetting it with an appetizer. In such cases, people desire not only to eat, but also to have a desire to eat. Someone may even want to have a desire to do something without wanting to do it. A psychiatrist dealing with drug addicts may come to believe that he could better understand his patients if he knew what it was like to have a craving for drugs, while retaining the conviction that drugs are extremely harmful. As a result, he may desire to have a desire to take drugs while desiring not to take them.[11] There are cases too in which people desire *not* to have desires.[12] Dieters abound who realize that it would be easier to stick to their diets if they did not have an appetite. Some take drugs like Dietac containing an appetite suppressant.

Volitive desires can also be directed upon volitive desires. Someone who believes that desiring to do what is right is necessary and sufficient for being virtuous may well desire to desire to do what is right and desire not to desire to do what is wrong. The psychiatrist mentioned above may also want to want drugs (without wanting them!), for the same professional reason. And appetitive desires can be directed on appetitive desires: an appetite is often appealing, particularly when we have just overeaten. Finally, it is difficult but not impossible to imagine cases in which appetitive desires are directed upon volitive desires. The prospect of wanting to do what is right may appeal to the sinner in his weaker moments. The distinction between volitive and appetitive desire therefore yields four distinct types of "*second-order*" desire. The first — volitive directed on appetitive — is the most common.

A major difference between volitive and appetitive desires is their "rationality." Volitive desires are typically based on *reasons*. Your reason for wanting to eat may be to get nourishment. Then your desire to get nourishment both explains and motivates your desire to eat. Appetitive desires, in contrast, are not the sorts of thing we have reasons for or against. There may be reasons why we have a desire to eat (such as food-deprivation), but we do not have reasons for having a desire to eat. "Why do you have an appetite?" is a legitimate question; "What are your reasons for having an appetite?" is not. Appetitive desires can be explained but are not motivated. In this respect, appetitive desires are more like aches and pains, while volitive desires resemble beliefs.[13] We may of course have reasons for wanting to have an appetitive desire. One common reason for wanting an appetite for food is to be able to enjoy eating. But reasons for wanting to have a desire are not reasons for having the desire. Similarly, while we may have reasons for wanting to have a tingling sensation, say, we do not have reasons for having a tingling sensation.

While volitive and appetitive desires are different mental states, they are not unrelated. For one thing, *an appetitive desire to do something tends to generate and motivate a volitive desire to do it.* An appetite for food tends to make people want food. The more appealing food is, the more likely a person is to want it, and the more he is likely to want it. Moreover, having an appetite is in itself a typical reason for wanting to eat. A further reason may be the pleasure to be gained from satisfying the appetite. While appetitive desires are not themselves influenced by reasons, they generally provide reasons for volitive desires.[14] Appetitive desires provide reasons even when we have no "*particular*" reason for wanting to do something (such as sing while walking alone on a beautiful day), when we "*simply*" want to. The action is appealing, which is our reason for wanting to perform it. Note that volitive desires are never self-motivating. My wanting to sing could not be one of my reasons for wanting to sing, any more than my believing that it will rain could be one of my reasons for believing that it will rain.

A corollary is that physical drives tend to generate and motivate volitive desires. Hunger tends to make people want to eat, and is a typical reason for wanting to eat. Eliminating the discomfort of being hungry is a further reason. The principle that appetitive desires tend to generate volitive desires entails that if a person with a desire to do something does not want to do it, there must be some *countervailing factors*. A woman with a ravenous appetite may not want to eat because she wants to lose weight. A man with an urge to commit adultery may not want to because he believes that it is immoral. We may have a strong desire to stay in bed in the morning, yet not want to because we have to go to work. The stronger the appetitive desire, however, the harder it is to resist, and so the less likely it is that any given countervailing factor would be effective. At the extreme, an appetitive desire may be *irresistible*, in which case no countervailing factors would be effective: the individual would volitively desire to satisfy his appetitive desire no matter what reasons he had for not satisfying it.[15]

Volitive desire is a more reliable indicator of action. It holds for both volitive and appetitive desire that *the desire to do A tends to result in doing A*. Appetitive desires influence action *indirectly*, however, by generating volitive desires. A person who has an appetite will not eat unless and until he wants to. Since there is an extra link in the chain, appetitive desires have a lesser tendency to result in action than volitive desires. For that link can be broken, as indicated in the previous paragraph.

Appetitive desire, on the other hand, is a more reliable indicator of enjoyment. It holds for both volitive and appetitive desire that *the satisfaction of a desire tends to be enjoyable*. The tendency is stronger, however, for an appetitive desire.[16] Let us imagine that Bob has a desire to listen to music, but does not want to. Imagine in contrast that Bill wants to listen to music even though he has no desire to. Imagine finally that both Bob and Bill do listen to music, perhaps because John turned on the stereo. Given only this information, who is more likely to enjoy listening to the music, Bob or Bill? Bob, surely. Look now at John, who wanted to depress the power button in order to turn on the stereo. It is unlikely that John enjoyed depressing the button. It is equally unlikely that he had a desire to depress it. Children often have such desires, but not normal adults.

Value judgments have a powerful influence on volitive desires.[17] A person who believes that something is or would be good, right, obligatory, just, prudent, and so on, tends to want it to exist; he at least has a reason for wanting it to exist. Indeed, volitive desires can almost be identified with one sort of value judgment: *The volitive desire to do A tends to result from the belief that it is desirable to do A*,[18] which is implied by the belief that one *should* or *ought* to do A, that A is *the (best) thing to do*. We are concerned with the belief that it is desirable *all things considered* to do A, where "all things" includes morality, law, prudence, etiquette, and whatnot. Suppose Bob believes that it is desirable to pay back his student loans. Then we could infer that Bob probably desires to pay them back. Any reasons Bob has for believing that it is desirable to pay back his loans should also be reasons he has for desiring to do so. Furthermore, we would expect that Bob desires to pay back his loans because he believes it is desirable. The reverse direction of explanation is conceivable, but unlikely. It would be a rather gross manifestation of irrationality. Now suppose Tom wants to buy a Porsche. Then we could predict that he probably believes it is desirable to buy a Porsche. Tom's reasons for desiring to buy a Porsche should be his reasons for believing it desirable to buy one.

Value judgments are not similarly associated with appetitive desires. The inference that Bob has a desire to pay back his loans — that he hungers or yearns or has an urge to do so; that he views the prospect with pleasure or finds it appealing — would be completely unwarranted. And from the fact that Tom has an urge to buy a Porsche, we could not infer that he believes it is desirable to buy one. Indeed, Tom may believe firmly that he should resist such a foolish urge.[19]

Weakness of will is often displayed when appetitive desires and value judgments conflict: when an individual has a desire to do something he believes he shouldn't do, or has a desire not to do something he believes he should. For example, John may have a ravenous appetite even though he is on a diet and believes he shouldn't eat. Three stages can be distinguished, depending on whether the value judgment or the appetitive desire determines what is volitively desired. *Stage I:* Value judgment determines volitive desire. At first, John does not want to eat because he believes he shouldn't. As a result, he refrains from eating. Appetite is tugging on the will, which is resisting the force. *Stage II:* Appetitive desire determines volitive desire. Appetite eventually wins out. John eats. Of course, he eats by choice, voluntarily and intentionally. So at this time, due to the strength of his appetitive desire, John wants to eat even though he believes he shouldn't.[20] *Stage III:* Value judgment again determines volitive desire. After having eaten for a while, John stops. He no longer wants to eat, and indeed regrets having done so. John continues to believe that he shouldn't eat, and perhaps still has an appetite. Concerning Stage II, we would say that if the individual had more *willpower*, he would not have given in to his appetitive desire. Whatever reasons had led him to the conclusion that he shouldn't eat would have kept him from wanting to eat and so from eating. Strength of will is displayed as long as the individual remains in Stage I. Willpower is the ability to resist such forces as appetitive desires which act to divorce volitive desires from value judgments. It is the antidote to irresistibility. Weakness of will shows that value judgments only *tend* to generate volitive desires,[21] while strength of will shows that appetitive desires only tend to generate them.

Impulsive action is another case where volitive desires do not result from value judgments.[22] Here, an appetitive desire arises and generates a volitive desire, which in turn leads to action, all before the agent has time to stop and consider whether he *should* act that way. There is no conflict between appetitive desire and value judgment because there is no value judgment. For example, after hitting a lousy shot, Clay had a sudden urge to smash his tennis racket into the court and did so. He wouldn't have smashed his racket if he hadn't wanted to. But he obviously did not believe that it was desirable to destroy an expensive racket. Indeed, if Clay had thought the matter over, he would have realized that he shouldn't smash his racket and would not have wanted to do so. But Clay acted without thinking. Some impulsive actions do not involve even a potential conflict between appetitive desire and value judgment. After making the toss on one of my serves today I had an urge to smash the ball with all my might and did so on the impulse. I had not formed any judgment about the desirability of the action, but I would have believed that it was desirable (to catch my opponent off guard) if I had considered the question. Impulsive action seems to be one case in which appetitive desires generate volitive desires *without motivating them*. If Clay had had a reason for wanting to smash his racket, then it would seem inaccurate to describe his action as impulsive, even if his reason were simply that he had an urge to do it.

Consider, finally, *arbitrary choices*. Jane faces numerous identical cans of tomato soup in the supermarket, and picks one. She wants to pick it, but it is unlikely that she believes that it is desirable to pick that one rather than any of the others. It is also unlikely that she has a desire to pick that particular can. So arbitrary choices provide examples of volitive desires that result from neither value judgments nor appetitive desires.

4. INTENTION AND DESIRE

In the introduction I mentioned the thesis that an intention to do something entails a desire to do it. It should now be clear that *intention entails volitive rather than appetitive desire*.[23] If I intend to eat, I must want to eat, but I need not have an appetite or view the prospect of eating with pleasure. I must desire to eat, but I need not have a desire to eat. Similar examples are provided by actions that are motivated by obligation or necessity rather than by desire. I may intend to teach today solely because I feel obligated to. I desire to teach even though I have no desire to. Cases like these can pull us one way then another unless we realize that "desire" is ambiguous, which explains I believe why many philosophers have thought it obvious that intention entails desire,[24] while others have thought it obvious that intention does not entail desire.[25]

The principle that intention entails desire can be expressed as follows: someone intends to do something only if he is *motivated* to do it. But "S is motivated to VP" is also ambiguous, meaning either that S volitively desires, or that S has an appetitive desire, to VP. In one sense I am not motivated to teach, since I have no desire to. I may need to "get motivated" in order to lecture effectively. In another sense, though, I am motivated to teach, by the fact that I am obligated to. Intending only entails being motivated in the sense of volitively desiring. This does not mean that all intentional action is motivated by desire. For an action to be motivated *by* desire, it is not enough that the agent want to perform it. His motivation, that is, his *reason* for wanting to perform it, must be that he has a desire to perform it. I want to teach, but my action will be motivated by obligation rather than desire. For my reason for wanting to teach is that I am obligated to rather than that I have a desire to (that I find the prospect appealing or view it with pleasure).

Some have contended that the sense in which people desire to do whatever they intend to do is abnormal, extended, or even contrived.[26] The following sort of dialogue, though, is quite common and perfectly normal. Imagine that a stockbroker and one of his clients have just completed a series of transactions.

> *Broker:* What do you desire to do next?
> *Client:* Sell 10,000 shares of GN.
> *Broker:* Why on earth do you want to sell GN? It's your best stock!
> *Client:* I have to pay off a gambling debt.
> *Broker:* If you want to pay off that debt, it would be better to use your money-market funds.
> *Client:* True, but I also promised my wife I'd get out of the stock market.
> *Broker:* Are you under a court order to liquidate your holdings or something?
> *Client:* No, I could keep the stock if I so desired.
> *Broker:* Well, the market for GN is thin; we may have trouble finding buyers.
> *Client:* I hope not.

Note in particular that the client's second and fourth remarks served to answer, not reject, the broker's questions. (Contrast: *"Broker:* Why do you desire to sell GM? *Client:* I don't; it's G*N* I wish to sell." Here the client's response rejects the question without answering it.) What *would* be abnormal and completely inappropriate for the client to say is: "I *don't* want to sell GN; what made you think I did?" Just imagine the look that would produce on the broker's face! Of course, the client might answer "I don't *want* to but I must." However, the emphasis on "want" changes its meaning to "really want" (see sec. 5). Emphasis often affects meaning.

Note also the appropriateness of "What do you want?" when asked of anyone who intrudes. The answer might be "To deliver a message," even though the intruder is embarrassed to interrupt and does so only because he feels obligated to. The answer "Nothing" would be extraordinary to say the least. "For him to say 'I don't want anything, I simply have an obligation to deliver a message' would at best be irrelevant pedantry."[27] Similarly, suppose you have to do something unpleasant that you don't know how to do, such as commit your wife to a mental institution, file for bankruptcy, or get to the city morgue. You could always ask for instructions by saying "I want to do such-and-such; how do I go about it?" The response, "How could you *want* to do something like that?" would at best be puerile humor.[28]

Reflect also on cases where a man refrains from doing something out of a sense of obligation even though he "really wants" to do it. Suppose Alan refrains from kissing Jill, even though he has a burning desire to kiss her, because he feels he ought to be faithful to his wife. Later, in order to show just how virtuous Alan was, we might observe that he had the ability and the opportunity, so that he could have kissed Jill if he had wanted to. The use of the *counterfactual* subjunctive here—if he *had* wanted to—presupposes that Alan did *not* in fact want to kiss Jill.[29] Note finally that any reason for doing something can be said, in perfectly standard English, to be a reason for wanting to do it. Suppose Bob announces that he is going to the store. If we wanted to know his motivation, we could ask either "What is your reason for going?" or "What is your reason for wanting to go?" Both questions could be answered "I promised my wife I'd do the shopping." In contrast, if Bob had announced that he is going to *jail*, then presumably neither question could be answered.

It might at this point be suggested that "desire," in the sense in which intention entails desire, is simply a synonym of "intention."[30] This is not true either. Intention, unlike desire, entails belief. I desire to make a fortune today, but cannot be said to intend to because I am certain I won't. Even belief plus desire is not the same as intention: I want and expect the sun to rise tomorrow, but could hardly intend it to rise. Finally, it has been objected that if "desire" is understood in the way I've indicated, then the principle that intention entails desire is trivial or tautological.[31] I do not regard this as an objection.

Intending, and therefore volitive desire, is involved in intentional action. Someone who intentionally flipped the switch must have wanted to, but he need not have had a desire to flip it. Volitive desire is similarly implicated in decision. Deciding to do something entails forming the intention to do it, which results in desiring to do it. If someone has decided to eat, he must want to eat, but he may have no desire to. Decision-making changes volitive desires, but has no effect on appetitive desires. Suppose Alan has an hour free. He has a desire to play tennis and a desire to play squash. He chooses tennis. Before deciding, Alan did not know what he wanted to do. Afterward, he wanted to play tennis, not squash. Even after choosing not to, however, Alan should still have a desire to play squash. Deciding to do something does not make it appealing, and deciding not to do something does not make it unappealing.

I selected the term "volitive" because volitive desires are the ones involved in intention and decision, that is, in volition. They are manifestations of the will, which most generally is the power or capacity to desire volitively. Appetitive desires, on the other hand, are inner forces acting on the will, pushing or pulling it in certain directions. Value judgments are other inner forces influencing the will. Sometimes such forces pull the will in different directions, as when a person has a desire to commit adultery while believing that adultery is immoral. But sometimes they pull together, as when a person's reason for believing that he should eat is that he has a ravenous appetite.[32] As I said above, willpower is the ability to resist when appetitive desires act to divorce volitive desires from value judgments.

5. REALLY WANTING

There are several distinct senses in which an individual may be said to *really want* something. In one, "really want" means *actually* want. Suppose we see John bidding on an old painting at an auction. We would naturally infer that he wants to buy it. John's close friend Bill, though, may tell us that appearances are deceiving: John does not really want to buy the painting, which he could not afford anyway; what John actually wants to do is make sure the painting fetches a high enough price for his aunt, who is selling it. Similarly, suppose Mr. Smith, explaining a new machine at school, says, "That light means it is overheated and wants to cool off." (Here, incidentally, is a genuinely extended use of "want.") An overly serious student might interrupt with, "That machine doesn't *really* want anything, does it? Do machines have minds?"

In another sense, "really want" means want *very much*. We might infer that Bob really wants to play tennis, in this sense, from the fact that he has not exercised in a week, and that he gave up a day's pay to play. We might infer that he doesn't really want to win, in this sense, from the fact that he is not making much of an effort to chase down difficult shots. What we really want, in this sense, is opposed to what we *merely* wish for. In a third sense, what you "really want" is what you *should* want, that is, what you would want if you were rational, had sufficient information, and thought things over with proper care. Thus in a friendly game of chess, as you are reaching to take my bishop, I may remark, "You don't really want to do that! I could take your queen. See?" You might retort, "Yes I do! Take my queen and I'll checkmate you in two." A parent may tell her boy, who is clamoring for a new toy, that he doesn't really want it, on the grounds that he would be bored with it in a few minutes. And, after having demolished his racket, Clay may remark, sadly, that he didn't really want to do that.

In a fourth sense, what we really want is what we have an *appetitive* desire to do. Chris came by my office to ask me to play tennis. "I really want to play," I said, "but I have to teach." A short while later Mark asked me whether I wanted to play tennis, and I replied, "No, I have to teach." My reply to Chris indicated an appetitive desire to play, while my reply to Mark indicated a volitive desire not to play. After placing an ad in the "Work Wanted" column, Ed may tell us that he doesn't really want to work, but he needs the money. Later, when an employer calls to ask whether he still wants the job, Ed may reply, "Yes, very much." Ed's statement that he does not really want to work indicates that he has no appetitive desire to work. His answer "Yes, very much" and the fact that he placed an ad in the "Work Wanted" column indicate that he volitively desires to work. What we want and what we really want may coincide. Suppose I ask what you want to do today. You answer that you want to play tennis in the morning, visit Mary in the hospital in the afternoon, and see a show in the evening. I then ask, "Do you really want to visit Mary, or do you want to purely out of a sense of obligation?" You might reply, "I really want to visit her. I enjoy her company. Besides, I am thinking of asking her out."

Emphasizing the word "want" can have the same effect as putting "really" before it. Ed might say that he doesn't *want* to work, and I might say that I *want* to play tennis. This despite the fact that Ed *does* want to work and I do *not* want to play tennis. Emphasis, of course, has other functions, such as drawing attention to a particular choice of words, as in "I *want* the sun to rise, but I don't *intend* it to."

"Really want" is often followed by a but-clause, which explains why a possible implication of really wanting in that sense does not hold. Thus if Bob heard us talking about his failure to chase down difficult shots, he might say, "I do really want to win, but my ankles were recently injured." His injury is supposed to explain why he is not running hard, something we would naturally expect if he wanted very much to win. Similarly, suppose Jill says, "I did not really want to kiss Alan, but he made me." The statement that she had no appetitive desire to kiss Alan might suggest that she did not kiss him. The statement that Alan made her explains why that suggestion is erroneous. Finally, Bill might say, "I really want to see Pat, but she is out of town," intending Pat's absence to explain why he will not see her even though he really wants to. "Really" in this example could have any of its senses.

Let us focus on the fourth, appetitive sense of "really want." The principle that appetitive desire tends to generate volitive desire implies that we tend to want what we really want in this sense. A but-clause is therefore often used—as in my examples three paragraphs back—to indicate that volitive desire diverges from appetitive and to explain why. My reason for not wanting to play tennis, despite my appetitive desire to do so, is that I have to teach. Ed's reason for wanting to work, when he has no appetitive desire to do so, is that he needs the money. In one use, then, "S really wants to do A, but (he believes that) *p*" implies:

(1) S has a desire to do A;
(2) S does not desire to do A; and
(3) S's reason for not desiring to do A is that *p*.

In its parallel use, "S doesn't really want to do A, but *p*" implies that S has no desire to do A yet nevertheless does desire to do A for the reason that *p*. Note the "he believes" in parentheses. This is always understood (in this use), but it may be deleted except when the speaker does not himself believe that *p*. "Bill really wants to kiss Jill, but it is immoral" would be a misleading thing for me to say unless I too believe that Bill's kissing Jill would be immoral. If I don't, then I would have to say, "Bill really wants to kiss Jill, but he believes it is immoral." In any case, (3) entails that it is Bill's *believing* that kissing Jill is immoral which explains his not desiring to kiss her.

Given conditions (1) and (3), it will generally be true that S *would* desire to do A *if he did not consider the fact that p*. I would want to play tennis if I ignored the fact that I have to teach. Similarly, Ed would not desire to work if he disregarded the fact that he needs the money. What we really want, in this sense, is typically what we would want if duty, necessity, and the like were disregarded.[33] As I put it above, appetitive desires generate volitive desires in the absence of countervailing factors. S's belief that *p* is just such a countervailing factor. The counterfactual "S would desire to do A if he did not consider the fact that *p*" will not hold, however, in cases where S's not desiring to do A—condition (2)—is overdetermined.

Two further implications hold in the typical case: *S wishes that not-p*, and *S's reason for wishing that not-p is that he has a desire to do A*. Thus I wish that I did not have to teach, and my reason for wishing this is that I have a desire to play tennis. Note that there is no incompatibility or conflict between desiring to teach and desiring not to *have* to teach. Similarly, Ed wishes that he did not need the money, since he has no desire to work. These further implications are not universal, however. For example, when asked whether he is coming to your party Saturday night, Mike might reply, "I really want to, but I will be in Hawaii." The sincerity of Mike's statement does not require that he wish he were not going to Hawaii. A somewhat weaker condition is nearly universal, however: *that he has a desire to do A is a reason S has for wishing that not-p.* Mike's desire to attend the party is at least one reason he has for wishing that he would not be in Hawaii, even though it is not a sufficient reason. We often have reasons for wanting to do something without in fact wanting to do it. Even this implication may break down, however, in extreme cases. Suppose Mary-Theresa really wants to commit adultery, but believes adultery is prohibited by God. She may regard God's prohibitions as a given, something not to be questioned, and so consider nothing a reason for wishing they were different.

Unlike the word "desire," "want" all by itself is not ambiguous—it only means volitive desire. To express appetitive desire, emphasis or "really" must be added.[34] Sentences like "He really wants it" are genuinely ambiguous,[35] however, and can be understood in any one of the four senses outlined above. "He is really tall," "She really runs," "That is really expensive," and "There's a real car" are ambiguous in some of the same ways.[36] Note that it is only in the first sense of "really," when it means actually, that wanting and really wanting are equivalent.

It is commonly said, though, that "want" is ambiguous.

> The words "want" and "desire" are used in wider and narrower senses. . . . Thus, in one sense of "want," "He didn't *want* to do that yard work" is compatible with "He got up early in order to get the yard work done." But in a wider sense of the term, the latter is equivalent to "He got up early because he wanted to do yard work." (Alston, 1967b, p. 401)

It is incorrect to say that one sense of "desire" is *narrower* than another. There are, to be sure, many cases in which we want something without really wanting it. But there are also cases in which we really want something without wanting it. Volitive and appetitive desire are logically *independent.*

It has been suggested that "want" expresses *intrinsic* wanting in its "narrow sense," and *intrinsic or extrinsic* wanting in its "broad sense."

> Suppose that x is visiting y in New York for a weekend and that on Saturday morning y asks x what he wants to do that day. In reply, x might say that he wants to see the paintings at an art opening, go shopping, eat at a Chinese restaurant, and spend the later evening at y's home. By contrast, if y asks x, as x is about to get out of y's car at the gallery, whether he really wants to see such garish stuff, x might

honestly say, "No, but it's a duty." Must we suppose that x's wants have changed? I think not. For y's question, in the context, might well be aimed at finding out whether x intrinsically wants to see the paintings. But in the morning y, as a good host, was concerned to help x accomplish as much as possible of whatever x wanted to do, regardless of whether the wants were intrinsic. . . . (Audi, 1973b, pp. 389ff.)

What we really want is not the same as what we intrinsically want. First of all, it is debatable whether anyone genuinely regards looking at art as an end in itself rather than as a means to the pleasure or enrichment or knowledge to be gained from looking at it. Wanting something *for the pleasure of it*, in contrast to wanting something *for its own sake*, is extrinsic wanting. It cannot be questioned, though, that people sometimes really want to look at art. Second, the fact that Mike really wants to attend the party is perfectly compatible with the claim that his desire to attend is based entirely on his desire to see Michele, who will be at the party. The intrinsic-extrinsic distinction cuts across the want-really want distinction.

6. SUMMARY

To summarize, my major claim is that the word "desire" is ambiguous, expressing two logically though not causally independent states. Volitive and appetitive desires are very similar: both are propositional attitudes; both tend to generate action, to spread from ends to means, and to yield pleasure when satisfied. But there are important differences: appetitive desire influences volitive desire, but not vice versa; volitive desire is a better index of action, appetitive desire of pleasure; only volitive desires are based on reasons, influenced by value judgments, or entailed by intentions. Of much less importance are my claims concerning how these states are expressed in English. Volitive desires are expressed by "to desire, want, or wish," appetitive desires by "to have a desire," "to *want* or really want," and "to yearn or long." The sharp linguistic differences that I believe mark the two senses of "desire" can be blurred without serious consequences, so long as the senses themselves are clearly differentiated.[37]

NOTES

1. This might suggest that wants are future-directed desires. But "I want it to be the case that I got up earlier" is both well formed and true.
2. See Ezorsky (1960); Gauthier (1963), p. 40; Brand (1970), p. 945; Radford (1970), pp. 56ff.; Audi (1973a), p. 19; and Anscombe (1976), p. 36.
3. But not exactly equivalent. Gordon shows that being happy that p entails not only being certain but also *knowing* that p; and hoping that p entails a special sort of uncertainty, uncertainty not based on indecision. See Gordon (1969; 1973, sec. 4; 1974, sec. 5; and 1980, sec. 4).

4. Cf. Gosling (1969), p. 97.

5. Contrast Gosling (1969), pp. 11, 102, 124.

6. This was observed by Gosling (1969), p. 97. Schiffer (1976, p. 198, n. 4) therefore misunderstood Gosling's discussion of the senses of "want."

7. "S *likes* the prospect of VP-ing" means "S is pleased by the prospect of VP-ing," which in turn means "S is pleased by the fact that he will or might VP." None of the three expressions, therefore, is equivalent to "S views the prospect of VP-ing with pleasure." One further difference might be noted. S can view with pleasure the prospect of making a fortune today even though he realizes there is absolutely no prospect of his doing so. But in that case, we could not say that he is pleased by the prospect of making a fortune today. I discuss liking and being pleased in "Pleasure and Happiness" (Davis, 1981a).

8. Remarkably similar examples were used by Daveney (1961, p. 142) to distinguish "inclinational" from "intentional" wanting.

9. Cf. Frankfurt (1971), pp. 7, 12.

10. See Brandt and Kim (1963), p. 426; von Wright (1963), p. 103; Alston (1967b), p. 401; Goldman (1970), p. 50; Norman (1971), pp. 19ff., 26ff.; Snare (1972), p. 397; Audi (1973b), p. 389; and Harman (1976), p. 436. Similar distinctions are drawn in Menger (1871), pp. 56ff., 228; Birck (1922), p. 28; Lewis (1946), pp. 382-388; and Narveson (1967), p. 71.

11. This case is due to Frankfurt (1971, p. 9).

12. Schiffer (1976) has argued that these cases lead to paradox unless two sorts of desire are distinguished.

13. Nagel (1970, pp. 29ff.) distinguishes motivated from unmotivated desires. Note that intrinsic volitive desires, as well as appetitive desires, are unmotivated.

14. The distinction between volitive and appetitive desires therefore seems to coincide with Schiffer's distinction between "reason-following" and "reason-providing" desires (1976, sec. 4). On "reason-following" desires, see also Locke (1974), pp. 172-176.

15. Cf. Neely (1974), pp. 46ff.

16. This fact is compatible with the claim I have made elsewhere (Davis, 1981a, 1981b, 1982) that pleasure or enjoyment *consists in* the *net* satisfaction of volitive desires. It is possible, for example, that the satisfaction of one appetitive desire is correlated with the satisfaction of a greater total number of volitive desires than the satisfaction of one volitive desire.

17. There is an enormous literature on the relationship between value judgments and desires. For an excellent review, see Frankena (1958).

18. Cf. Gauthier (1963), pp. 33-43, and Gosling (1969), pp. 97, 102.

19. Watson (1975, pp. 210ff.) has some excellent examples here, but he fails to distinguish volitive and appetitive desires. Contrast Gauthier (1963), pp. 36-38.

20. Such a change of volitive desire against a constancy of appetitive desire enables a simple resolution of the paradox of desire discussed by Schiffer (1976). Specifically, Schiffer's paradox disappears if before the change the agent desires *not* to have a desire to eat (because he wants

to avoid eating) while after the change the individual desires to *have* a desire to eat (because now he wants to enjoy eating as much as possible). Schiffer's apparent assumption that the agent's desires are constant makes it hard to explain why the agent's actions change (from noneating to eating).

21. Cf. Gauthier (1963), pp. 12-17 (but see pp. 33ff.); Bond (1974), sec. 3; Watson (1975); Schiffer (1976), sec. 5; and Stocker (1979); contrast Hare (1952), chaps. 1, 11; and Davidson (1970).

22. Cf. Gauthier (1963), pp. 36-38.

23. Of course, if expected but unwanted consequences of intended acts are themselves intended, then intention does not even entail volitive desire. I argue that they are not intended in "A Causal Theory of Intending" (Davis, 1984a).

24. Daveney (1961); Churchland (1970), p. 231; Goldman (1970), p. 50; Nagel (1970), p. 29; and Audi (1973b), p. 389.

25. Jenkins (1965), p. 165; Rachels (1969), p. 10; Baier (1970), pp. 651ff.; Chisholm (1970), p. 645; Hare (1970), p. 46; Meiland (1970), p. 117; and Lawrence (1972), p. 86.

26. Norman (1971), p. 19; Lawrence (1972), p. 88; Hampshire (1975), p. 40; Neely (1974), pp. 32ff.; and Miller (1980), p. 339.

27. I am indebted here to Audi (1973b), p. 390. Another of Audi's examples is quoted below in section 5.

28. Cf. Gosling (1969), pp. 93, 105.

29. Cf. Gosling (1969), pp. 87ff.

30. See Daveney (1961); Sellars (1963), p. 217; Fleming (1964), p. 304; Bedford (1966), pp. 654ff.; Chisholm (1970), p. 645; von Wright (1971), p. 103; Foot (1972), p. 204; and Miller (1980), p. 339. Contrast Meiland (1970), p. 74; Audi (1973b), pp. 390-391; Harman (1976), p. 432; and Davidson (1978), pp. 58ff.

31. See Fleming (1964), pp. 307ff.

32. Watson (1975) has an interesting discussion of the view, which he traces back to Plato, that appetites and values are two different sources of wants.

33. Cf. Daveney (1961), pp. 138-143.

34. In correspondence, Audi pointed out an apparent exception to this rule. "Want" can certainly express sexual desire in "He wants her." Even here, though, I tend to "hear" emphasis.

35. Contrast Gosling (1969, pp. 18ff.), who seems to treat "really wanting" as univocal, expressing a "full-bodied, unqualified case of wanting something"—an amalgam of all the different senses distinguished above, while treating "wanting" as equivocal ("shifty").

36. See Goldstein (1973) and Davis (1981b) for a discussion of "really happy."

37. This essay is an expanded version of "The Two Senses of Desire" published in *Philosophical Studies* 45 (1984): 181-195 (copyright © 1984 by D. Reidel Publishing Company, Dordrecht, Holland). I would like to thank Robert Audi and Joel Marks for their comments.

The want of a thing is perplexing enough,
but the possession of it is intolerable.
— SIR JOHN VANBRUGH

Desire and Time

Ronald B. de Sousa

Abstract. This paper defends the thesis that there is a relation of correspondence between desire and its object, analogous to that between belief and truth. Specifically, some events have an intrinsic organization in time, and desires can represent their object under corresponding temporal aspects. "False desire" results when these don't match. This is especially likely to occur when we confuse "consummatory" and "play" desires, and it explains some instances of the "dust and ashes" phenomenon, viz., the disappointment which sometimes attends the nominal satisfaction of our desires.

1. THE PARADOX OF CONTINGENT SATISFACTION

That one can want something, and then not enjoy it when one gets it, is just a piece of melancholy common sense. Nevertheless it is sometimes paradoxical. It is not simply that satisfaction of a desire doesn't guarantee the satisfaction of its *owner*. To be sure, having any one thing that I wanted may leave me dissatisfied and unhappy, if only because there may be many other things that I lack. Moreover the desired event may have repellent features I had never dreamed of. What is surprising is that even when the desire and its object are considered in isolation from their context, and there seems to be nothing in the description of the outcome that would have been disavowed by the desiring imagination, still anticipation can seem betrayed, leaving only the proverbial dust and ashes. The meal I so wanted to repeat may taste exactly as I remembered it, yet I find this time that I just get little pleasure from it. There can be *technical satisfaction* (the truth of p) of a desire that p, without *phenomenological satisfaction* — actual enjoyment of p. That fact makes a mystery of the connection between the object posited by a desire and what will actually satisfy it. Is it purely accidental? Russell (1921, p. 72) once proposed the extreme empiricist view that since a desire and its condition of satisfaction are separate, contingently related states, the best

way to gratify any particular desire can only be discovered by experience. That view has a certain mad charm. Even if it were true,
however, it presupposes that there is some real and regular correspondence for experience to turn up. So one might grant that the connection between the desire that *p* and its satisfaction by the truth that *p* is
logically contingent, but stop short of inferring that it is just accidental. And that is just as well, because if it were just accidental then
acting to secure the object of our desires would seem a hopeless
gamble.

But if there is a relation of contingent correspondence between
desire and object, what does this relation consist in? The question
resuscitates a concept first introduced – to still enduring scandal – in
Plato's *Philebus:* the concept of a *false desire.* That concept will gain
some legitimacy if we can outline at least one set of correspondence
conditions to account for the paradox of contingent satisfaction. That
is what I propose to do in this paper.

The hypothesis I shall put forward is that at least one source of fit or
lack of fit between desire and object relates to the way that the desire
represents the temporality of the object. Some events have an intrinsic organization in time; if desire represents them as having another,
there will be a mismatch between the desire and the event. To explain
the type of organization involved, I first need to introduce the notion
of *temporal aspect*, a technical term from traditional grammar.

2. TEMPORAL ASPECT: TIME-INDEXED AND
IMMEDIATE DESIRES

The reader brought up on some old-fashioned notions of grammar,
especially of Greek, will remember a distinction between tense and
aspect. Aspectual distinctions are not concerned with whether the
event is past, present, or to come. Instead they concern how events
are envisaged in time. The possibilities are roughly the following (they
are all, for convenience, exemplified with reference to a time past,
though all, as we shall see, can apply equally to the present or future).

> 1. An event may be viewed as enduring through a stretch of time. In
> terms of that ugly but accurate current barbarism, it is viewed as
> *ongoing.* This is the *continuous* aspect. The imperfect tense in Indo-
> European languages usually expresses continuous aspect as well as
> past tense. Example: *She was rich, but she was honest.*

> 2. An event can also be viewed as occupying a certain location in time.
> This is the *punctual* aspect. The Greek aorist and the French *passé
> simple*, although usually called past tenses, actually express punctual
> aspect. Example: *On the third day she won the jackpot.*

In English the distinction between imperfect and aorist has no clear morphological markers, but it is readily expressed: it is the difference between *she laughed* (when I brought up the aorist), and *she was laughing* (when I brought up the rear).

> 3. The *perfect* is also commonly but mistakenly thought of as a tense. The perfect "tense" indicates that an event is considered as fully achieved or terminated. The "perfect" event, past, present, or future, can in addition be presented from the point of view of the imperfect, indicating that the perfect was appropriate over a lasting period of time, or from the point of view of the punctual, i.e., of an instant in time. These are somewhat subtle nuances which the reader may dispute. But as examples I propose respectively: *By the time of adolescence, I had already learned many a trick*, and *At noon, he had gone.* The time referred to in the perfect aspect can be present, as in *I have done it*, or past, as in *I had (already) done it* (e.g., when you inquired).

> 4. Finally there is the *frequentative* aspect. This views an event or action as taking place repeatedly or habitually in some period of time under consideration. Example: *Sundays I play golf.*

In normal use the present tense is frequentative. Locutions such as "I am doing it" are used for the continuous, which can be stressed with the phrase "I am in the process of...." But it is almost impossible to express a punctual present, perhaps because it is difficult to think of the present as anything but the "ongoing" specious present. One might expect the "simple" present—"I do it"—to express the punctual aspect. In fact, however, the only context in which it does so is where it functions as the "historic present," which is really an aorist. The historic present is a narrative "tense," with both colloquial and literary uses, that no longer carries any connotation of relative temporal location. Instead it suggests that events are being viewed as points beaded serially on the string of time. "So he comes in. I says to him: 'Where have you been?' 'Nowhere special,' he says..." In all other contexts it has lost its punctual nuance, if it ever had one, and is used almost exclusively as a frequentative. "Yes, I play tennis" means something like "I am in the habit of playing tennis."

As for the future, the morphological system of English shows even less interest in the nuances of time and aspect. But it is possible by circumlocution to indicate whether one is envisaging a future event as "ongoing" or as simply occupying a point of future time. ("I'll be doing it all through next week" versus "I'll do it next week.")

3. THE ASPECT OF DESIRE

I now wish to argue that desires have important aspectual features. To
clarify this idea, let me first set aside a related but different distinction
with which the aspectual might be confused. That other distinction is
the familiar one between *standing* and *occurrent* desires. Occurrent
desires, it might be suggested, are desires viewed in the punctual
aspect. They are dated events occurring at a particular point in time,
with causes and effects, if any, that could also be dated. Standing
desires, by contrast, are viewed either from the continuous or from
the frequentative aspect. They are supposed to be dispositions giving
rise to occurrent desires when activated by the right triggering occasion. Whether we should admit the existence of any standing desires
is largely a terminological question. One reason for resisting the usage
is that we might find it useful to have a special word for that class of
wants that can exist only in full actuality. Suppose that for my birthday you present me with a specially desirable widget. If I truly exclaim
that *this is the widget I have always wanted*, I have chosen my words
sensibly: my sincerity would have been suspect had I claimed instead
that I had always *desired* it. Reserving the word *desire* for the occurrent, conscious, and actual state in terms of which dispositions must
be defined, therefore, has the advantage of putting a tiny bit of order
into a chaotic field.

For this reason, I shall confine myself to the occurrent sense of the
word in this discussion. But this is not the sense in which I am
interested in aspectual distinctions. The occurrent-dispositional distinction is concerned with the temporal aspect of the *experience* of
desire. I am interested rather in the aspect of the *object*.

My suggestion is that the intentional objects of desire, like analogous objects of belief, may be *viewed aspectually*. Moreover, again as
in the case of belief, *actual* objects of desire — i.e., the real event-types
in the world which the desire sets up as its technically satisfying
condition — are of different types, to which different aspects may be
variously appropriate. Corresponding to these two suggestions, I must
now make two sets of distinctions.

The first distinction separates those desires that focus on a specific
point in the future ("I want to come and see you Sunday") from those
that do not ("She's just dying to see you"). I shall call them, respectively, *T-desires*, for "time-indexed," and *I-desires*, for "immediate"
desires.

As a first approach to this distinction, note that T-desires are typically specified in terms of propositional objects (Sam desired that
Steve would come), whereas immediate ones typically have direct
objects (Sam desired Steve). This test gives some of the flavor of the

distinction, but it is unreliable and superficial. A better test is that I-desires, but not T-desires, are unproblematically attributed to animals. This is related to a third criterion, which is that T-desires may involve reference to particular temporal locations. T-desires are possible only for beings capable of framing a reference to some particular time.[1] A corollary is that T-desires, but not I-desires, are closely bound up with the possibility of planning. They are the sort of desires that we can *intend* to realize: that is to say, they are the sort of desires for the realization of which it makes sense to establish a timetable.[2] I-desires come without any such time index: they are always, phenomenologically, desires for something *right away*. But even that is misleading, because it seems to imply just what I am denying, namely, that in I-desires the subject is conscious of some point in time (namely, *right away*) to which the desire applies.

I shall take for granted without discussion here that the object of desire is necessarily referred to the future in either case. But this is a requirement of intelligible description, not of the phenomenology of desire itself. The third-person description of Sarah's desire must refer, *de re*, to some vague region of time later than the onset of the desire. But the I-desire's *own* representation (or our description of it *de dicto*) contains no time reference at all. I-desire is in this respect more "primitive," without however lacking the essential structure of desire. I-desire, like T-desire, explains action in the context of a desire-belief pair, from which the action's claim to rationality or irrationality can be inherited. But that structure is extremely minimal. I-desire can figure out immediate means, but not make elaborate plans.[3]

So much for the distinction between T-desires and I-desires. It takes care of one side of the correspondence between desires and their object. To see how that correspondence can break down, by analogy to the breakdown in correspondence we call *falsity* in the case of beliefs, let us now move to the other side — the side of the potentially satisfying event.

This is the second of the promised distinctions. It is one that Aristotle first made, and rightly thought crucial to his analyses of virtue, pleasure, and happiness. It is the threefold distinction between *states*, *activities*, and *achievements*. States are passive and activities are actively engaged in, but both states and activities endure indefinitely through time. Neither needs any specific completion. They contrast in this with achievements, which have a natural end. Achievements may take time from their beginning to their completion, but they do not exist as achievements until the moment of their completion. *Winning a race* thus contrasts with *walking about*, as Aristotle puts it, in that it can be truly said that you *have been walking about* as soon as you have started, whereas merely beginning to run a race, even if you are "in the process" of winning it, does not make it true that you have won it yet.

The following remarks, then, relate three categories, or parameters. (a) Whether the desire is *time-indexed* or *immediate*; (b) the *temporal aspect* under which it is desired: continuous, punctual, perfect, or frequentative; and (c) the *category of the actual object* of desire: here the alternatives are state, activity, and achievement.[4]

The hypothesis I offer can now be made explicit in terms of the distinctions made so far:

> For each *aspectual type* of object as defined in Aristotle's taxonomy, there is a natural or *privileged aspect* of desire.

The requirement that the temporal aspect of desire match the aspectual category of its object is a requirement of rationality. Here, as in the case of other rules of rationality, these constraints are bordered by constraints on what can be *consistently ascribed*.[5] Here, then, are some illustrations of the constraints involved.

First, notice that only T-desire can view the desired object in the *frequentative* mode. This follows from my assumption that there is no representation of temporal location available to I-desire. When we envisage the desires of other animals, we must assume that all their desires are immediate. Because we don't know how to attribute to them any references to future time, we can't make a difference between their desiring something "right away" and their desiring it to be repeated indefinitely in the future.

Second, we can desire to feel excited or kindly, as well as to walk or play. But since these are states or activities enduring through time, the suitable aspects of I-desires for them are only the continuous and perhaps the perfect. To envisage a state or activity as object of I-desire under a punctual aspect, we must have in mind the *onset* of the state or activity rather than the activity itself. It is possible to envisage a state or activity punctually in the context of a T-desire, since we can treat a period of time in the future as a point. But that doesn't make sense in the context of an I-desire.

Third, achievements, such as *winning*, can be desired only in the punctual or the perfect aspects in the mode of I-desire. Aristotle points out that a *kinesis* "moves toward a goal, and becomes complete only when what it aims at has been produced" (*Nicomachean Ethics*, bk. 10, chap. 4). So the continuous aspect can make sense only in relation to some activity or state that is conducive to the achievement, and not in relation to the achievement itself. This is because the moment of completion cannot be decomposed into parts (although sometimes the part of the process that led up to it can). And whereas it is possible to view some period of time as a point when we take the long view allowed for by I-desire, it isn't so easy, outside of typography, to view a point as a period.

Fourth, it may seem that one can desire anything in the perfect aspect. But—this is a feature to which I shall return below—there is a peculiarity attending achievements. These are most naturally desired punctually, as in "Calvin desires *to win the race.*" Does it not seem equally natural, though, to desire *to have won?* It does indeed. But these are not merely two different temporal aspects of the same desire. As we shall see later, they are distinct desires, and this fact turns out to have important consequences. States and activities, on the other hand, may be the objects of continuous or punctual I-desires, but if they are desired in the perfect aspect this amounts to the desire that *they cease to exist.* For consider what it can mean for me to desire *to have felt excited.* If we are talking about the mode of T-desire, it might mean that I wish to have had the experience, at some time or other in my life. In the mode of I-desire, on the other hand, the presumption is that I can only want to have experienced something if I am now experiencing it. And this means in effect that the desire in question is for the cessation of that experience. To desire in the perfect aspect in the mode of I-desire, in other words, is *to desire the experience to stop.* And this seems very different from a mere aspect under which the experience is desired. This, too, is a fact the importance of which will become clearer below.

To represent these facts compendiously, we can use a three-dimensional table, corresponding to the three categories of facts that I distinguished above. In Table 1, the four aspects are listed in consecutive columns, while the categories of events are listed in rows. Beneath each row, representing the third dimension, is an additional row in which the question is answered, whether that type of event in that temporal aspect is susceptible of being the object of I-desire (ID). Asterisks mark dubious or impossible items.

The interest of this table lies in this: much of the criticism of the ways of desire by philosophical or religious moralists, including the attacks on pleasure and desire by Plato, by the Stoics, or by Buddhists, or for that matter by the sort of moralist who writes books about how to get the most out of your sex life, can be construed as claiming that some categories of desire are inferior in virtue of their instrinsic aspectual properties, or in virtue of the aspectual category to which their typical object belongs. Most intriguing are those cases where the category to which a given pleasure belongs is disputable. Many of the moral disadvantages under which sexual desire has seemed to labor down the ages might be traced to its end having been mistaken for an achievement when in truth it should be viewed, like Aristotelian

Table 1
Three Dimensional Table of Aspects, Object Categories, and Desire Types

DESIRE TYPE AND OBJECT CATEGORY	TEMPORAL ASPECTS			
	Continuous	**Punctual**	**Perfect**	**Frequentative**
I. State	*I was feeling excited.*	*I felt excited.** (inception only?)	*I have felt excited.** (= *I have experienced excitement?*)	*I used to feel excited.*
Can be object of ID?	Yes (*I desire to be excited*).	No.	No (but cf. *I desire it to stop,** which is a centrifugal desire*).	(no ID possible)
II. Activity	*I was walking.*	No (but cf. *I went for a walk,** which is an achievement*).	*I have had my walk.*	*I walk after dinner.*
Can be object of ID?	Yes (*I desire to walk*).	No.	No.	(no ID possible)
III. Achievement	No (but cf. *I was winning,** which refers to the process leading up to the win*).	*I won.*	*I have won.*	*I (usually) win.*
Can be object of ID?	No (but cf. *I desire the feeling of having won,* which is a perfect*).	Yes (*I desire to win*).	Yes (*I desire to have won*).	(no ID possible)

Note: Asterisks denote dubious or impossible items.

contemplation, as an activity. Leaving aside the *moral* side of the strictures bestowed upon sexual desires, I think they rest on a sound *semantic* point. I shall return to say more about this after introducing yet another related distinction.

4. OBJECTIVE AND SUBJECTIVE DESIRES

When we desire food, drink, or sleep, it is usually obvious to us that the desire will last, at most, only as long as it is not gratified. But other desires—those associated with love, or beauty, and perhaps also jealousy, grief, or revenge—seem to come with a secondary desire for their own continuation: it is painful, while one is in their grip, to think of them as ephemeral (Schiffer, 1976). This difference appears to mark a deeper distinction, between *subjective* and *objective* desires. That distinction goes back to Plato's *Euthyphro*, in which Socrates asks, in effect, whether when we desire something we desire it *because it is desirable*, or whether on the contrary its desirability is simply the projected shadow of our desire. Rather than demanding an answer valid for all desires, it seems more sensible to suppose that there are two classes of desire, which I shall refer to as *subjective* and *objective* desires.[6] The contrast between them is grounded in the issue of whether there is a possibility of disagreement: for disagreement carries a presumption of objectivity. (If you are expressing purely subjective preferences or reactions, I can fail to sympathize, but it makes no sense to claim I *disagree*.) But from the first-person point of view another criterion might be used: subjective desires are those which *we do not mind thinking of as liable to change*. By contrast, when a desire appears to us to be for something objectively good, any future change will seem a betrayal:

> Nay, if I wax but cold in my desire,
> Think heaven hath motion lost, and the world, fire.[7]

Some desires, then, seem to come with accompanying second-order desires. Typically, the second-order desire is for the continuation of the first-order one. Let us call these *positive* second-order desires. But there are also *negative* second-order desires: desires that the first-order desire *not* continue.

As a first approximation, second-order desire might be identified with judgments of objective value, or endorsements of the first-order desire as having such value (see Frankfurt, 1971). But this won't always work. One can imagine wanting a certain desire never to stop (thus having the positive second-order desire) but knowing, at the same time, that this second-order desire is merely incontinently caused by the first-order desire. Such perhaps was the case with Augustine, when he uttered his prayer: *Give me chastity, but not yet.*

Still, we might deal with such apparent exceptions to the rule that objective desires are accompanied by positive second-order desires by appealing to yet another level. Suppose my first-order desire $D1$ (a simple physical desire, let us say) generates a second-order desire $D2$ that $D1$ continue. The test of a sincerely negative evaluation of $D1$ is that there be a desire $D3$ for $D1$ (and perhaps also $D2$) to disappear. In this way, then, we might still make the distinction between objective and subjective desires in terms of higher-order attitudes to the temporality of the desire.

But there is a simpler means of doing this, which is to appeal not just to the future but also to the past. Attitudes to *past* changes of desire are almost exactly the inverse of attitudes to future changes. Objective desires are those with respect to which we view change with equanimity, whereas we may (though we need not) regret a change in subjective desire. The explanation is the same in both cases. Where there is a presumption of objectivity, one can do no better than assume that one is right *now* (for if one does not think one is right now, then one is caught in Moore's belief paradox, holding something like "*p*, but I don't believe that *p*"). Hence when facing the future one requires (or hopes for) constancy; but one's past commitments, if they now seem just objectively wrong, one is understandably willing to dismiss.

The possibility of marking the distinction in terms of higher-order desires is a useful rule of thumb. But it is based on a symptom rather than being itself explanatory. The symptom, however, confirms the hypothesis for which I am arguing: namely, that the underlying explanation lies in a presumption of objectivity made by a certain class of desires.

5. CONSUMMATORY DESIRES AND PLAY DESIRES

The distinction between "objective " and "subjective" desires, by the present criterion, is common to both T-desires and I-desires. But chief among the I-desires that come with a *negative* second-order desire are what I shall call *consummatory desires*. The mark of a consummatory desire is that *its end is its end.* To put it slightly more perspicuously, the goal or (teleological) end of a consummatory desire may be identified with its termination or (temporal) end.

Obvious paradigms of consummatory desires and pleasures include hunger (eating) and a certain sort of sexual desire — specifically the desire for male orgasm, which typically represents the cessation of desire, leading for that very reason to the proverbial postcoital *tristitia*. And the negative second-order desires associated with these, as well as any regret that follows their satisfaction, may be taken as an indication of their repudiation as sources of objective value. This explains the bad press which bodily pleasures and desires have characteristically received from certain moralists. But it does not prove the correctness of their assimilation to the pure cases of consummatory desires: ones in which there is nothing more to the object of desire than its own annihilation. Desiring the pain to stop may be such a pure case if anything is, but even then, as we shall see in a moment, there may spring up a kind of derivative but separate desire for the pleasure of relief.

Consummatory desires contrast with those that come with an implicit desire for indefinite continuation, without regard to any consummation or satisfaction. The paradigm of nonconsummatory pleasures and desires is *play*, and especially the undirected and nonteleological play of a child. It is that "pottering about," the intellectual form of which Aristotle dignified with the title of *contemplation*. It is also the psychological ancestor of those pleasures that Plato called "pure" pleasures, of which he cited smelling a rose as the paradigm. Rather puzzlingly, Plato then went on to identify these with the intellectual pleasures. What smelling a rose and intellectual pleasures seem to have in common is that their anticipation is not necessarily linked with pain. They cannot therefore be afflicted with that self-destructive character that Plato thought essential to desire.

Let us look a little more carefully at the structure of consummatory desires. Their identifying mark, I have said, is that *their end is in their end*. We cannot assume that only I-desires are, properly speaking, consummatory, for one can presumably look forward to some particular point of future time at which relief will come. But if the desire is actually an occurrent one, which I have stipulated, *and if it is purely consummatory*, then it is difficult to see why immediate satisfaction would not always be preferable, *other things being equal*, to the more remote.

Both the italicized conditions are important, as can be seen from the following putative counterexample. As a child I admired a certain girl as a kind of hero of hedonism, because she would postpone micturation for as long as she could stand it, for the sake of the greater pleasure in ultimate relief. Is this a counterexample? No, for although she did turn an I-desire into a time-indexed one by virtue of the hedonic calculation that led her to this practice, the *ceteris paribus* clause was not satisfied. For she presumably thought the increase in pleasure worth the wait. (Note that in the Augustine case, which might also seem to offer a counterexample, what is wished for is not the satisfaction of a consummatory desire but the end of a certain class of such desires.) It will do no harm to proceed, then, as if we were speaking only of I-desires.

Even a pure consummatory desire is not merely a desire *for* its own termination, for some terminations are preferable to others. Which is which depends on your ideology: Plato and the Buddhist will prefer the itch just to cease, the sybarite will prefer to scratch. So these desires are not merely *for their own termination*. Freud was mistaken, then, when he proposed as a general characterization of satisfaction the mere cessation of stimulation (a characterization, originally, of the pleasure principle, but later rather more appropriately transferred to the Death instinct).[8] The question, then, is this: If consummatory desires are not literally *for* their own annihilation, do they necessarily come with a second-order desire for that end? Schiffer has argued that the desire for the desire's own termination, the desire for relief, and the desire (say) for a drink must all be *one and the same desire*. His argument is that this is necessary in order to avoid a paradox, which goes as follows:

> To act on an r-p [i.e., reason-providing] desire to ϕ is to ϕ only because one has that desire, but it is also to ϕ only because of one's desire for the pleasure and relief of discomfort ϕing affords. . . . Now there are . . . r-f [i.e., reason-following] desires to gain pleasure and to relieve discomforts . . . [but] r-p desires are not among them. . . . It would be altogether a mistake to suppose that a thirst was an r-f desire to drink; for then it would have to be a desire one had because one expected drinking to be pleasurable and relieving, . . . [but] the desire to drink itself is what is discomforting and the anticipated pleasure is itself the pleasure of gratifying that desire. (Schiffer, 1976, p. 198)

Schiffer concludes that

> there is one and only one way of avoiding a contradiction . . . : one's desire to ϕ, one's desire to gain the pleasure of satisfying one's desire to ϕ, one's desire to relieve the discomfort of one's desire to ϕ — these are all one and the same desire. An r-p desire is a self-referential desire for its own gratification. (Schiffer, 1976, p. 199)

To rephrase this rather abstruse argument, I take Schiffer to be saying the following: There would exist no pleasure, if it weren't for the (reason-providing) desire. So the second-order object would have no target. The conditions of existence for first- and second-order desires are therefore identical. So they must be one and the same.

If Schiffer were right, this might provide an explanation for the Paradox of Contingent Satisfaction, at least for the limited class of consummatory pleasures. The reason we are disappointed, we might infer, is that we thought there were two desires up for satisfaction, the first-order and the second-order, when indeed there was only one. If so, then consummatory pleasures would systematically provide us with only half of what they had seemed to promise.

But Schiffer's view can't be right. For if all those different formulations refer to the same desire, then even if we concede that a single desire does not have to be describable in terms of a single propositional object, still there must be a single measure of the *intensity* of that single desire. Schiffer rightly points out that we sometimes have

> the frustrating but not unheard of experience of an intense desire for chocolate, or whatever, the satisfaction of which brings and was expected to bring only a little pleasure. (Schiffer, 1976, p. 202)

He should be more disturbed by this case than he is. For if the pleasure desired and the relief from desire are objects of the same desire, then the *measure* of relief should be a measure of the pleasure. And in turn the relief, and the pleasure, should be proportional to the intensity of the desire. This is precisely what does not hold in the case described. Quite the contrary: One could even envisage a sort of hedonic calculus based on the distinction between the "relief pleasure" and the simple pleasure. I might sometimes say: I desire this passionately, though I am aware that the pleasure it will afford me is likely to disappoint me. Still, I prefer the relief of this painful desire *with* the disappointment, rather than the avoidance of disappointment if it means this continuing torture. Or on the contrary, if one is equally passionate but given to resentment, one might prefer to suffer the desire rather than the disappointment.

I conclude that a second-order desire for satisfaction of the first-order desire rides piggyback on top of the latter, but is not identical to it. We must therefore look for another way to understand the contingency of satisfaction.

The key, I suggest, lies in applying two notions introduced above: one is the aspectual features of desire; the other is the model of desire as quasi-cognitive or perceptual, that is, capable of a kind of fit or failure of fit analogous to truth and falsity. Recall that desire can envisage its object in various temporal aspects. Not anything can be desired in just any aspect, however. An "achievement," for example, cannot be desired in the continuous aspect, because it necessarily involves an undecomposable instant of time at which the achievement is consummated. This limitation, which I speculate may be rooted in our biological dispositions, introduces an element of objective correctness or incorrectness in the conception of a desired event implicit in the aspectual character of the desire. In the case of the chocolate craving, for example, the discrepancy arises because of a mistake in the desire as to the character of its own object. Eating chocolate appears to be an activity. It seems to be the sort of thing that one might enjoy doing, and therefore desire in the durational aspect. But in the case of a mere craving, *all that is actually desired is the consummation itself.* That is why the pleasure of it is so disappointing: such consumption of chocolate is, indeed, a *vice.* The nature of vice is frequently misunderstood, because (like weakness of the will) it is assumed to be a *moral* concept, whereas in fact it is a *psychological* one. The proper psychological definition of a vice is: *something that one craves to do even though it no longer brings any pleasure.* Or, in terms of the notions introduced above, a vicious desire is a *punctual* or *perfect* desire for a *state* or *activity.* And we now have an explanation of how that can come about, in terms of the notion of *naturally suitable aspects* for certain categories of objects of desire. We need not grant Schiffer's implausible thesis that a desire for chocolate can be *the very same desire* as a self-referential second-order desire for itself to end.

The difference between consummatory and play pleasures and their corresponding desires is an important one, which looms large in many fundamental disputes about human nature and the concepts of happiness and satisfaction. If the apparatus I have sketched is sound, there should be many other sorts of cases based on different kinds of mistaken assessments of the temporal aspect of desire most appropriate to a given target. Here is one which is the converse of the last. It is the case of the *harried tourist.*

The discomfort of the harried tourist comes from the fact that in actuality the viewing of memorable sites and works of art is, if pleasurable at all, pleasurable as an *activity.* But the harried tourist makes the mistake of desiring to tour only in the perfect, or perhaps sometimes in the punctual, aspect. She wants not to see, but to have seen.[9] ("Have you *done* the Uffizi?" "Not yet, but we have done the Duomo.") The trouble is that it is in the nature of sightseeing to take time, and the sightseer who is only interested in having done it will get little profit for a lot of work.

Much sexual activity is no doubt construed as the harried tourist construes sightseeing. Witness the dismal view of "Lust in action" as "Th' expense of spirit in a waste of shame" so powerfully expressed in Shakespeare's famous sonnet:

> Past reason hunted and no sooner had,
> Past reason hated. . .

This can now be seen for what it is: the result of an aspectual mistake about the nature of sexuality. If the real nature of sex demands that it be treated as an *activity,* there will be an inevitable discrepancy between it and a desire for it that is aspectually perfect rather than continuous. It amounts to taking sex for an achievement instead of an activity. Such a mistake is always likely to prove disappointing. For it amounts to construing *play*, which is *valuable activity* (that is, done for its own sake), as *work*, which is *useful* (that is, done for the sake of some end outside itself).[10] There is nothing especially pleasant about the end of play. So if play is desired in the aspect appropriate to work, it will always seem more work than its ending is worth.

This, then, is how the quasi-cognitive perspective I have adopted makes room for the resolution of the Paradox of Contingent Satisfaction. One way to fix this moral in the mind is to advert to the *Platonic Theory of Advertising*. Plato thought you could never be satisfied by the ordinary targets of your ostensible desires, because those were not their *real* targets. So the pursuit of the wrong objects could only exacerbate desire. Similarly, the principle behind contemporary advertising is that you must be made to think you want (say) a Cadillac, when what you really want is some far more primal comfort. Thanks to this carefully cultivated mistake, there will be no end to your desire, and you will gratify the advertiser by coming back endlessly for more Cadillacs.

I have been assuming, in this section, that there is some objective fact of the matter about the nature of certain pleasures and activities. I have followed Aristotle, for example, in saying that *seeing* is by nature an activity, while the satisfaction of a craving is by nature an achievement. But how seriously can we take this idea? In my concluding section, I very tentatively sketch a sanguine position.

6. TIME AND RATIONALITY

I have spoken of a distinction between objective and subjective desires, and I have speculated that we have biologically determined inclinations to view certain sorts of events in some preferred aspect. This suggests that there might be a biological basis for some of the mechanisms that govern the temporality of desire. While I think this is true, two qualifications must be made.

First, like any claim about what is natural, a thesis about the naturally correct aspect in which to think of some sort of action or experience will be inherently controversial. The claim just made about sexual pleasure, for example, is admittedly tinged with a particular ideology. That ideology can be argued for, nevertheless, and the use I have made of it in attempting to explain some of the traditional dissatisfaction which moralists have expressed with sexual experience constitutes one such argument.

My second qualification is that even if it is granted that there are relevant biological facts, these may not determine the psychological facts in any simple way. This is, of course, a commonplace. But the way that it applies in the present context is worth noting. It is, in brief, that *biological consummations and psychological consummations need not coincide*, so that a simple inference from the former to the latter will not in general be valid. It is one manifestation of this that some desires can be, so to speak, *biologically centripetal, but psychologically centrifugal* — and vice versa. By this I mean simply that from the point of view of our experience, a certain pursuit may be motivated by the desire to avoid a painful situation; bodily needs such as the avoidance of extreme temperatures or of hunger may be of this sort, where biologically speaking there is some definite positive goal being pursued. At a deeper level of analysis, the opposite may be the case. There is no *real* teleology in nature, and so what is experienced as a centripetal pull to a certain fulfillment may, biologically speaking, be driven by a purely causal mechanism.

Consider the question of whether there is a naturally correct category of sexual pleasure and desire. The vulgar sociobiological account of the sexual instinct may well be basically correct: male orgasm is a consummatory activity[11] which, biologically speaking, needs to be carried out as often and as quickly as possible. Nevertheless, Freud (1905) may also be right, from the psychological point of view, in speaking of the fusing of a number of very different "component instincts" into the "mature" sexual instinct. These other "instincts," which include looking, touching, etc., may participate more in the nature of playful activity than in that of achievement. This may explain the fact that we have the *capacity* to experience sexual activity as play, even though from the point of view of its strict and immediate biological goal it should be a consummation. Much the same holds for the processes that Plato took as the paradigms of bodily pleasure, namely, those that are generally associated with the restoration of some sort of homeostatic balance. These include some forms of nutritional replenishment, and some forms of the elimination of waste. They are also from the biological point of view consummations, or achievements. And they are associated with pleasure, just exactly insofar as we can exercise voluntary control over behavior that can bring them about. (Hence, just as we would expect, pleasure and desire are associated with elimination through defecating, but not with elimination through sweating.[12]) But this does not mean that we must view these bodily functions, and experience our desires for them, strictly in terms of punctual or perfect consummations. It is a further question, and an open one, whether for the sake of maximizing pleasure, of for the sake of happiness, or morality, we *ought* to view them in one way and not in another.

To some extent, in the matter of our desires and their satisfaction, thinking (or desiring) makes it so. But as the cases of Vice, Tourism, and Sex have, I hope, made clear, our construals of the nature of our desires and their objects do not always lead to satisfaction, let alone happiness. In those cases it is at least a hypothesis worth considering that there are natural limits to our capacity to construe things as we please.[13]

NOTES

1. Cf. Wittgenstein's remark: "One can imagine an animal angry, frightened, unhappy, happy, startled. But hopeful? And why not? A dog believes his master is at the door. But can he also believe his master will come the day after tomorrow?... Can only those hope who can talk? Only those who have mastered the use of a language. That is to say, the phenomena of hope are modes of this complicated form of life" (Wittgenstein, 1958, p. 174).

2. Annette Baier discusses the case of Corlissa, who orders flowers on Friday to be delivered Sunday, in apology for the insult of which she rightly *predicted* that she will be guilty on Saturday night, though she now neither intends nor desires it: "What feature of intention is lacking [in the expectation of insult]? I suggest that what is lacking is precisely what is present in Corlissa's Friday intention to apologize, namely an implementation-plan, a *timetable* linking the present with the intended future" (Baier, 1985, p. 15).

3. This is apparently the situation of the desiderative part of Plato's soul. See Penner (1971), especially pp. 103-116.

4. See Aristotle, *Nicomachean Ethics*, bk. 10, chap. 4, and bk. 11, chap. 5. I follow Ryle in using "achievement verbs" to correspond roughly to Aristotle's *kineseis* (Ryle, 1964). See also Vendler (1967). Vendler adds a fourth category of *accomplishments*, which includes *running a mile, drawing a circle, etc.* Accomplishments seem designed to comprise both the winning of the race and the running that leads up to it: a phase of activity limited by some punctual completion. Aristotle means to include them in his *kineseis*; I prefer to view them as composite. Nothing rides on this for my purposes here.

5. I have called this the "Principle of Minimal Rationality." For more details, see de Sousa (1980).

6. The distinction corresponds roughly to ones made by others in different terms. Compare, for example, Nagel (1970), Parfit (1984), and Schiffer (1976). Nagel talks of reasons versus (merely) "subjective reasons"; Parfit contrasts "agent-relative" and "agent-neutral" reasons; and Schiffer uses "reason-following" for what I call the objective, and "reason-providing" for the subjective. These categories are not exhaustive. A fuller treatment would include a third category which I call *self-related* desires. These are intermediate between the other two, in that they claim a degree of objectivity but only relative to certain

requirements of an ego-ideal or self-concept.

7. John Donne, Elegy XII: "His Parting From Her." Note that the presumption of objectivity in these latter desires does not commit us to a Platonic view: it does not imply that nothing is objectively valuable except for what is eternal. It implies only that the *value* of what is valuable is timeless, not that what is valuable must exist forever. (Compare: the truth of what is true is timeless, though the things and events of which it is true need not be.) To take an extreme case, one of the things we might prize as having objective and timeless value is *fleeting pleasure:* "Death is the mother of beauty," as another poet has written (Wallace Stevens, "Sunday Morning"). By definition, fleeting pleasures would lose their identity, and therefore their value, if they were to persist forever.

8. For the early view, see Freud (1895); for the later, see Freud (1920).

9. In the course of explaining the difference between the two categories of activity and achievement or process, Aristotle gives *seeing* as an example of an activity, and remarks that "when you see, you have seen." The harried tourist's mistake is to reverse the formula.

10. Some things can be both valuable and useful, but only what is useless can be wholly and purely valuable. This, rather than the usual disingenuous mumblings about careers in law, is the proper retort to students who question the usefulness of philosophy.

11. Both in my sense, and in the sense in which N. Tinbergen (1969) uses the phrase.

12. Not that one can't enjoy sweating, or even desire it. But "I want a pee" and "I want a sweat" seem to express wants that bear different relations to their corresponding needs. The sweat isn't *experienced* as a mode of excretion.

13. This paper is an advance draft of part of a chapter of the author's *The Rationality of Emotion*, forthcoming from MIT Press (Bradford Books). Thanks are due to the editor of the present volume for his judicious encouragement to greater clarity. Believe me, it used to be worse.

The Circle of Desire

Robert M. Gordon

Abstract. There appears to be a reflexive circle of justification: Having a particular desire provides one with a justification for having just such a desire. For, given a desire for a state of affairs s, one would seem to have a pragmatic reason to have a desire for s: namely, that having such a desire increases the likelihood that one will do something that brings s about, which in turn increases the likelihood of s. Some desires (among them, the "appetites") fail to close the circle, for they presuppose their own existence and fail to cover times and possible worlds at which they do not exist. To close the circle a desire must move one as follows: to do x, without regard to whether one happens to be moved to do x. But if there are desires that have this feature of preaching independence from all desire, then perhaps we lose some of the theoretical motivation for postulating practical reason as separate from one's desires.

1. DESIRES THAT CLOSE THE CIRCLE

Like money, much of what we desire doesn't grow on trees: we have to work for it. The work may be as trivial as snapping one's fingers or making a wish, as natural as an infant's cry, as pleasant as eating strawberry jam. But trivial, natural, or pleasant, it is an instance of *doing something* that gets us what we want. Desiring a state of affairs s, we do something that brings s about (or helps bring s about);[1] for otherwise it is unlikely, or not likely enough, that s will obtain.

It need not be an instance of doing something *in order to* get what we want. The early cries of infants may have a communicative *effect* though they lack communicative *intent*. A genetically preestablished harmony with the receptive faculties of adults would suffice to produce attributions of desire that make probable the right nurturing and care at the right time. But older children and adults don't have it so easy. "Natural" actions, actions done without intent, rarely suffice to get us what we want: rarely does one hit the target without aiming. It greatly increases the likelihood that one will do the right thing—an action that brings about a state of affairs that one desires — if one acts *with the intention of* bringing about the desired state of affairs.[2]

But *acting with intention* in turn requires *desire.* Or so a number of philosophers have argued.[3] Moreover, even if one does not accept a desire analysis of intentional action — e.g., on the grounds that a *sense of obligation* cannot be reduced to a kind of desire — one can grant that as a rule A's having a desire for a state of affairs *s makes it more likely* that A will act with the intention of bringing *s* about. And by making this more likely, A's having the desire makes it more likely that *s* will be brought about.

Given either a desire for *s* or a sense of obligation to bring *s* about, one would seem to have therefore *a pragmatic reason to have* a desire for *s:* that is, having such a desire increases the likelihood that one will do something that brings *s* about, which in turn increases the likelihood of *s.* I speak of a "pragmatic" reason for desiring something as an analogue of the familiar notion of a pragmatic reason for *believing* something. Such a reason would tend to justify *choosing or allowing oneself to have* (insofar as it is a matter of choice or assent) a particular desire or belief (i.e., one with a specified content) at a particular time solely in terms of the (more or less probable) *causal consequences* of having the desire or belief at that time. That having a desire increases the likelihood of what it is a desire for would seem to be a very important causal consequence, typically the most important of all — *given, of course, that one desires* what it is a desire for. And so someone who desires *s* would have a reason to choose to desire *s,* were desiring it a matter of choice; or to assent to desiring it, were it a matter of assent. This would be a special application of a generalization that appears to be universally true (x-ing ranges over actions and states that are at least to some degree a matter of choosing or allowing oneself to x):

> Given a desire for *s,* the fact that x-ing would increase the likelihood of *s* constitutes a reason for x-ing.

For example: I desire to be healthy and

> (1) my desiring to be healthy makes it more likely that I will be healthy.

In that case (1) would be a pragmatic reason for me to desire to be healthy. Insofar as it is *up to me* whether or not I shall have a desire to be healthy, (1) provides me with some justification for *having* such a desire. Suppose I were given the option of *not* having my desire to be healthy: a button to push, connected appropriately to the brain, or a perfectly harmless drug. There is a reason for me not to push the button or take the drug, namely, that *I am more likely to be healthy if I do not.*

What this amounts to saying is that a desire to be healthy provides one with grounds for a *second-order* desire, viz., a desire *that one have a desire* to be healthy, and not just have it but *be moved by it to do something* that brings (or helps bring) it about that one is healthy.[4] Desiring to be healthy, one has reason to *desire to desire* to be healthy: namely, as a means of increasing the likelihood that one will in fact be healthy. (What *other* grounds might there be for a second-order desire? Possibly one might desire to have [not to have] a certain desire on the grounds that one is or would be in some respect a better person for having [not having] such a desire. But the more usual grounds, I believe, are that the *behavioral consequences* of having [not having] the first-order desire would be good.)

Since we are presuming that one already *has* a desire to be healthy, a second-order desire to have such a desire might seem to be functionally otiose. But it is not. For one thing, it gives one reason to be *glad* or *thankful* that one has the desire one has. I am glad (someone may say) that I am one of those who cares, and has cared, about being healthy, physically fit, well-informed, and so forth: for as a result I am now and will continue to be *better off*—healthier, more fit, better-informed— than I would otherwise have been. More important, there are times when such a second-order desire will affect one's actions in a crucially important way, as I shall show in the final section of this paper.

There appears, then, to be a reflexive circle of justification: Having a particular desire provides one with a justification for having just such a desire.[5] This circle is reminiscent of one that obtains among beliefs. There is a notorious short answer to questions of the form, "Why do you believe that *p*?" It is this: "Because *p*." For example:

I believe Satan exists "because he does."

I believe the new Mercedes is the best car ever made "because it is."

Such an answer does indeed furnish a justification for believing something, even if in general the answer would be conversationally pointless, except as a way of forestalling inquiry into one's evidence or grounds. *Already presupposing* belief that *p*, it appeals to the principle, "It is best (or right) to *believe to be* so what in fact *is* so." There is, I submit, a comparable short answer to, "Why do you desire *s*?" It is this: "To bring about *s*." *Given* a desire for *s*, this would indeed be a justification for having a desire for *s*; though again the answer would be conversationally pointless, except as a way of forestalling inquiry into one's grounds for desiring *s*. Along these lines we can invent a conceptual joke:

Q: Why do you want a Mercedes?

A: How else will I get one?[6]

I must note that it is not *universally* true that desiring *s* increases the likelihood of *s*. In some instances it may even get in the way, *decreasing* the likelihood of *s*. For one thing, there is probably some substance to the often-mentioned "hedonic paradox," viz., that striving for pleasure (often) interferes with the attainment of pleasure. More generally, the *emotional* effects of some desires, e.g., anxiety and nervousness about attaining what is desired, may interfere with its attainment. Finally, one can easily devise stories in which the environment is rearranged with the very aim of frustrating someone's desires, whether by a malicious external agent or by a component of the individual's psyche. (Apart from stories: aren't prisons at least in part an embodiment of this aim, tailor-made to frustrate many of the desires of the majority of their inmates?)[7]

For the most part, however, desires tend to promote, to make more probable, what they are desires for. And yet many of these desires, too, *fail* to furnish pragmatic reasons for themselves. This might seem impossible: For didn't we say that, given a desire for *s*, the fact that *x*-ing would increase the likelihood of *s* constitutes a reason for *x*-ing? These desires do tend to promote what they are desires for. Isn't this a pragmatic reason for having the desire?

Consider this example, however. After a heavy midday meal I feel sleepy; I want nothing more than to sleep. Suppose that (as is often the case)

(2) my desiring to sleep makes it more likely that I will sleep.

(For one thing, my desire to sleep leads me to lie down, and without lying down I am unlikely to fall asleep.) Is (2) a pragmatic reason for me to desire to sleep? Given a choice in the matter, would (2) be a reason to opt for having a desire to sleep?

On the one hand, it would appear that the answer must be "Yes." For this would seem a straightforward instantiation of the generalization above, viz.,

Given a desire for *s*, the fact that *x*-ing would increase the likelihood of *s* constitutes a reason for *x*-ing.

That is, given my desire to sleep, the fact that my desiring to sleep makes it more likely that I will sleep constitutes a reason for desiring to sleep, insofar as it is up to me.

On the other hand, this answer strikes me as plainly false. Suppose again that I have the option of ridding myself of the desire. A cup or two of strong coffee might even do the job. It would be absurd for someone to suggest that I had a reason not to take the coffee and thereby to rid myself of my desire to sleep: namely, that I will be *less likely to sleep* if I do this. It would be equally absurd to suggest that I have a reason for being *glad* or *thankful* that I have a desire to sleep, namely, that it makes me *more likely to sleep.* "But you *do* desire to sleep, don't you?" Yes. "And you're much more likely to *get* what you desire if you lie down, and much more likely to lie down if you desire to sleep." Granted. "So it's a good thing to have a desire to sleep: Why get rid of it?" Something is wrong.

Matters might be different if I wanted to sleep also for the sake of my health, or so that I will be more alert when I wake up, or as a means to some other end.[8] Where I desire to sleep for the sake of my health, for example, I might be thankful that I also have the spontaneous, nonderivative sort of desire one gets when one just "feels sleepy." For a desire of this spontaneous sort can be useful as a conative *signal* that one's body needs sleep; further, as a *motive* that actually helps insure that one's body will get what it needs whether or not one correctly interprets the signal. But we are considering an example in which someone has, at a particular time, *only* the spontaneous sort of desire one gets when one just "feels sleepy." Such a desire furnishes one with no pragmatic reason for having such a desire and offers no grounds for a corresponding second-order desire. The same can be said of the desire to eat that is characteristic of hunger, and of the various desires characteristic of the several so-called appetites. It can also be said of hedonically motivated desires, i.e., desires for something in virtue of its being pleasant or enjoyable, and desires to avoid something in virtue of its being unpleasant. This is not an exhaustive taxonomy.

There is, then, a difference between one class of desires, exemplified by the typical desire to be healthy, and a second class of desires, exemplified by the desire that is characteristic of "feeling sleepy." Desires of the former class close the circle, furnishing pragmatic reasons for themselves; those of the latter class do not. We shall inquire now into the difference that accounts for this difference.

2. DESIRES THAT PRESUPPOSE THEIR OWN EXISTENCE

Many of our desires regarding our own future state and behavior give no deference to our *future* desires. I desire to be healthy into my eighties (if I live that long). But I believe there is a possibility that at age eighty I will not care about my health, or at least not care sufficiently to promote my health. My present desire to be healthy at eighty is very clearly a desire that I be healthy at that age *whether or not* I should happen *then* to desire to be healthy. If I do not, then (as I might express it) let me be healthy *in spite of myself!* Likewise, of my desires to be mentally active, to have companionship, and so on: Let these desires be fulfilled into late old age, even if I have by then lost all interest in such matters. Such desires may be expressed in the form of *categorical imperatives addressed to the future.*

The same is true of certain desires governing actions toward others: desires to keep my promises, to treat others decently and fairly, and so on. It is of course at least odd to say of a type of action: Let me act in that way *intentionally*, even if I then have no desire to act that way. As mentioned earlier, on some views of intentional action one never acts a certain way intentionally without desiring to act that way. So the point is better restricted to desires regarding states and conditions (being healthy, being mentally active, having companionship) and to desires regarding acting a certain way intentionally or not. For example: Should the day come when I do not care about keeping promises, treating others fairly, and so on, then let me act in these ways notwithstanding, fulfilling at least the "letter" of these desires, even if unintentionally or by sheer force of habit.

But much the same is true of my desire to be healthy, etc., at the *present* time. Like my desire to be healthy at eighty, my desire to be healthy *now* is a desire that I be healthy at a particular time *whether or not I should happen at that time* to desire to be healthy. The question, "Do I now care about my health?" has no greater rational bearing on my present desire to be healthy now than the question, "Will I care about my health when I am eighty?" has on my present desire to be healthy when I am eighty. The typical desire to be healthy may be expressed by a categorical imperative addressed to the present as well as to the future:

> Let me be healthy whatever my desires in the matter may be (at future times *or* at present)!

Or as a transcendent or objective evaluation:

> It would be good (for me) to be healthy, whatever my desires (or attitudes or evaluations) regarding my being healthy may be (at future times *or* at present).

People generally regard their own health as a *transcendent* or *objective* value, i.e., as desir*able* even when and if it is not desired. This is not to say that they believe the property, *being healthy,* to possess the second-order property, *objective value or desirability;* but rather, only that they have a *desire* of a certain kind, namely, one whose fully explicit expression would contain a stipulation to the effect:

> whatever my desires [or attitudes or evaluations] regarding my being healthy may be [at future times *or* at present].

On the matter of *rational bearing* or *relevance* it should be noted that most if not all desires are in a sense "blind" to much of the world. One's desire to be healthy, or to have companionship, or to sleep, sits comfortably with gross ignorance of the world in which, were one's desire satisfied, one would be healthy, or have companionship, or sleep. Is it a world in which Jupiter has twelve moons, or thirteen? (I forget.) In which Europe is larger than Australia? (I believe so, but I may be wrong.) In which Calvin Coolidge was a philanderer? (I have never thought to inquire.) One desires that one be healthy, or have companionship, or sleep no matter what the answer to these irrelevant questions.

I find it helpful to represent these as desires to be healthy, or to have companionship, or to sleep *relative to a set of possible worlds:* worlds in which Jupiter has twelve moons as well as worlds in which it has thirteen, worlds in which Europe is larger than Australia as well as worlds in which it is not, and so on. Of these, some are worlds in which the desire is *satisfied,* i.e., its satisfaction condition is *true.* All others are worlds in which the desire is *frustrated,* i.e., its satisfaction condition is *false.*

But one desires to be healthy, etc., relative to a set that *excludes* some possible worlds. For one thing, the desirer doesn't exist in all possible worlds; for another, he may have no body of a sort that would make it intelligible for him to be called "healthy" or "unhealthy," "asleep" or "awake," and so on. The satisfaction condition for the desire is neither true nor false in such worlds. Hence we may say that the desire does not "cover" or "extend to" such worlds.

Now to the main question. Consider possible worlds in which *one has no desire,* e.g., to be healthy. Does one's present desire cover at least some worlds of that sort? I noted earlier that one desires that one be healthy no matter what the answer to certain irrelevant questions. The issue, then, is as follows: Is *this* question—whether one has a desire to be healthy, or not—among those irrelevant questions?

In the case of desires to be healthy, to be mentally active, to have companionship, to keep one's promises, etc., the answer, at least for typical instances of such desires, was "Yes." The question, "Do I desire to be healthy?" has little or no more relevance to the typical desire to be healthy than the number of Jupiter's moons. Are all desires alike in this regard? If I want to sleep, for example, is the content of my desire comparable to that of wanting to be healthy: that I sleep, period — irrespective of my desires in the matter? When hungry do I have a desire to eat (edible food), period?

The answer, for the "appetites" generally, is "No." Consider an opposing view: what might be called the *itch-scratch* theory of the appetites. The appetites, it might be thought, are just distinct forms of discomfort or malaise, global or partially localized, that "aim" merely at *their own cessation*. They are differentiated chiefly in that they are typically caused by one or another type of deprivation or deficit; hence typically *relieved* by ending or removing the deprivation or deficit. The *objective* "object" (to eat food, to sleep, etc.) is desired merely as *a means of quenching the appetite*. (Sometimes also to obtain pleasure in the bargain.)

But neither of these simple conceptions of the appetites is satisfactory. Suppose I am hungry and want (as I might express it) "to eat." Although food deprivation (with resulting metabolic deficits) may be the typical cause of hunger, it causes hunger only against a background of other causal conditions. Thus by removing one of the other causally necessary conditions one would get rid of the hunger just as effectively as by eating (perhaps even more reliably). But if I take a pill (or have an injection, etc.) that immediately takes away my hunger, my former desire has not been *frustrated*, notwithstanding the fact that *I do not eat*. And if a moment later *I do eat* (say, because someone forces me to), my former desire has not been *satisfied*, notwithstanding the fact that *I do eat*. Hence the satisfaction condition for the desire was not simply that *I eat*. Nor was the satisfaction condition simply that *I quench (extinguish) my appetite*. The pill or the injection extinguished my appetite, but did not do so by *satisfying* my desire.

(Contrast the typical desire to be healthy. If I take a pill that takes away my desire to be healthy, and with the consequent neglect I become unhealthy, my former desire *has* been frustrated; and if, luckily, I am healthy despite the neglect, my former desire has been satisfied.)

In short, the object of the appetites resists atomization. In worlds in which the whole is split asunder — e.g., one quenches the appetite without eating, one eats but fails to quench the appetite, or one eats at a time at which one no longer has the appetite — the desire is neither satisfied nor frustrated: the satisfaction condition for the desire (or: the statement of the satisfaction condition) is neither true nor false. The satisfaction condition may be said to *presuppose* that one eats (etc.) and by doing so quenches the appetite; a fortiori it presupposes that one *has* the appetite, and indeed has it up to the time at which one eats (etc.).[9] By a slight extension we may say that the appetite or desire itself presupposes this. Desires that presuppose their own existence fail to cover times and possible worlds at which they do not exist; and desires that do not presuppose their own existence do cover times and possible worlds at which they do not exist. So, just as a desire to be healthy does not cover or extend to times or possible worlds at which the *desirer* doesn't exist (specifically, in a body that might intelligibly be called "healthy" or "unhealthy"), an appetite does not cover times or worlds at which *it*, the very *desire* itself, doesn't exist.

The complexity of the object of an appetite is surely not to be attributed to conceptual sophistication. On the contrary, it is likely to be a sign of the relatively primitive character of these desires, particularly their origin in a system (or systems) that *makes no distinction* between inner and outer, subjective and objective, and so forth. In fact, our inability to atomize the object of an appetite gives evidence of being neurologically hard-wired, "informationally encapsulated," and mandatory: in short, the work of what Fodor would call a "vertical faculty" or "module" (1983). It would not be hard to find a plausible evolutionary story that could explain why this is so.

There are likely to be desires of types other than the appetites that exclude possible worlds in which they themselves do not exist. To mention one other type, whenever we *enjoy* something, we have, I believe, such a desire. If one is enjoying some activity—fishing, for example—one simultaneously desires to be engaged in this very activity; and further, the desire to be engaged in it is *caused* by the activity itself (see Warner, 1980). I would suggest that the object of such a desire resembles the object of an appetite in its refusal to be atomized. The objective activity, fishing, and the subjective state that results from it—including the desire itself—are welded together, jointly constituting the object of one's desire "to be doing what I am doing." Had one been fishing but doing so joylessly, *without* one's present desire to be fishing, that would not have sufficed to satisfy one's present desire. Putting the point in terms of *evaluations*, what one *finds good* about what one is doing cannot be located simply in the objective activity, considered apart from the resulting psychological reaction to the activity, *including one's finding it good.*

3. EXPLANATION OF THE DIFFERENCE

A quick glance at the examples discussed suggests that the distinctions introduced in sections 1 and 2, respectively, are coextensive. It appears that a desire closes the circle, furnishing a pragmatic reason

for its own existence and thereby furnishing a reason for a corresponding second-order desire, just in case it is a desire that covers possible
worlds at which it, the desire itself, does not exist. An extrapolation
from so small a sample is of course a weakly supported hypothesis.
But a brief investigation will reveal an underlying *conceptual depen-
dency* that would explain why the two distinctions are coextensive.

Suppose Alf desires to be healthy but contemplates the way things
would have been if he *had not had* such a desire. He reasons: "It would
have been bad, for I probably would have neglected my health, and as a
consequence been unhealthy." This is a reason for him to be thankful
for his present desire. Then he contemplates the way things would be
if he did not *continue to have* such a desire. Given a *choice* as to
whether or not to sustain his desire, he reasons: "It will be bad if I
don't continue to have it, for then I will probably begin neglecting my
health, and as a consequence become unhealthy." This would be a
reason for him to choose to sustain his present desire.

His reasoning may be represented by the following argument:

(1) Suppose I do not desire to be healthy: then I will neglect my health
and as a consequence will not be healthy.

(2) It will be bad if I am not healthy.

Therefore, (3) It will be bad if I do not *desire* to be healthy.[10]

What is crucial here is that in contemplating the possibility of not
having (or not having had) the desire, *he does not suspend the desire.*
Even though he is considering the way things would be or have been
without a desire to be healthy, he *uses* his desire—more accurately,
uses an expression of his desire—as an implicit premise in *evaluating*
the way things would be or have been without the desire. But this is
possible only because the typical desire to be healthy, as argued in
section 2, covers possible worlds in which one has no desire to be
healthy. Particularly to the point, I noted that it may be expressed by a
transcendent or *objective* evaluation:

It would be good (for me) to be healthy, *whatever my desires (or
attitudes or evaluations) regarding health may be (at future times or at
present).*

Hence the *supposition*, in (1), that one lacks the desire, leaves the
evaluation unaltered.

Turn now to the appetites. Suppose Beth feels hungry and is about
to eat. She sees no reason to eat now, other than to satisfy her hunger.
Suppose that, contemplating the way things would have been if she

had not felt like eating now, she reasons: "It would have been bad, for I probably would not eat. So I really should be thankful for my present desire to eat." Suppose that, given a choice as to whether to let her appetite continue or to take a pill that would immediately quench it, she reasons: "It will be bad if I take this pill, for then I will probably not eat. So I had better not take it."

The reasoning rings hollow. Yet it may be represented by an argument that is superficially parallel to Alf's:

(1') Suppose I do not desire to eat: then I will not eat.

(2') It will be bad if I do not eat.

Therefore, (3') It will be bad if I do not *desire* to eat.

The problem is that what is being supposed in (1') contradicts a *presupposition* of (2'). (Or, if one is a purist about presupposition, it contradicts a presupposition of *a statement of the satisfaction condition* for (2').) As pointed out in section 2, an appetite would be neither satisfied nor frustrated—its satisfaction condition would be neither true nor false—if one were to eat, fall asleep, etc., at a time at which one lacked the appetite, or a fortiori if one had not had the appetite in the first place. (In other words an appetite does not cover times or worlds at which *it*, the appetite, doesn't exist.) Despite its superficial resemblance to (2), (2') must *not* be understood as an objective evaluation, to be expanded as follows:

It is (will be) good if I eat, *whatever my desires (or attitudes or evaluations) regarding eating may be at the time.*

In short, the fallacy in Beth's argument is her use of (an expression of) an appetite as a premise in evaluating the way things would be or have been *without* the appetite—as if it were of no consequence whether she has the appetite or not.

Our brief discussion of enjoyment suggests that it would in similar fashion be fallacious to reason:

It's fortunate that I find fishing enjoyable: for if I didn't, I probably wouldn't go fishing very often—which would be too bad, since it's so enjoyable.

4. BEARING ON TRADITIONAL ISSUES OF
REASON AND WILL

In the first section of this paper I described the circle of desire and noted that, whereas some desires close the circle, furnishing pragmatic reasons for their own existence, others do not. In section 2 I drew a distinction between desires that presuppose their own existence, failing to cover times and possible worlds at which they do not exist; and desires that do not presuppose their own existence, and thus do cover times and possible worlds at which they do not exist. In section 3 I tried to show that the distinction drawn in section 2 *accounts for* the difference noted in section 1.

What bearing has any of this on traditional philosophical problems concerning desires? In this concluding section I shall briefly discuss some consequences for a set of issues concerning the relationships among *desires, reason, and the will.*

To many philosophers of the past, "reason" designated a faculty that is capable of standing in opposition to any and all of one's desires. In Kant's version, practical reason issues, among other things, apodictic or categorical imperatives that enjoin the will wholly without regard to the agent's desires; it requires or forbids actions without consideration of the agent's subjective ends, without regard to whether his desires happen to "go along" with its dictates.[11] And it not only *tells* one to act in certain ways but (in those possessing a good will) *moves* one to act in these ways.

A quick and superficial glance at this conception of practical reason might lead one to think it incoherent. One might urge that if reason were to dictate that one act in certain ways *without regard to whether one happens to be moved or inclined to act in these ways*, then reason would cut itself off from all possible *incentives* to follow its dictates. If that were so, then reason could not *move* one to do its bidding.

This reasoning is fallacious. There is no inconsistency in the supposition that an agent A is *moved* as follows:

to do x, *without regard to whether I happen to be moved to do x.*

We saw in section 2 that there are *desires* with just such a content: e.g., the typical desires to be healthy, to be mentally active, to have companionship, and so on; to keep one's promises, to treat others decently and fairly, and so on. Such desires may be expressed by categorical imperatives that take no heed of the agent's desires in the matter. With regard to their content, such desires preach independence from desire; indeed, one is called upon to leave behind the *totality* of one's subjective leanings. Expressed as *evaluative judg-*

ments, they predicate transcendent or objective values that stand in stony independence of one's own subjective judgments of value.

But if there are *desires* that have this feature of preaching independence from all desire, then perhaps we lose some of the theoretical motivation for postulating a practical reason as a separate theoretical entity or faculty in contradistinction to one's desires. To express the point in bumper-sticker prose,

> *Content* independence does not entail *ontological* independence.

Thus one might after all identify reason with those "calm desires and tendencies" which, according to Hume's *Treatise* (1978 [1739], bk. 2, pt. 3, sec. 3), are vulgarly called one's "reason," viz.,

> certain instincts originally implanted in our natures, such as benevolence and resentment, the love of life, and kindness to children; or the general appetite to good, and aversion to evil.

Contrary to both Hume and Kant, there is justification in calling such desires "reason." The justification is not that they are "calm" desires, but that they would require us to act in certain ways whatever our desires in the matter; they predicate transcendent or objective values, against which we can evaluate our desires.

But we have other desires as well, our appetites and enjoyments among them. These do not always go along with the dictates, particularly the summary all-things-considered dictates, of that subset of our desires that constitutes our reason. The consequences are familiar. For one thing, such "unruly" desires sometimes move us to action. In such cases our acts will be inconsistent with our all-things-considered objective evaluations: We will fail to follow our own "best judgment." This would account for many, perhaps most, instances of what philosophers are wont to call "weakness of will."

To speak of these as "weakness of will" is of course to presuppose that those unruly desires, *even when they move us all the way to action*, do not constitute our will. If the argument of this paper is sound, we can begin to understand why our actions, though *intentional* under a given description, need not under that description *conform to our will*. The desires we see as constituting our will are just those desires that require us to act in certain ways whatever our desires in the matter, that predicate transcendent or objective values against which we evaluate our desires. For it is precisely those desires that *justify their own existence*, thus guaranteeing our *endorsement*. In sum, those desires we see as constituting our "will," as well as those we see as constituting our "reason," are precisely the ones that close the circle of desire.[12]

NOTES

1. The disjunct, "or helps bring about," is hereinafter to be understood.
2. I am ignoring the technical distinction between *likelihood* and *probability*.
3. Robert Audi and Donald Davidson, among others.
4. This corresponds to what Harry G. Frankfurt (1971) calls a "second-order *volition*" in his important paper on freedom of the will.
5. But we shall see that there are some very important exceptions.
6. Whosoever gets my joke gets my point. But perhaps not conversely.
7. Desires that get in the way of their own fulfillment pose a curious dilemma. Clio would be more likely to be elected to office if she didn't desire the office, perhaps even preferred not to hold it. And so, precisely because she desires it, she desires not to desire it. But once she has succeeded in fully eliminating the desire, her effort to eliminate it will have come to seem pointless: now she really doesn't want the office after all, perhaps even prefers not to hold it. A better strategy would be, where possible, to hang on to the desire while eliminating its self-frustrating *aspects*.
8. Matters might also be different if I desired to sleep *merely for its own sake*, as Larry Davis has pointed out to me. Perhaps I don't "feel sleepy," nor want to sleep for some further end; I want to sleep, just for the sake of sleeping.
9. This assumes a standard more or less Strawsonian understanding of presupposition.
10. This is not to be read as a "detached" conclusion. One might render it by qualifying the term *bad* in (3) by the phrase, *relative to (1) and (2)*.
11. This is of course only a small portion of Kant's teachings on practical reason. Most important, it fails to include his doctrine of *the* Categorical Imperative. In Kant's view, reason demands not only that one act in certain ways without consideration of subjective ends, but also that these ways — one's duties — be determined in a purely formal way.
12. This paper develops in greater depth some ideas broached in sections 6 and 7 of Gordon (1986a). There I am chiefly concerned with what I call "The Paradox of Unsuccessful Intervention," e.g., an unwilling cream pie addict, with one hand eating a pie, with the other hand pushing a button on an apparatus designed to quell the desire for cream pie, but on this occasion defective. His desire to eat the pie appears to be "stronger" in that it moves him to action; but his desire that he *not* eat the pie also seems to be the "stronger" in that it moves him to press the button.

    Thanks once again to the ministrations of Larry Davis, this is a better paper than it might have been. I am grateful to Joel Marks for some excellent editorial suggestions.

Actions, Emotions, and Desires

O. H. Green

Abstract. The active-passive distinction has a strong intuitive basis in our sense that what we do is in our control, as what happens to us is not, and seems important in its implications for our responsibility. Yet well-known ways of marking the distinction are fraught with difficulties. My contention is that an interpretation of the distinction between activity and passivity in terms of direct dependence on desires which are responsive to considerations of desirability is more adequate.

Actions and emotions have long been supposed to fall on either side of the distinction between what we do and what happens to us.[1] The motivation for drawing the active-passive distinction and applying it in this way is twofold. We have the sense that what we do is typically in our control, as what we feel is not. This is reflected in the appropriateness of commanding a person to perform an action, the inappropriateness of commanding a person to have an emotion. Also, the distinction appears to explain why we are generally taken to be responsible for the actions we perform, as we are not for the emotions we have, and why we are assessed accordingly.

The distinction between activity and passivity has been expressed most often in terms of the effects of volitions and the will. Actions are subject to the will and are the effects of volitions; not so emotions. Notwithstanding the weight of a tradition extending from the Stoics and Augustine to Descartes and onward, the very mention of volitions and the will became anathema to a generation of philosophers, largely owing to Gilbert Ryle's polemic in *The Concept of Mind.*

Ryle inveighs against "the Myth of Volitions" as an "extension of the myth of the ghost in the machine" (Ryle, 1949, p. 63). Understood in this way volitions turn out to be spiritual causes of bodily events, and all the problems with Cartesian interactionism present themselves. Ryle also takes volitions to be mental acts of will. Accordingly, he asks whether acts of will are themselves supposed to be voluntary or subject to the will, and in doing so reveals a dilemma. If acts of will are not subject to the will, they can hardly account for voluntary action; if acts of will are subject to the will, an infinite regress of such acts is started (Ryle, 1949, p. 66). These objections to the theory of volitions can be set aside. The theory need carry no commitment to dualism; it is quite possible to hold that volitions are realized in the brain. And in the second objection, Ryle has simply given us reason to deny that volitions are acts, not to deny that there are volitions.

What remains of Ryle's case against the theory of volitions amounts to this. Volitions are not empirically identifiable nor can they legitimately be introduced as theoretical entities. It is Ryle's contention that we are unable to answer questions about volitions which should be answerable easily if they were items of our experience. "If we do not know how to settle simple questions about their frequency, duration or strength," he remarks, "then it is fair to conclude that [the existence of volitions] is not asserted on empirical grounds" (Ryle, 1949, p. 65). Ryle also holds that the theoretical introduction of volitions is blocked by explanatory failure. He writes:

> Though volitions were called in to explain our appraisals of actions, this explanation is just what they fail to provide. If we had no other antecedent ground for applying appraisal-concepts to the actions of others, we should have no reasons at all for inferring from those actions to the volitions alleged to give rise to them. (Ryle, 1949, p. 66)

From these considerations, Ryle's conclusion is that we have no reason to suppose that our actions are the effects of volitions. Unlike the other objections, this is an argument which must be taken seriously if the active-passive distinction is to be made in terms of volitions. Thus, it is fair to say that this is Ryle's central objection to the volitional theory.

As an alternative to a volitional account, we might attempt to make out the distinction between what we do and what happens to us in terms of the circumstances of the occurrence. Such an approach has been favored by Ryle and others influenced by him, but the idea goes back at least to Book Three of the *Nicomachean Ethics*. The circumstance most clearly determinant of the distinction, on this view, is the imposition of external force. In going out to sea, the captain is passive if swept by a storm; in the absence of any such circumstance, he is presumably active. The bearing of other circumstances, such as coercion or the absence of information, on the distinction between activity and passivity is, of course, less clear-cut. They are usually arrayed more or less closely around compulsion.

It is hardly deniable that circumstantial considerations are relevant to the active-passive distinction, but it is clear that this approach fails to yield an adequate account of the distinction. For one thing, pointing out that compulsion and related factors render one passive does not explain why this is so or how one is active when such influences are absent. Even more important for our purposes is the fact that an account of the distinction between activity and passivity which is focused on the imposition of external force has no application to emotions. As Irving Thalberg puts it, "When I am said to be transported by joy or buffeted by despair, nothing analogous to a flood or a gale will be found" (Thalberg, 1984).

The active-passive distinction presents us with a problem. On the one hand, we have a distinction which is well motivated and supported by an important philosophical tradition; on the other hand, we find that there are difficulties about how the distinction is to be made. The problem is pressing because the distinction seems to have an important bearing on our understanding of the nature of actions and emotions. The solution which I find most plausible is one which turns on the relation of actions and emotions to desires.

1. DESIRE DEPENDENCE

My idea is that actions are dependent on desires as emotions are not and that in general the active-passive distinction is to be understood in this way.[2] If volitions are identified with the desires in question, it is in fact one interpretation of the traditional way of making the distinction in terms of volitions and their effects. Still, I think that it has some advantages over other possible interpretations.

To begin, I should say something about my conception of the intentional structure of desires. I take desires to be mental representations of states of affairs as ones which are to obtain. They have world-to-mind direction of fit and are successful only if the state of affairs represented obtains. Satisfaction is the success condition for desires. The rationality of desires is a function of the agent's beliefs about the feasibility and desirability of their being satisfied. This conception of desires is meant to capture the representational and rational properties of a class of mental states. For this reason, it is broad in its extension, taking in not only desires ordinarily so-called but intentions as well.

The intentional structure of desires contrasts with that of beliefs, which I also conceive broadly, in terms of the representational and rational properties of a class of mental states. Beliefs I take to be mental representations of states of affairs as ones which obtain. They have mind-to-world direction of fit and are successful only if the state of affairs represented obtains. Truth is the condition of success for beliefs. The rationality of beliefs is a function of the likelihood of their being true, given the agent's evidence and perceptions.

Now consider the case of intentional actions. Intentional actions are actions the agent intends to perform, at least at the time of performance. The state of affairs which consists in the agent's performing the action is represented by him as one which is to obtain. Thus, on the broad conception of desires, intentions are desires of a kind, and intentional actions are actions the agent desires to perform. Actions depend causally and rationally on the agent's desires that he perform them and are identified by reference to those desires.

When I take a walk, I take a walk at the time I do because I desire to take a walk at that time, and if I did not have the desire I would not take a walk. In this way, actions are causally dependent on the agent's desire to perform them.

Actions are also rationally dependent on desires. Rationality requires representation. The representation of states of affairs as ones which obtain or are to obtain sets the conditions of success for cognition and conation, and rationality is a function of the likelihood of success. In general, however, actions are not representational. The action of kicking a field goal does not represent the kicking of a field goal; it is the intention to kick the goal which represents the action as one which is to be performed. The rationality of actions is determined by the intentions with which they are performed, and intentions are generically desires. Thus the rationality of going for a field goal depends on that of the desire to go for a field goal. If the desire is rational, so is the action.

The desire dependence of actions is reflected in the fact that they are identified by reference to the intentions with which they are performed. My action in bringing the ax down upon the log is one of chopping wood because in so doing it is my intention that I chop wood. Apart from that intention there is only intentionally indeterminate bodily movement.

I will argue that emotions are not causally or rationally dependent on desires that one have them as actions are dependent on desires that one perform them and are not identified by reference to such desires. It will be useful, however, to consider first the cases of beliefs and desires, which are also not dependent on desires in the relevant ways.

Beliefs and desires are different from actions in that they are not causally dependent for their occurrence on desires that we have them. To have the belief that p or the desire that p when I do, I need not in general have the desire that I have those beliefs and desires at that time. In fact, such a desire is typically ineffective in bringing about the belief or desire. Also, while actions are rationally dependent on desires to perform them, beliefs and desires could hardly depend for their rationality on desires that we have them. If someone believes that p because he desires that he believe that p, we have a case of self-deceptive irrationality. Desiring that *p* because one desires to desire that *p* is hardly less irrational. (Of this, more later.)

Unlike desire-dependent actions, beliefs and desires are intrinsically representational and are identified by reference to their content as the belief that *p* or the desire that *p*. They could hardly be identified by reference to the desire to have them. My belief or desire that *p* must have content independent of any desire that I have them for that desire itself to have its content, that I believe that *p* or that I desire that *p*.

That emotions are not causally or rationally dependent on desires as actions are can be explained in the light of what has been said about beliefs and desires. In *Emotions and Rational Representation* I develop and defend a belief-desire theory of emotions (Green, in preparation). On this theory, emotions are intentional structures of beliefs and desires. Thus, in joy A believes that *p*, and A desires that *p*; in sorrow A believes that *p*, and A desires that not-*p*; in hope A believes that it may be the case that *p*, and A desires that *p*; in fear A believes that it may be the case that *p*, and A desires that not-*p*; and so on.

Emotions are not causally dependent on desires just as beliefs and desires are not. Certainly one doesn't have to desire to be sad to be sad. Indeed, emotions are notably resistant to desires that we have them. Were it otherwise we could be happy all the time.

Also, like beliefs and desires, emotions are not rationally dependent on desires that we have them. The rationality of emotions depends on that of the beliefs and desires which constitute them. If it is rational to believe that *p* and to desire that not-*p*, it is rational to be sorry that *p*. Since the rationality of the constituent beliefs and desires does not depend on desires that we have them, neither does the rationality of emotions depend on desires that we have them.

Like beliefs and desires, emotions are intrinsically intentional and are identified by reference to the content of the beliefs and desires which constitute them. Thus, A is glad that *p* in that A desires that *p*, and A believes that *p*. Though the content of the emotion depends on the constituent desire in this way, it does not depend on a desire that one have the emotion. For a desire to be the desire to be glad that *p*, the gladness must have its content independent of the desire.

In the cases of actions, beliefs, desires, and emotions, considerations of desire dependence enable us to draw the line between activity and passivity where intuitively it seems it should be drawn. There is, however, a more basic motivation for making the active-passive distinction in this way. To see this, the causal dimensions of mental representation must be considered.

Biologically speaking, perceptual beliefs about the surroundings and intentions or desires to act on the surroundings are the elementary forms of mental representation for an organism. In its causal interaction with the environment, the survival of the organism depends on the success of these representations.

The success of our perceptual beliefs depends on our being affected by what we perceive and thus precludes direct dependence on desire. The success of our intentions or desires to act depends on our effecting what we intend and so requires desire dependence. In this way desire dependence ties in with our being active, nondependence on desire with our being acted upon. These notions, of course, are at the heart of the active-passive distinction.

While the connection between dependence or nondependence on desire and causal direction is, I think, of basic importance for understanding the distinction between activity and passivity, it requires careful handling. For one thing, problems with causal theories of cognition in epistemology and difficulties about deviant causal chains in action theory indicate that even in the case of perceptual beliefs and intentions or desires to act, the relevant causal relations with the world may be hard to describe. Still, that appropriate causal connections with the environment are required for the success of perceptions and intentions is hardly subject to doubt.

Another thing is this. The causal constraints on the success of perceptual beliefs and intentions or desires to act do not apply to beliefs and desires generically. General, abstract, and mathematical beliefs, for example, evidently need stand in no particular causal relation to the state of affairs represented. The same holds true of intentions and generic desires. A distinction may be made between *performative desires* that one perform an action and *optative desires* that a state of affairs obtain which does not consist in one's performing an action. Unlike performative desires, optative desires are generally indifferent to the causal path to their satisfaction. Nevertheless, beliefs generally are analogous to perceptions in that their success depends on the way the world is; they have the same input-oriented direction of fit. Desires generally are analogous to intentions in that their success depends on how the world comes to be; they have the same output-oriented direction of fit. Thus representational direction of fit is established in cases in which success is causally constrained and generalized to cases without the same causal constraints. The analogy captures a real feature of beliefs and desires because representational direction determines the mode of rational functioning, and beliefs and desires do have distinctive roles in the rational economy of mind.

The input-oriented constraints on the success of beliefs extend to desires and emotions. The rationality of desires is a function of that of beliefs concerning the feasibility and desirability of their satisfaction. In this way desires are also constrained by the state of the environment. Emotions, too, are subject to similar constraints, since they are constituted of beliefs and desires.

What we find in considering the causal dimensions of mental representation is that the functional rationality of our beliefs, desires, and emotions is constrained by the way the world is. It is for this reason that these representations are not desire dependent. Dependence on desires would not insure that they have the required relation to the environment. It is in action, which is desire dependent, that representation is output-oriented.

This result is reinforced by the fact that where there are no cognitive constraints on mental representation, there may be desire dependence. Imaginative representations, which include besides imaginings, dreams, seeings as, and suppositions, represent states of affairs as obtaining without any commitment to truth. There are thus no cognitive constraints on imaginative representations. On this account, they may be, but need not be, desire dependent. Imagining and supposing are things we often do.

The desire dependence of actions ties in with our being causally effective on the environment, the lack of desire dependence of beliefs, desires, and emotions with our being causally affected by the environment. This is what underlies the active-passive distinction interpreted in terms of desire dependence.

There are certain respects in which this account of the distinction requires more development. This will come in further discussion. Meanwhile, it is already evident that this view of activity and passivity has advantages over alternative accounts. For one thing, it affords a plausible explanation of the control and responsibility we have regarding our actions, as opposed to our passive states. Actions are causally and rationally dependent on desires. This means that they are a function of how the agent would have the world be, and typically that is up to him. Beliefs, desires, and emotions, on the other hand, are not desire dependent. They are, at least in part, a function of how we take the world to be and subject to causal and rational constraints. How we take the world to be is, in this way, typically not up to us.

In the second place, we can readily answer Ryle's central objection to the volitional theory if it is interpreted in terms of desire dependence. According to that objection, volitions are not items of our experience nor can they be introduced legitimately for explanatory purposes. Casting desires in the role of volitions, the answer is that volitions are items of our experience. We may be conscious of our desires in that they occupy our attention and we believe that we have them. Questions about their frequency, duration, and strength may be easily answerable. Also, volitions have a legitimate explanatory role. Rather than presupposing control and responsibility in our actions, our desires help to explain these features of actions.

Finally, the desire-dependence interpretation accounts for the relevance of external force to our activity or passivity. Compulsion blocks the effectiveness of our volitions and affects us in ways we do not desire. The account also has a clear application to emotions. As structures of beliefs and desires, emotions are taken to be paradigms of non-desire-dependent states in which we are passive.

Though the volitional theory understood in terms of desire dependence has advantages as an account of the active-passive distinction, it is also evident that it encounters certain difficulties. In the first instance, I shall concentrate particularly on two of these. The first concerns slavery to desires. There are cases, notably cases involving addictions, in which desires can be irresistible. Though the addict's drug use reflects his desire, it is natural to think that he is not free or active in what he does. If this is so, desire dependence seems not to insure activity. The second difficulty concerns deciding to believe. On the Cartesian view, believing is desire dependent, something we do and in which we are active. A related problem concerns our activity in having emotions. According to Sartre and others, we make ourselves have the emotions we do, so that they are presumably desire dependent. If these positions are sound, ordinary actions are not alone in being desire dependent.

Central to the position that we are active in having beliefs and emotions, as I interpret it, is the claim that they are dependent on desires that we have them. Perhaps the most prominent solution to the problem about slavery to desires also turns on desires about desires. Thus, these second-order intentional states require attention.

2. ITERATED BELIEFS AND DESIRES

The appeal to second-order beliefs and desires in dealing with problems about activity and passivity may seem to be unproblematic in principle. Daniel Dennett asserts without argument that "the iteration of beliefs and other intentions is never redundant" (Dennett, 1978, p. 273). Second- or higher-order beliefs and desires may not be redundant relative to the first-order beliefs and desires they are about. Dennett is right about that. My belief that I believe that p, for example, is obviously not equivalent to my belief that p; it stands to the first-order belief as an introspective representation of it. There are other ways in which redundancies may arise in the iteration of beliefs and desires, however, and a consideration of them is crucial for the active-passive distinction.

The iterated beliefs and desires which concern us are second-order beliefs and desires, beliefs about beliefs or desires and desires about beliefs or desires. We need to make a distinction between two types of these second-order beliefs and desires.[3] First, there are *success-oriented second-order beliefs and desires*, or *S-beliefs* and *S-desires* for short. These are beliefs that the related first-order beliefs and desires are successful or desires that they be successful. In the following cases we have S-beliefs and S-desires:

A believes that he has the true belief that *p*.

A believes that he has the satisfied desire that *p*.

A desires that he have the true belief that *p*.

A desires that he have the satisfied desire that *p*.

In the second place, there are *non-success-oriented beliefs and desires*, to be dubbed *N-beliefs* and *N-desires*. These beliefs and desires are indifferent to the success of the related first-order beliefs and desires. Cases of N-beliefs and N-desires may be obtained by deleting reference to the success of the first-order representation in the cases of S-beliefs and S-desires just given.

With respect to the first-order belief or desire that *p*, an N-belief or desire focuses on the attitude, on *having* the belief or desire, rather than on the content, on *what* is believed or desired. For instance, I may believe that I have the desire that *p*, leave alone whether what I desire obtains. On the other hand, an S-belief or desire regarding the first-order belief or desire that *p* focuses not only on the attitude, but on the content as well. I may desire, for example, that I have the belief *p* but also that what I desire to believe be the case. The distinction between S-beliefs and desires and N-beliefs and desires is easily overlooked because of the attitude-content ambiguity of "belief" and "desire," which may be used to refer either to the mental representation or to what is represented. Still, the distinction is one which must be made in order to discern the scope for redundancies in the iteration of beliefs and desires.

Beliefs and desires are individuated by their contents and success conditions, as the belief that *p*, the desire that *q*, and so on. A redundant belief or desire is one which has the same content and success conditions as the beliefs or desires relative to which it is redundant. Typewise, they are the same representation. Redundant representations do no work in the rational economy of mind. Having the same content and conditions of success as the representations relative to which they are redundant, they can have no independent part in cognitive and conative operations which are success-functional.

N-beliefs and N-desires are not redundant. In each case the first- and second-order representations have different success conditions and contents. The success of the first-order belief or desire that p requires that it be the case that p. The success of the second-order belief or desire, which is indifferent to the success of the related first-order representation that p, does not require that it be the case that p; it requires only that the first-order attitude be instantiated.

The N-belief that I have a first-order belief or desire is the form which intentional self-consciousness takes. The standing of N-desires that one have first-order beliefs or desires is more dubious. To desire that one have a belief regardless of its truth or to desire that one have a desire regardless of its satisfaction is an indirect form of irrationality. This is due to the fact that the belief or desire which one N-desires that one have, would be irrational, there being, so far as one is concerned, no likelihood of its success. Still, since its conditions of success are different from those of the desired first-order representation, the N-desire need not be directly irrational.

As with N-beliefs and desires, the content and success conditions of S-beliefs are different from those of the first-order beliefs and desires to which they are related. The specification of the content of the S-belief or desire makes reference to the related first-order representation and to its success. Neither is referred to in the specification of the content of the first-order representation itself. This gives rise to the impression that, like N-beliefs and desires, S-beliefs and desires are not redundant. The impression is deceptive. Further consideration must be given to what must be the case for S-beliefs and desires to be successful.

S-beliefs and desires have a content which is compound. If A believes that he has the true belief that p, A believes that he has the belief that p and that what he believes — namely, that p — is true. If A desires that he have the true belief that p, A desires that he believe that p and that what he desires to believe be true. This means that, in each case, the content of the S-belief or desire is equivalent to the N-belief or desire that A have the belief that p and the first-order belief or desire that p. The content-individuated S-belief or desire effectively reduces to the related N-belief or desire and first-order representation. For this reason, there are in general no nonredundant S-beliefs and desires. S-beliefs are redundant relative to N-beliefs and first-order beliefs; S-desires are redundant relative to N-desires and first-order desires.[4] The critical importance of this redundancy for considerations of activity and passivity turns out to be substantial.[5]

3. SLAVERY TO DESIRES

In cases of hardcore drug addiction, someone is hooked on a drug. His desire for the drug is irresistible. He has lost control in his drug use and, no doubt, in much else that he does. Here, it seems, we have desire dependence with a vengeance, but without the control which marks activity in general. The problem is how these cases are to be described.

My critical concern is with two approaches to this problem. Both are couched in terms of the freedom of the agent with respect to an irresistible desire. Freedom of agency is such an overburdened notion that I prefer to give it rest. In considering the positions which concern me, I shall continue to speak of the agent's control over what he does.

The first approach to describing cases involving an irresistible desire has been particularly influential and is due to Harry Frankfurt. Frankfurt's contention is that whether an agent has control over what he does depends on "volitions of the second order." A second-order volition, for Frankfurt, is a desire that a first-order performative desire be effective, that it be a desire which issues in action. On this view, the addict's loss of control is due to the fact that his desire to use the drug is not endorsed by the second-order desire that it be effective but is contrary to his second-order volition that it not be so (Frankfurt, 1971).

Despite its initial appeal, this approach runs into a standard objection. The problem is that dependence on higher-level desires is an infinitely repeatable relation. If control over first-order desires is a function of the second-order desire dependence, control over second-order desires should be a function of third-order desire dependence, and so on and on (see Watson, 1975).

I think that both the second-order desire-dependence thesis and the standard objection fail for the same reason. The second- or higher-order desires in question are S-desires, desires that first- or lower-order desires be satisfied. S-desires, however, are redundant relative to first- or lower-order desires. Frankfurt's free agent has the desire that p and the S-desire that he have the desire that p. The S-desire effectively reduces to the N-desire to have the desire that p and the desire that p. Frankfurt's conflicted addict has the desire to take drugs and the S-desire that he have the desire not to take drugs. The S-desire effectively reduces to the N-desire that he have the desire not to take drugs and the desire not to take drugs. In neither case can the success-indifferent N-desire do the work Frankfurt expects of the S-desire in the endorsement of the related first-order desire. Effectively, we have to do with first-order desires. Appealing to higher-order desires is similarly futile.

The second approach to the problem of describing cases involving irresistible desires appeals not to higher-order desires but to the agent's evaluative beliefs. Such an approach is taken by Gary Watson. For Watson, an agent is in control when his performative desires and actions are those which, all things considered, he thinks it best that he have or perform. The conflicted addict's problem, on this view, is that he thinks it best that he not use the drug but using the drug is just what he most wants to do and does (Watson, 1975).

If an agent's performative desires and actions are contrary to his considered beliefs about what is desirable, they are, on his own view, irrational. On the other hand, an agent will regard as rational those of his desires and actions which accord with his evaluative beliefs. Thus, on the view under consideration, agent control is a function of subjective rationality. That one is not in control of what one does when what he does is not what he thinks it best to do is an intuitively implausible idea. It has an implication that is even harder to accept. Typically, one is not responsible for what is not subject to one's voluntary control. On the evaluative conception of voluntary control, this would mean that one is not responsible for actions one does not take to be those it is most desirable to perform. This, I think, is absurd.

While not acceptable as it stands, the attempt to account for voluntary control in terms of the agent's beliefs about what is desirable seems to be on the right track. Having stressed the importance of dependence on desires for making the active-passive distinction, I must now stress the responsiveness of desires to reasons. The point to be made is not that a person has voluntary control over what he does to the extent that his performative desires answer to his beliefs about what is desirable. A person may have voluntary control in impulsive, akratic, or perverse actions in which he acts without considering what is desirable, or acts in some way contrary to what he considers desirable. In these cases, at least counterfactually, the agent's desires may be responsive to reason. The notion of an irresistible desire that we want is that of a performative desire which would not respond, whatever internal or external criticism or persuasion is brought to bear, to considerations of desirability.[6] A desire of this type is such that in having it and acting on it, the agent lacks voluntary control. When an agent lacks control owing to an irresistible desire is an empirical question. No doubt it can happen in cases of drug addiction. This, I think, is how to handle cases of slavery of desires.

4. DECIDING TO BELIEVE

Arguments that beliefs and emotions are desire dependent represent a challenge to the intuitive plausibility with which the desire-dependence thesis draws the line between activity and passivity. On the Cartesian view, to believe that *p* is to assent to the truth of the proposition *p*, and assent is subject to the will. In terms of our analysis, this means that belief is desire dependent.[7] This view would seem to be rooted in an analogy with verbal assent to a proposition. Verbal assent is certainly subject to the will. How could mental assent be less so? From the outset, this analogy should be regarded with suspicion. Verbal assent hardly amounts to belief. Why should mental assent be different? Still, much more remains to be said about the voluntarist conception of belief.

For the Cartesian, volition is the pivotal step in the transition from evidence to assent or belief, as it is in the transition from practical reasoning to ordinary action. We may or may not have adequate grounds for believing or acting; our beliefs and our actions may be rational or irrational. In any case the mediation of the will is necessary. Neither our beliefs nor our actions are directly input dependent or stimulus bound. On the face of it, it cannot be denied that this is a position with a certain appeal. Even so, there are problems.

An influential line of objection to the voluntarist conception of belief has been developed by Bernard Williams (1973, pp. 149-150). (Following Williams, similar arguments have been used by David Wiggins [1970] and Arthur Danto [1973, chap. 6].) Williams's argument proceeds in two steps. He first argues that, in virtue of certain features of belief, the idea that A could believe that he believed that p because he desired to believe that p is incoherent. For Williams, the concept of belief is such that, if A believes that p, A must take his belief that p to be true, and, in the case of empirical beliefs at least, this means that A must take his belief that p to be caused by the state of affairs which it represents. If A believed that he believed that p because he desired that he believe that p, he could not take his belief that p to be caused by the state of affairs which it represents and so could not take his belief that p to be true. Since necessary features of belief would be absent in this case, Williams draws his first conclusion. Williams next argues that if A could believe that p because he desired to believe that p, he would believe that he could do so. This would require that he believe, at least on some occasions, that he believes that p because he desired to believe that p. This, by the first step in the argument, is impossible. Thus, Williams concludes in the second step that A cannot believe that p because he desires to believe that p.

It is fairly clear that there are difficulties with Williams's argument. It involves the claim that for every first-order empirical belief, one must have two second-order beliefs, one regarding its truth, the other its etiology. This is a very dubious thesis. Williams seems to have taken representational and rational features of belief to be the contents of related beliefs. Also, the argument incorporates the idea that to have a voluntary capacity, one must believe that one has it. This, too, I find very doubtful. Counterexamples are easy to find.

These, however, are not the objections I mean to press. There is a much more fundamental point to be made.

Before getting to that point, we should consider the application of Williams's argument to the Cartesian position. It turns out to be less sweeping than might be expected. The argument does apply to the case of irrational belief formation, where one wills or desires to believe or assent to a proposition without having evidence connecting the belief with the state of affairs it represents. In this case, the etiological belief Williams requires is absent, and so will be a truth assessment based on it. The case of rational belief formation is different. Here the desire to believe the proposition is based on evidence of the proposition's truth. There is room for the second-order beliefs which Williams's argument requires. At most, then, Williams's argument would seem to show that irrational belief formation, as understood by the Cartesian, is impossible—a result which might yield a curious comfort to rationalistic seekers after certainty.

The point which I am most concerned to make in considering the voluntariness of belief is one which simultaneously undercuts both the Cartesian position and Williams's objection. The voluntarist's position is that the rational individual wills or desires to believe or assent to what is clearly true. The operative desire is the desire to have true beliefs. This, of course, is a truth-oriented S-desire. Williams argues that it is not possible that one should believe that p because of the desire, including the S-desire, that one believe that p. On either hand, we are concerned with S-desires. S-desires, however, are redundant. The second-order desire that one have the true belief that p is redundant relative to the first-order desire that p.

The redundancy of S-desires has devastating implications for the voluntarist's view. Since it is redundant relative to the first-order desire that p, believing that p because of the S-desire to believe that p amounts to believing that p because one desires that p. This, of course, is a form of self-deception. This form of self-deception, then, is precisely what we have in cases of irrational Cartesian belief formation. Here one believes that p because of the desire that p without adequate evidence that p. Cases of rational Cartesian belief formation are also self-deceptive and turn out to be doubly irrational. Here one believes that p because one desires that p, and one desires that p because one believes there to be evidence that p. This involves the irrationality of self-deception in believing that p because one desires that p, but it also involves the irrational perversity of desiring that p because one believes there to be evidence that p. So, the redundancy of S-desires to believe that p means that on the Cartesian view all irrational belief formation is self-deceptive and rational belief formation is not only self-deceptive but doubly irrational.

The implications of S-desire redundancy are hardly less devastating for Williams's objection. In arguing that one cannot believe that *p* because of the S-desire to believe that *p*, Williams is in effect arguing that self-deception which consists in believing that *p* because one desires that *p* is not possible. Believing that *p* because one desires that *p* is of course irrational. It involves believing that *p* without any reason to believe that *p*. Believing without reason, however, is not the same as not believing. Self-deception of the kind Williams's argument commits him to denying is, I think, common enough.

Truth-indifferent N-desires to have a belief are not redundant, and it is worth considering whether a voluntarist might construct an account of belief based on such desires. In this event, there is a problem about rationality. If we believe that *p* only because of an N-desire to have the belief, the belief will be irrational, since for us there will be no likelihood of its truth. If beliefs were generally based on N-desires in this way, beliefs would always be irrational. This, then, could hardly be a position proponents of the Cartesian view would take.

There is another possibility. The N-desire to have the belief that *p* may motivate us to inquire whether it is the case that *p*. Here we have a more reputable case of believing that *p* because of the N-desire to believe that *p*. Still, what should be noted is that in this case the operative desire motivates not the belief but the inquiry. The belief itself is formed subject to rational and causal constraints of evidence. Thus, this is not a case of direct desire dependence. Actions, however, are directly desire dependent. For this reason, once again the case for a voluntarist view of belief fails. Beliefs are not dependent on either S-desires or N-desires. Hume was right when he said that belief is "something which depends not on the will."

The view that we are active in having emotions is akin to the voluntarist conception of belief. It is prominent in Sartre's account of emotions; he holds that we make ourselves have the emotions we do, so that they are presumably desire dependent (Sartre, 1962 [1939], pp. 44-45). Sartre is followed in this view by Robert Solomon (1976).

I shall treat the voluntarist view of emotions with dispatch. For one thing, it is set out by its proponents with very little attention to detail. More importantly, what has been said about desire dependence and belief enables us to see readily that a voluntarist view of emotions won't work, regardless of the details. Practically all emotions theorists, myself included, hold that having an emotion involves having a belief. Sartre and Solomon hold that emotions are beliefs or ways of viewing the world. Either way, it follows that if emotions are desire dependent, beliefs must be so as well. But beliefs are not desire dependent. More could be said about voluntarism and emotions, but for the present, perhaps this will suffice.

5. RESPONSIBILITY

I have suggested that interpreting the active-passive distinction in terms of desire dependence helps us to understand the control and responsibility we typically have regarding our actions, as opposed to our passive states. This suggestion can lead to difficulties, and I should say something, at least briefly, to forestall them.

It might be objected that the active-passive distinction does not coincide with that between what we are and are not responsible for. There are actions for which we may not be accountable, and we may be accountable for our beliefs, desires, and emotions. The best way to meet the objection is to grant it; it is, after all, true. Desire dependence does not provide a necessary or a sufficient condition for responsibility. However, this does not mean that it is not useful in answering questions about responsibility.

The importance of desire dependence in understanding some cases in which a person may not be responsible for what he does has already been noted. In cases involving compulsion and related impositions, the effectiveness of our desires may be blocked. And the addict's desire on which his drug use is dependent may not be responsive to considerations of desirability.

Cases in which we may be accountable for our beliefs, desires, and emotions, which are not directly desire dependent, remain to be considered. Among these cases are ones in which we may be taken to task for an absurd belief, a perverse desire, or a grossly inappropriate emotion. Even here the indirect role of desire dependence is important for understanding responsibility. What we are responsible for in the cases I have in mind is the irrationality of a belief, desire, or emotion. This is a matter of the lack of likelihood of cognitive or conative success and is due to the absence of supporting considerations. The irrationality for which we may bear responsibility is, I am suggesting, indirectly responsibility for inattention to available evidence or want of care in inference. And these are operations which are desire dependent.

6. CONCLUSION

The active-passive distinction has a strong intuitive basis in our sense that what we do is in our control, as what happens to us is not, and seems important in its implications for our responsibility. Yet well-known ways of marking the distinction are fraught with difficulties. My contention is that an interpretation of the distinction between activity and passivity in terms of direct dependence on desires which are responsive to considerations of desirability is more adequate.[8]

NOTES

1. It should not be thought that the distinction between doings and happenings is quite coextensive with that between activity and passivity. Only usually are we fully active in our doings, as the case of tossing and turning in one's sleep suggests. Such discrepancies should be explained in an account of the active-passive distinction.

2. Robert Gordon makes the superficially similar suggestion that emotions are not responsive to evaluations of having them as actions are to evaluations of performing them and that this helps explain the active-passive distinction. Gordon, however, does not distinguish between desires and beliefs about desirability. This is a distinction which must be made to understand the importance of desire dependence. Neither emotions nor actions are directly dependent on beliefs about their desirability (see Gordon, 1986a).

3. A similar distinction is drawn by Bernard Williams in the case of second-order desires about beliefs (Williams, 1973, pp. 149-150).

4. It should be observed that this conclusion applies only to indexical S-desires and beliefs in the first person. Nonindexical and second-person S-beliefs and desires are not redundant. The former cases, however, are our concern in considerations of an individual's activity or passivity. Even our actions are not directly dependent on the desires of others but only on our own desires.

5. Irving Thalberg also argues that problems of free agency can be resolved without recourse to higher-order desires but without the backing of an account of redundancy in iterated desires (Thalberg, 1978). Robert Gordon does suggest that redundancy may be involved in appeals to iterated desires and recommends that we appeal instead to desirability judgments. However, Gordon's failure to distinguish between desires and desirability judgments undercuts the position he advocates. Desirability judgments about desires and beliefs are not redundant (see Gordon, 1986b).

6. I take substantially this suggestion to be made by Wright Neely (1974). Like many others, however, Neely does not separate desirability beliefs from desires, so that his position does not stand out as basically different from Frankfurt's. The separation of desirability beliefs from desires is obviously something on which I mean to insist.

7. Descartes himself distinguishes between volitions and desires, so that this statement of the position does not accurately represent his view. I think that my criticism of doxastic voluntarism could be revised to apply to Descartes's own version, but historical criticism is not my purpose.

8. This paper was written while I was a participant in the National Endowment for the Humanities Institute on Human Action held at the University of Nebraska at Lincoln in 1984. The support provided by this grant is gratefully acknowledged. I should also like to express my gratitude for helpful comments to Institute Director Robert Audi, to Institute participants James Montmarquet, Michael Robins, Edward Sankowski, Donald Sievert, and Michael Zimmerman, and also to Barry Loewer, Joel Marks, and Irving Thalberg.

The Difference between Motivation and Desire

Joel Marks

Abstract. This is a defense of the reality and importance of desire in explanations of action and analyses of emotion, including moral action and emotion. Recent objections by Thomas Nagel, Don Locke, and Mitchell Staude center on a distinction between two senses of "desire." This distinction is accepted but shown to be benign. In the process, important differences are brought out between being in a motivational or a feeling state on the one hand and, on the other, being in a state of desire.

Mary eats an apple. Why? A traditional view in philosophy has it that at least one of Mary's desires is an essential component of the explanation of her behavior;[1] for example, she may eat the apple because she is hungry, i.e., desires to eat some food. Let us call this position "conativism."

In this essay I shall defend conativism against a group of attacks in the recent literature,[2] which take their common impetus from a distinction: "desire" is found to have more than one sense, and this fact is used to undercut the significance (if not literal truth) of conativism. I shall call my opponents "cognitivists" (or "the cognitivist") because they characteristically champion belief over desire in the explanation of action.[3]

In section 1, I will recapitulate the cognitivist's argument. In section 2, I will turn the tables on the cognitivist and use the distinction between two senses of "desire" to vindicate conativism. Finally, in section 3, I will draw some parallels between the present debate in theory of action and another ongoing controversy in theory of emotion.

1. THE CONATIVIST FALLACY

A great many writers have discovered ambiguities in "desire";[4] but in the recent literature three writers stand out who use such a discovery to *denigrate* desire in the explanation of action, viz., Thomas Nagel, Don Locke, and Mitchell Staude. The particular ideas of these three differ. In this section I will extract what I take to be the common essence of their arguments.

Whenever a person does something, he or she may be said to *want* to do that thing. For example, if Mary eats an apple, it is perfectly acceptable to say that Mary *wants* to eat the apple. After all, if Mary did not want to eat the apple, why would she eat it? On the other hand, it is equally proper to say, "But of course she didn't *really* want to eat the apple. (Mary hates apples!) She ate one only because she was hungry and there was nothing else available to eat."

Furthermore, it is possible to draw behavioral and phenomenological distinctions between Mary's *eating the apple even though she didn't really want to eat an apple* and, say, Mary's *eating the apple because she craved an apple.* For example, in the former case she may do so with annoyance, in the latter with gusto. In the former case she may entertain images of various foods in her mind and rummage the cupboards and only then the refrigerator and finally the vegetable bin and then experience some disappointment when she finds (only) the apple; in the latter case she may imagine apples specifically in her mind and go straight to the vegetable bin and feel delighted when she discovers the apple.

The upshot is that there is what Locke calls a "formal" sense of desire, which is properly employed whenever a person acts intentionally, and a "genuine" sense, which has more restricted application. Conativism is true in this sense: formal desire is always involved in the explanation of action. It is always correct to say that one did such-and-such because one wanted to. But, as the contrasting apple-eating examples show, desire in this formal sense can be tantamount to no desire at all in any *significant* sense of desire; for Mary can, in the formal sense, desire to eat an apple even when she does not *really* ("genuinely") desire to eat an apple (indeed, even when she really desires not to eat an apple).

So to say that it is always true, as conativists do, that desire is involved in the explanation of action is as empty of significance as the assertion that being unmarried is essential to bachelorhood. When someone asks why John is a bachelor, the answer, "Because he is unmarried," is singularly unsatisfying. The question remains, "Yes, of course, but *why* is he unmarried?" Similarly, when someone asks why John got married, the answer, "Because he wanted to," may only prompt a rephrasing of the original question; "Yes, of course, but what I want to know is *why* he wanted to get married (after all these years of bachelorhood!)."

Conativism is thus reduced to an analytic thesis (if it is true); it is to be understood as the thesis that "every act is motivated." Desire, in the sense which makes conativism true, means "motivational state"; to desire to do something is simply to be motivated to do it.

But the question remains, motivated *by what?* By *desire?* Not necessarily, if desire is taken in what Locke calls its "genuine" sense. As shown in the contrasting examples above, Mary may eat an apple *even though she really does not want to.* Hence, although she is surely *motivated* to eat the apple (for how else could she eat it intentionally?), it is clear that in this case she need not "genuinely desire" to eat the apple, or an apple, or even any food at all. Mary may be very ill and experiencing a complete loss of appetite, i.e., desire for food. She eats the apple only because she knows she has to eat something in order to get well, and the apple is the only food available.

Therefore, concludes the cognitivist, if desire is understood in the sense of genuine desire, conativism is obviously *false.* What is always true is that an action is (must be) *motivated;* and since desire has as one of its senses, "motivational state," it is always true that desire *in this sense* is involved in action. But presumably this is not the sense of desire which concerns the true conativist, for then conativism would be true simply in virtue of the meanings of words and fail to embody a significant psychological thesis. Yet when desire is taken in its stronger sense, referring to a particular *kind* of motivational influence, conativism is seen to be false; for genuine desire is just one kind of motivational influence. Other kinds of things can motivate as well, for example beliefs.

In effect, the conativist commits a fallacy. From the analytic truism that action is always motivated—which is the content of the claim that people only do what they want to do—the conativist infers that people always have a (genuine) desire *to do what they do* (and that they act the way they do because of what they desire). We can call this the Conativist Fallacy. It is a fallacy of equivocation if the two senses of "desire" are employed in the premise and conclusion. Pointing out and articulating this distinction between two senses of "desire" is, therefore, the cognitivist's strategy for undercutting what appears to be the main argument in support of conativism.

In sum, Nagel, Locke, and Staude have distinguished two senses of "desire," a formal and a genuine sense (to adopt Locke's terminology). Desire in the formal sense is the mere analytic shadow of action; although always attributable to an agent, it serves no truly explanatory purpose. Genuine desire, on the other hand, while capable of functioning as a true motivator of action, seems inadequate to support the conativist thesis on what may be taken to be empirical grounds; consideration of everyday cases of motivation apparently refutes the contention that such desires are *always* party to the production of action. Thus, on these accounts, conativism is either trivially true or obviously false.

2. DEFENSE OF CONATIVISM

My defense of conativism accepts, and is in fact premised upon, the distinction between two senses of "desire" which is the cornerstone of the cognitivist's argument. I consider this distinction to be a genuine contribution to our understanding of mind and action. Furthermore, I concede that it is fallacious to infer from the *motivation* to perform some act to a *genuine desire* to perform that act, and I am willing to grant, for the sake of the argument, that Mary does *not* require a genuine desire to eat an apple in order to eat an apple.

But the question remains: does the presence of motivation imply the presence of genuine desire? This question remains because, for all that the cognitivist has shown, there may yet be a genuine desire (from now on I shall just say "desire") *other than* the desire to do whatever a person happens to be motivated to do. And at first glance this does seem to be the case; for example, although Mary may indeed lack a desire *to eat an apple*, must she not still desire *something*, say food or health, in order to be motivated to eat some particular apple which is available to her? (Else, why would she eat of it? — the familiar conativist refrain.)

What I will do in this section is defend an affirmative reply to that question. We may call this thesis, "weak conativism," to distinguish it from the strong variety which insists that every motivation *is* a (genuine) desire. It is clear from their writing that the critics of conativism are opposed to it in both dilutions.

It is easy to understand why a philosopher might find any form of conativism distasteful. If a desire is always required for action, then certain kinds of ethical action become problematic, for example acting in the face of countervailing (malevolent or imprudent) desires or merely absent (benevolent or prudent) desires. Furthermore, certain ideal styles of behavior, such as the stoic's or Buddhist's or karma yogi's or Kantian's "dispassionate" or "desireless" action, would be in need of rescue from conceptual self-destruction. The favored philosophical recourse is the rationalist one: rational animals are capable of acting on the basis of *reasons* alone, which can substitute for and even override desires. In the present context, reasons appear in the guise of beliefs; hence cognitivism.

But since, prima facie, desires *are* always involved in behavior, the burden of proof lies with the cognitivist. The argument against desire which was presented in the preceding section only addresses *strong* conativism. I have pointed out that additional argument is required to refute weak conativism (from now on simply "conativism"). The critics of desire seem to have overlooked this logical gap in the presentation of their case.

My strategy, therefore, will be to extend the cognitivist line of argument to cover the whole range of desire and thereby illustrate its ultimate failure.

Let us extend the cognitivist argument by taking a closer look at the examples cited earlier.

> 1. Mary eats an apple, but she has no genuine desire to eat an apple (not to mention this apple). Mary is simply hungry.

In this example, the "desire to eat the apple" drops out; it is psychologically spurious, as argued above.[5] But note that another genuine desire has been substituted for it, viz., Mary's desire to have food in her belly. Thus, while this example does serve to establish the distinction between two senses of desire, it does not help to refute conativism.

However, the cognitivist goes on to argue that Mary need not be hungry, i.e., need not have a genuine desire for food, in order to be *motivated* to eat. It would be to commit the Conativist Fallacy to think otherwise. Example 2 bears this out.

> 2. Mary eats an apple, but she has no genuine desire to eat the apple and she is not hungry. Mary is ill and is experiencing a loss of appetite. She eats the apple because she knows she needs to eat something in order to get better and the apple is the only food available.

In this example, the attempt is made to circumvent any mention of a genuine desire. Mary's act is explained by reference to her beliefs (what she "knows").

But a response to such an attempt is to point out that a genuine desire must surely be *presumed*, for why else would these beliefs move Mary to action? We have it on Humean authority that "Reason being cool and disengaged, is no motive to action, and directs only the impulse received from appetite or inclination . . ." (Hume, 1975 [1751], app. 1).

But aside from that, there is the simple argument that the very same beliefs could be present in Mary's mind, and with the same degrees of conviction and "vividness," yet Mary not eat the apple (and not because of some external intervention or failure of physiology, etc.). The conativist concludes that we must (in light of Mary's loss of appetite) postulate some such desire as Mary's desire *to get better* in order to explain the motivating force of her belief that *eating the apple will help her get better.*

But the cognitivist counters that a genuine desire is not a necessary component of Mary's motivation to eat the apple. Again, only the Conativist Fallacy would make one think so. What is necessary is that Mary be *motivated* to do what she believes will help her get better, but it is an open question whether this "desire" involves a (genuine) desire such as the desire *to get better.* An alternative to desire is given in Example 3.

> 3. Mary eats an apple, but she has no genuine desire to eat the apple nor is she hungry, nor does she have a genuine desire to recover from the illness from which she is suffering. Mary's illness is so debilitating that Mary has not only lost her appetite but even her desire to get well. Nonetheless she eats the apple because, while recognizing her own deficiency of desire, she believes that she ought to do whatever is necessary to recover her health.

The latter belief is what Don Locke has called a "sufficient-reason belief" (Locke, 1982, p. 247). It is a meta-belief which has motivational force or which confers motivational force on some other belief; in other words, it functions in just the way the conativist supposes only desire does. In this example we may suppose that Mary has the belief that *she ought to try to recover her health* on the basis of some principled belief such as that *health is a good* or that *she has an obligation to be healthy for her children's sake,* and her belief that *eating something may help her regain her health* thereby takes on the power to cause her to eat the apple.

The notion of a sufficient-reason belief is an attractive one. As explained above, it is uplifting to think that beliefs, especially principled ones, can override or substitute for desires. Alas, desiring does not make it so. The conativist will point out, analogously to Example 2, that even a sufficient-reason belief can fail to have or provide motivational force. For example, there are the notorious cases of "weakness of will" when a person such as Mary believes, genuinely believes, that she ought to do a certain thing, and yet cannot bring herself to do it. Mary must at the very least retain the general desire *to do what she believes she ought to do* if her behavior in Example 3 is to be intelligible and possible.

The natural response of the cognitivist — for it would involve no new principle or argument — is that conativists once again commit a fallacy when they infer from the presence of a motivated state to the presence of a genuine desire. Clearly, Mary must be *motivated* to do what she believes she ought to do if she does eat the apple because of her sufficient-reason belief that she ought to. But it does not follow from this that Mary has a *genuine desire* to do what she believes she ought to do.

In sum, the dialogue between the cognitivist and the conativist keeps repeating the following form. (1) The cognitivist poses an example which is intended to show that genuine desire need not be present in the motivation of a particular act. (2) The conativist objects that the act in question would not and could not have occurred unless a genuine desire were present at some point in the causal chain. (3) The cognitivist replies that the conativist commits the fallacy (the "Conativist Fallacy") of inferring that a genuine desire is present from the mere fact that motivation is present. The cognitivist concedes that the agent in the example must be motivated, but insists that it is at least an open question whether her motivation consists of or involves a genuine desire.

I will now show that this pattern of argument cannot continue indefinitely, and that the buck stops only at a genuine desire. I will show this by asking the reader to consider exactly what the cognitivist means by "motivation" or "being in a motivated state." And to see that, we can take another look at the three examples.

In Example 1, Mary was motivated to eat an apple because she was hungry, i.e., had a genuine desire for food although not for an apple in particular. What did Mary's motivation consist of? Clearly, the desire for food was part of it, for ex hypothesi Mary would have had no reason to eat had she not been hungry. But the desire for food cannot be the whole story. One can be hungry and not eat, even in the presence of food. Mary must have *cognized* the presence of food; Mary *believed* that the apple was food (or that the only food available was this apple, or some such proposition). So Mary's motivated state consisted of desiring something *and believing* something; *together,* a belief and a desire constituted her motivational state.

It will not surprise the reader that Mary can be in a state of conviction (i.e., belief, even strong belief) with respect to the proximity of an apple and yet be completely unmotivated; after all, Mary may simply not be hungry. What is perhaps controversial is my claim that Mary is not necessarily in a motivated state *even if she has a desire*, even a strong one, even an "occurrent" one, *if belief is absent*. Take the desire specified in Example 1, viz., the desire for food; exactly what would Mary be *motivated to do* if she had this desire, *belief absent?*

Granted, Mary has a great deal, indeed an infinite amount, of *hypothetical* motivation. For instance, if Mary desires food, then *were* she to believe that an apple is the only food present, she *would be* motivated *to eat the apple*. But if Mary happens to believe nothing (relevant to her hunger desire), then I do not see how she can be said to be in a "state of being motivated," no matter how strong her desire.[6]

One general principle at work here, which I wish to defend, is that motivation is conceptually tied to action, while *desire is not*. For example, one cannot be motivated that it be a nice day, for its being a nice day is not a possible act. One can only be motivated to do or try to do something which may have or may be thought to have some influence on the niceness of the day; for example, one may be motivated to pray, or to spray the clouds with silver halide crystals.

But one can certainly *desire* that it be a nice day. This is because the proper (intentional) object of a desire is a *state of affairs*.[7] This state of affairs *may or may not* be an act (of the desirer's).

This is one way we could have established that Mary's being hungry, in Example 1, is a desire rather than a state of motivation. Although we may casually speak of being hungry as a desire to eat, literally it is a desire to have food in one's belly;[8] i.e., it is a desire that *a state of affairs that is not an act* obtain. Hence, it cannot be that the sense of "desire" at work in the example is the sense which is equivalent to *motivation*; hence, the desire must be a *genuine* one.

But the point is even more general than my interpretation of *being hungry* suggests. What I have just argued is that desires need not take acts as their intentional objects, while motives (if I may use this term as equivalent to "motivations") must. Now I will also maintain that desires which *do* take acts as their intentional objects—call such desires "practical desires"—need not (causally) yield (those) acts, even under "normal circumstances," whereas motives must (ceteris paribus). For example, suppose Mary desires to eat an apple, i.e., specifically to enjoy the *activity* of consuming (tasting, crunching, etc.) a piece of fruit. Is Mary thereby motivated to eat an apple? It seems to me that *she is not* unless she happens to *believe* something, for example that there is an apple readily available to her. Otherwise Mary simply is not motivated with respect to eating an apple, albeit her desire may be intense (and, along with other beliefs, help motivate her to do *other* things, such as walk to the grocery store).

The upshot of all this is that desire turns out to be very like (Humean, not Nagelian) belief in its *inefficacy* to generate action. It is only desire *in combination with belief* which yields action, or *motivation*. (The Humean point is the complementary one, that it is only belief *in combination with desire* which yields action.)

And cognitivists should have no quarrel with this because it is implicit in their distinction between two senses of "desire" and their indictment of conativism as either vacuous or false. For conativism is vacuous precisely if desire is conceptually tied to action, i.e., is equivalent to motivation; while it is false, cognitivists argue, if desire is not conceptually tied to action. And it is the latter sort of desire which, if any, is the "genuine" sort. So in effect the cognitivists have asserted that desire is not conceptually tied to action, while motivation is. (But I will use this distinguishing feature to "save" conativism.)

The preceding discussion can be summarized in the form of three criteria for distinguishing motivation from desire.

(1) Motivation involves belief, desire does not.

(2) Motivation is conceptually tied to action, while desire is first and foremost tied to a state of affairs.

(3) Motivation is sufficient to produce action, "other things equal," while desire is powerless to produce action in the absence of relevant belief.[9]

What emerges from these criteria is a sense of the *practical impotence* of desire. Nonetheless, I shall use this feature of desire to vindicate the role of desire in the generation and explanation of action.

Let us move on to a reexamination of Example 2. Does this example bear out the conceptual conclusions drawn from our reexamination of Example 1? Two interpretations of Example 2 were offered earlier. The conativist suggested that Mary ate the apple because she had a genuine desire to get well. On this interpretation, Mary's motivation once again consists of a belief and a desire, for in addition to the desire postulated by the conativist, there must presumably be some such belief as, "Eating this apple will help me to get better."

The cognitivist countered that Mary may not have had a genuine desire to get well, but only have been motivated to get well. But notice that here, too, we can say that Mary's motivation consists of a belief and a desire, although now the desire is of the "formal" sort, the "empty" sort, a "mere" motivation rather than a genuine desire. Thus, there is now a *hierarchy* of *motives* wherein a "surface-level" motive (to eat an apple or to eat something) partially consists of a "deeper-level" *motive* (to get well).

(Note also that the intentional content of Mary's desire is possibly different between the two interpretations. If Mary's desire to get better is formal, hence a *motivation*, then what she "desires" is *to do* something, viz., *to do* whatever is reasonably necessary to get well. Whereas if her desire is a genuine one, it may be just for a non-act state of affairs, say, being healthy again.)

In sum, analyses of Mary's motivation in Examples 1 and 2 suggest that motivation consists of *either* a belief and a genuine desire *or* a belief and a formal desire (i.e., a belief and another motivation). The stage is now set for my answer to the cognitivist.

Consider Example 3. Here the cognitivist draws his trump card. Having argued that Mary may merely be motivated to do what is necessary to get well, rather than have a genuine desire to get well, the cognitivist spells out a possible alternative account of Mary's nonconative motivation (to eat the apple); Mary has a "sufficient-reason belief," which serves adequately to explain her behavior.

But now we see that this cannot be the whole story. Motivation, even on the cognitivist's interpretation, consists of *two* components, viz., a belief and a desire. The desire component may itself consist of *either* a genuine desire or a formal desire (we have granted this to the cognitivist); but the model of motivation derived from Examples 1 and 2 calls for a desire *of some sort*. Therefore Mary's sufficient-reason belief cannot provide the total explication of her motivation. We will need to say that Mary ate the apple because she believed she ought to *and* she desired (on the conativist interpretation) or was motivated (on the cognitivist interpretation) to do what she believed she ought to do.

Suppose we accept the cognitivist interpretation. Then, once again (as with Example 2), Mary's motivation (to eat the apple) partially consists of another motivation (in this case, to do what she believes she ought). But this time the cognitivist is stymied, I submit. For at this point it becomes implausible for the cognitivist to offer a still finer-grained analysis of Mary's motivation. He has simply exhausted his (or Mary's!) cognitive resources. The backstop of his account was supposed to be Mary's sufficient-reason belief. But now it looks as if the cognitivist will have to postulate some still more fundamental belief, to help constitute Mary's *motivation* to act in accordance with her sufficient-reason belief.[10]

And there is more. So long as cognitivism continues to offer motives (motivations) in place of genuine desires in the descent into the springs of action, it will have to offer yet "deeper" beliefs. Not only will these belief attributions appear less and less plausible, but they are also incorporated in a regress which is vicious because unending (whereas the human psyche is clearly finite).

I conclude that if the regress is to stop, a genuine desire must be postulated at some point in the analysis of motivation.

3. DESIRE AND EMOTION

Throughout this essay I have paid deference to the cognitivist's theoretical accomplishment of distinguishing two senses of "desire." I have tried to show, however, that far from undercutting a crucial role for desire in theory of action, the distinction can be used to vindicate that role. In this final part of my essay I would like to make a similar point about the role of desire in theory of emotion.[11]

In recent theory of emotion, as in recent theory of action, belief has been in the ascendant over desire.[12] The situation for desire in theory of emotion has been, if anything, more pathetic than in theory of action, since in the former context desire has not so much been attacked as ignored.[13] But fortunately for conativism a healthy "lobby" has sprung up very recently among emotion theorists.[14]

What I will do here is present a problem case for an analysis of emotion in terms of desire.[15] Then I will show how the two senses of desire can be used once again to "save" conativism (this time "emotional conativism" rather than "practical conativism").

Consider a straightforward conativist analysis of an emotion like fear. *Jim is afraid of the dog = Jim believes that he is about to be maimed by the dog + Jim desires that he not be maimed.* An objection to this analysis would be that Jim could be in the identical belief-desire state, yet not be afraid.

In particular, suppose Jim's desire *not to be maimed* is purely instrumental; Jim desires *not to be maimed* solely because he desires to compete in a beauty contest. (We may suppose the latter desire to be intrinsic for the sake of the example.) Then, if Jim believed he was about to be maimed, it would make more sense for him to be, say, disappointed or annoyed or angry than for him to be afraid.

Now, any of the three former emotions would indeed be in keeping with the character of Jim's *intrinsic* desire (to compete in the contest). But how, the objection continues, can the conativist analysis dispose of Jim's *instrumental* desire (not to be maimed) in its account of what Jim must be feeling? That is, why is not a conativist account obliged to attribute some composite fear-annoyance state to Jim, rather than just an annoyance state?

An intrinsic (or "basic") desire is a desire that something be the case for no further reason. For example, if one desires to jog "for its own sake," for "the joy of jogging," then one has an intrinsic desire to jog. An instrumental (or "extrinsic") desire is a desire that something be the case because one desires that something else be the case. For example, if one desires to jog because it will promote one's health, then one has an extrinsic desire to jog (and perhaps an intrinsic desire to be healthy or to do that which promotes one's health).

Prima facie, intrinsic desire and extrinsic desire are both desire plain and simple. But the cognitivist's distinction of senses of "desire" should alert us to the misleading possibilities of desire talk. And I now think the answer to the present problem is that, properly speaking,

Jim has no (genuine) desire that he not be maimed. What Jim desires is that he be able to compete in a contest. The case is analogous to Example 1 wherein Mary has no real desire to eat an apple in particular, but rather only a desire to eat something (i.e., she is hungry). The conclusion there was that Mary is in a motivational state with respect to eating the apple, and *not* in a (genuine) desire state.

In the present case, the situation differs only in that no mention of an *act* has appeared in the description of Jim's intentional state(s). Therefore it would be inappropriate to speak of Jim's being *motivated* not to be maimed. The term of art left to us is "instrumentally desires" not to be maimed. But I think it can now be seen that instrumental or extrinsic desire is only a more general form of the phenomenon we call motivation. For a person is motivated to do something as a *means* to bring about a desired end, just as a person *instrumentally* desires what he or she believes will conduce to some desired end.

Indeed, it would be perfectly appropriate to speak of a motive as an instrumental desire. The term "motive" picks out those instrumental desires which take the desirer's own acts as their intentional objects; for example, Mary instrumentally desires *to eat an apple* because she is hungry. But, strictly speaking, instrumental or extrinsic desire drops out of our psycho-ontology altogether.

I leave the precise characterization of extrinsic desire to another time. Obviously, the three criteria of motivation developed above will not do to characterize extrinsic desire since, for example, extrinsic desire lacks the conceptual tie to action that motivation has. Nonetheless, I think the reader can sense the formal parallels. And these are sufficient to suggest the interesting thesis that extrinsic desire is just another variety of Lockean formal desire.

This interpretation of conativist analyses of emotion is also helpful in the realm of moral (and immoral) emotions (not to mention motives). For example, suppose Jim desires (in some sense) Mary's welfare; is Jim's attitude *altruistic?* It depends on the nature of his other-directed desire. In particular, is it intrinsic or extrinsic? If Jim desires Mary's welfare "for its (and her) own sake," then it seems clear that his intentions toward her are strictly altruistic.

Suppose Jim desires Mary's welfare solely because he believes his own happiness is contingent upon hers. In other words, let us say that it is a desire for his own welfare which is intrinsic in this case. Then I think we should say that the analysis (and moral evaluation) of Jim's psychological state toward Mary must pay heed to this self-directed desire, and *no heed at all* to the other-directed desire (if it is a *desire* at all). It counts for *nothing* that Jim "genuinely wants" Mary to be happy (as evidenced, say, by his being *highly motivated* to make her happy, or by his *feeling terrible* when she is sad); his attitude (or motivation with respect to his action) may be strictly egoistic, for all that.

A conativist analysis of altruistic and egoistic emotion and motivation would seem hard put to account for the phenomena of this case. Jim's instrumental other-directed desire would "get in the way" of a straightforward account (just as did his instrumental desire *not to be maimed* in the previous example). But if we acknowledge that extrinsic desire is desire in name only (really just Lockean formal desire generalized to cover nonmotivational as well as motivational cases), then I think we can see how a conativist account in terms of genuine desire will succeed.

4. CONCLUSION

I have presented a defense of desire in theory of action and theory of emotion. My defense has employed a distinction between two senses of "desire." Ironically, this is the distinction my cognitivist opponents used in their attempt to demolish conativism, but they have been hoist by their own petard. They argued that there are two senses of desire and *therefore* motivation need not involve genuine desire. I have countered that an understanding of the differences between formal desire and genuine desire demonstrates that the presence of motivation implies the presence of genuine desire.[16]

Also ironically, I attribute to my cognitivist opponents the same essential mistake they have attributed (correctly, I grant) to one brand of conativism, viz., conflating the two senses of desire. It is just that cognitivism conflates them "in the opposite direction." While conativism got into trouble by sometimes expecting genuine desires to do the job of formal desires, viz., function as motivation, cognitivism, I have argued, insists that formal desires do a job that only genuine desires can perform, viz., give motivation a foundation.

Yet another irony which emerges in the course of my defense of the crucial role of desire in generating action, is that desire differs from the ersatz variety precisely in its *in*ability to generate action "on its own steam." This feature of desire shows it to be essentially *independent* of action (at least as independent as belief is; and thereby hangs a puzzle: harking back to the title of this essay, we may now wonder just what is "The Difference between *Belief* and Desire"). Thus, in addition to motivational states, an avenue is opened to the analysis of nonmotivational states, such as emotions (i.e., those emotions which are not themselves motives), in terms of desire.[17]

NOTES

1. "Behavior" should be taken to mean intentional behavior throughout this essay; similarly for behavior words such as "do" and "act" and "jump." People can be said to *do* things which are "mere" behaviors as opposed to behaviors imbued with intentionality; for example, Mary is "doing something" when she sneezes as well as when she eats an apple. But *mere* behaviors are not my concern in this essay.

   There is also an ambiguity in the word "intentional." An act can be intentional because it is intended in a deliberate fashion; for example, Mary may go out for a walk as the result of "forming the intention" to get some exercise in this way. But an act is also intentional (in a special sense) if it is done with more direct control by the agent than your average sneeze; thus, Mary may start walking just on impulse and still do so *intentionally* in this sense. This essay is concerned with the whole range of intentional behavior.

   Yet another problem about action is how to identify and enumerate acts. For example, if it is five o'clock and Mary is driving her car to Ohio for a meeting, is Mary *driving to Ohio*, or is she merely *driving her car*, or is she *turning the steering wheel and also pressing on the accelerator*, etc.? This issue is certainly relevant to the concerns of my essay, but I cannot hope to treat it here.

2. My main sources have been Locke (1982), Nagel (1970), and Staude (1982). See also Locke (1974), Silver (1980), and Staude (1979). The basic criticism of conativism also receives passing mention in Hospers's (1967) discussion of laws of human nature.

3. "Conativist" and "cognitivist" are thus not symmetrical. The conativist claims that desire is a necessary condition of action, the cognitivist that belief is (at least sometimes) sufficient.

4. For example, see Alston (1967b), Audi (1973b), Davis (1984b), and Schiffer (1976). In the sequel I will speak of the word "desire" and of the phenomenon (or phenomena) of desire indifferently; also, I will not distinguish desiring from wanting.

5. Another argument, this one time-honored, is that such a desire—the conclusion of a practical syllogism—is simply superfluous. For a recent reference see Wheeler (1982).

6. Someone might object that Mary will never be in a condition of believing *nothing* that is relevant to her desire for food; for example, she will presumably at all times believe, however "latently," that food can be obtained at grocery stores. Therefore she will be in a motivational state, however rudimentary, *whenever* she has a desire for food. But this is not an objection to what I have claimed. It may be a matter of contingent fact that people are always in some motivational state corresponding to their desires. My claim is only that for a person to be in a state of desire is not, as a matter of analytic truth, for her to be in a motivational state. Furthermore, *which* motivational state(s) one is in will be completely belief dependent.

7. See Searle (1983), p. 30, for an argument that desire is always propositional.

8. Actually, there are all sorts of ways of being hungry; just grant me that this is one of them.

9. Criterion 3 may be too strong; sometimes desire alone seems to motivate (e.g., an intrinsic desire to shout) or desire plus something other than a belief (e.g., a desire to scratch an *itch;* or does this involve a "sensational belief"?). But *conativism* survives even if the *belief*-desire thesis does not.

10. Jerome Shaffer (personal communication, 1985) has pointed out that Don Locke may already have gone too far when he postulated the sufficient-reason belief itself. Recall that Locke criticized the conativist for postulating a desire *solely* because the action, which it is intended to explain, has occurred. But has Locke any better reason for postulating his favored substitute for that desire?

11. I am using "emotion" to refer to psychological (or "intentional") attitudes generally. In Marks (1982) I argued that, properly speaking, "emotion" refers only to attitudes containing a *strong*-desire component. But the word "emotion" is used more broadly in most of the recent literature, and the points I wish to make here pertain to emotion in this broad sense.

12. Recent cognitivist analyses of emotion include Lyons (1980), Neu (1977), and Solomon (1976).

13. Stocker (1983b) is an exception, though his argument is distinctive (and noncognitivist).

14. For example, see Davis (1981b), Green (1979, in preparation), Marks (1982), Robinson (1983), and Shaffer (1983).

15. It is not clear, however, that the case I will present would actually help a *cognitivist* account of emotion.

16. I leave it to the reader to figure out where my thesis fits on the analytic-synthetic continuum.

17. This essay has benefited from dialogue with Mitchell Silver, O. H. Green, the University of Connecticut Philosophy Department, and of course Mary.

Defining Desire

Dennis W. Stampe

Abstract. A definition of desire, in terms of its function in the determination of rational action, is examined. The question is raised whether this definition is adequate: whether it is not viciously circular, whether it explains the rationality of acting so as to satisfy one's desires, whether it distinguishes between what one wants and the possibly unwanted effects of getting what one wants, and whether it distinguishes desire from belief, on the one hand, and from intention on the other. Amendments are proposed which equip the definition to meet these requirements. The amendments would require the postulation of an autonomous mental faculty of appetition, and the recognition of the role of something's being good, in an adequate definition of desire. The question whether a definition employing that predicate can parade as "naturalistic" is addressed briefly, and its continuity with a conception of desires as representations of needs is asserted.

Desire would once have been thought irrelevant to the theory of belief. Perhaps this was because philosophers then tended to concentrate on their own, the first-person, case, and it seems that one knows what one believes, immediately, without considering what one's desires[1] may be. But the ascription of beliefs to another person must be made on the basis of evidence—the evidence, presumably, of his behavior. The notion was aired that perhaps to believe something, that it is raining, say, is nothing other than being disposed to behave in a characteristic sort of way: to behave *as if* it were raining.

This idea effectively fell to a point made by Geach: there is no such thing as behavior that can "be described as 'acting as if you held such-and-such belief' unless we take for granted, or are specially informed about, the needs and wants of the agent"—e.g., whether he wants to stay dry or not (Geach, 1957, p. 8). The ascription of beliefs, to other persons at least, is linked in such a way to the ascription of desires to them. But we may abandon the behaviorist idea that there are observationally identifiable kinds of behavior specific to a given mental state, and definitive of its content, without giving up the idea that what it is to be in a given state of mind, is to be disposed to behave in a certain way—so long as we recognize that the way one will be disposed to behave will be a function of other states of one's mind as well. Thus, one who believes it is raining is disposed to behave in a way he thinks will satisfy his desires, whatever they may happen to be: so as to keep dry, if that is what is wanted. And such "behavior" is more than that—it is rational action.

What, then, are desire and belief? They are, as Robert Stalnaker puts it, "correlative dispositional states of a potentially rational agent":

> To desire that *P* is to be disposed to act in ways that would tend to bring it about that *P* in a world in which one's beliefs, whatever they are, were true. To believe that *P* is to be disposed to act in ways that would tend to satisfy one's desires, whatever they are, in a world in which *P* (together with one's other beliefs) were true. (Stalnaker, 1984, p. 15)

Suppose I am being held prisoner in this study, and want to escape. My desire to escape is a disposition to do things, such as jump out the window, that would tend to bring it about that I do escape, if my beliefs, including my belief that if I jump I will escape, should happen to be true. And to have that belief is to be disposed to do things—such as jump out the window—that would satisfy such desires as I might happen to have—such as, perhaps, the desire to escape. That is, the belief is a disposition to do such actions as would satisfy my desires if the belief were true.

But to want to get out is not to want to get hurt, and yet the disposition to do what would tend to bring it about that I do escape, if my beliefs be true, is a disposition to risk injury: indeed, to break a leg, which is what I believe might happen if I jump. But I have no desire to break my leg.[2] The formula, then, does not—or apparently does not—provide *sufficient* conditions for my desiring that *p:* that is, the converse of the formula does not hold; for to be disposed to act in ways that would tend to bring it about that *p* (e.g., that I break my leg) in worlds in which my beliefs are true is not necessarily to desire that *p* (that I break my leg). But it is *logically* possible to escape, even to jump, without risking a broken leg, and perhaps this possibility is what keeps my desire to escape from being also a desire to break a leg. This, at least, is the notion that Stalnaker explores: desires are attitudes defined by their propositional contents, and propositions are functions from possible worlds to truth values. There are logically possible worlds in which it is true that I escape but not true that I am harmed, and it is its satisfaction in these possible worlds that determines that the desire is to escape, and not to risk injury. But this question of defining the objects of desire—that is, of what determines exactly what it is that will *satisfy* a given desire—this question must wait. First, we must consider what this "satisfaction" *is*, and whether the suggestion before us offers at least a necessary condition, and a partial definition, of the desire that *p*.

Now Stalnaker's formulations are well designed to bring out the correlativity of belief and desire—the way in which characterization of the one as a disposition to a certain kind of action makes essential reference to the other. Just because of this virtue, as Stalnaker himself points out (1984, p. 15), the formulas may seem unsatisfactory—if not circular, at least unfinished. For belief is defined in terms of the satisfaction of desire, and desire is defined in turn by reference to belief. We need, at least, an analysis of the "satisfaction" of desire, one free from reference to belief.

If states of mind are to be understood in terms of their functional roles in determining action, should we not hope to understand the satisfaction of a desire, somehow, in terms of the satisfaction of some *nonpsychological* state of the organism—some state such as the satisfaction of its needs? (*Needing it to be the case that p* is not a propositional attitude, and need, of course, is not a psychological state.) Might this be the way to supply the extramental grounding such definitions seem to require?

Perhaps. But it would be premature to launch out upon that adventure, inviting though I think it is. (The discussion will come back to needs in the end.) It would be premature here because there is, in fact, simply no difficulty in defining the satisfaction of a desire. In order for a desire, say, the desire that it be the case that *p*, to be *satisfied*, what is required, and all that is required, is that it be the case that *p*. My desire to have a peach is satisfied if and only if I have a peach. The *satisfaction* of a desire is not a psychological state, though the desire itself is. In particular, it is not a matter of the termination of the desire, or of the satisfaction of the *person* who has the desire. Neither is it necessary that it should involve the *satisfaction* of a nonpsychological state, like a need. For I can get what I want without my knowing it, or liking it, or being the better for having it. And my getting what I want is all it takes to satisfy my desire.

The satisfaction of a desire is to the desire the same thing as the truth of a belief is to the belief. It is a purely semantic property. It is nothing more than the truth of the proposition expressed by the complement of a sentence ascribing the desire, or the belief, to someone or something. It is the truth of *p* in the schema *S wants it to be the case that p*—just as the truth of a belief is the truth of *p* in the schema *S believes it to be the case that p*.

There is no circularity in the reliance of these definitions upon the notion of the "satisfaction" of a desire. "Satisfaction" is just truth by another name. But when the notion is shorn of unwanted connotations, a question is revealed.

Our desires and beliefs essentially dispose us to act in ways that will tend to satisfy the former if the latter are true, and *therefore* such behavior constitutes rational action. An adequate characterization of desire, or belief, should yield as a consequence the proposition that it is rational to act in the ways these states dispose us to act. But the dispositional characterization, as so far developed, fails to do this. Wanting to eat this peach, I am disposed to take a bite of it. For that is the only action which would satisfy that desire, in a world in which my beliefs are true. But why should I take a bite of the peach? That is, what reason have I to do so? The answer cannot be just that I am so inclined. Having jumped out the window, I will be inclined to accelerate at a constant rate: but my being so inclined is no reason for me to do so, and I *have* no reason to do so. (Of course there is a reason *why* I do so—that is to say, there is something that causes me to do so.) Wanting food, one is inclined to eat. But why should one—what reason does one therefore have—to do it?

It is not that the answer to this question is hard to come by. On the contrary, the answer is very obvious. One reason one has to do the things one's desires dispose one to do is simply that doing them will satisfy those desires. That, I think, is the full and correct answer to the question. The problem is not how to answer the question, but to understand why that answer *should* answer the question. That is not so obvious. Why should the fact that something will satisfy some desire I have be a reason I have to do that thing? Has explanation run out so soon? If it has, then the *difference* between desire and belief is inexplicable. For the satisfaction of the desire that something be the case is merely its being the case, just as the truth of the belief that something is the case is merely its being the case. But if my wanting it to be the case that p is my reason to do what will make it true that p, why shouldn't my believing it to be the case that p be equally a reason for me to do what will make it true that p? And of course, it is not. My believing that my food is poisoned is no reason for me to put some poison in it, so as to ensure that my belief is true. But *why* isn't it, if satisfaction is just truth by another name, and my wanting something to be the case is a reason to do what will satisfy that desire? (By the name "satisfaction," it seems truth has a sweeter smell.)

It should be emphasized that it is no objection to these functionalist definitions of desire and belief that they expose this simple question about how belief and desire differ. On the contrary. It is a good question, and one that can, I think, be given a good answer within this framework. And it is a question the functionalist should be required to answer, although, it might be noted, the behaviorist could not be required to answer it. Should the behaviorist hold, as he might, that being in pain is a disposition to squawk and moan, he could not be made to explain why one *should*, why it would be rational, to squawk and moan: his thesis would be just that that is the way one observably does behave, irrational though it may be to do so. And similar views even about belief and desire have been reported. But the functionalist recognizes that beliefs and desires are states essentially of rational agents. And this means, of course — for so are indigestion and pain and sleep "states of rational agents" — that beliefs and desires are states that enter into the rationality of the agent, states, that is, that rationalize the agent's thoughts and feelings and actions. So we must insist on an answer: if desire and belief are the dispositions to action these definitions say they are, why is it that one should do the things that one's desires and beliefs dispose one to do?

But there is a prior doubt as to whether the definitions are adequate to distinguish belief and desire. Each state is characterized in terms of the effect it tends to have under ideal conditions. But the effect that characterizes each state is *one and the same:* the satisfaction of desire. Both belief and desire tend, working in tandem, to cause behavior that tends to bring about *the satisfaction of desire.* Further, the conditions under which each tends to have that effect are also the same: the relevant beliefs must be true. Desire is a kind of mental state in which one is disposed to act in ways that will bring it about that the propositional contents of certain states of mind are true in case those of certain distinct states of mind are true. Belief is exactly the same kind of state. So what is the difference between them? Does it elude the definitions?

But on second thought, the formulas do identify a difference between the respective effects of the two states of mind: a desire tends to effect *its own* satisfaction, whereas a belief tends to effect (not its own but) a *desire's* satisfaction. And there is a corresponding difference in the conditions under which each tends to have this effect: a desire does so when states of another kind — viz., beliefs — *are true*, whereas a belief does so in case *it itself* is true. There is, then, a certain asymmetry between the two kinds of states.

Beliefs yield the satisfaction of desires and desires yield the satisfaction of themselves. This asymmetry is connected with another one, a difference between belief satisfaction and desire satisfaction. This emerges upon consideration of a belief and desire that have the same content — or that have, as nearly as this is possible, the same content.[3]

Suppose we have a tennis match set for tomorrow. I want to win and I think I will. These states of mind have the same content: my winning the match. But there is a difference: if my belief that I will win is going to turn out to have been true, then it will *have been* true — true, that is, even now, before the first point is played. (My belief that I will win, if it should be true, will not come to be true *when* I win.) My desire to win, however, if it is to be satisfied, will come to be satisfied only when I win—that is, only at match point; only my having won will satisfy that desire. So even if I will win, my desire to win is not now satisfied; but my belief that I will win is *true* now if I am going to win, and my having won won't make *it* true (won't make it true, that is, that I *will* win).

Now, by hypothesis this difference between desire and belief, i.e., between the satisfaction of the one and the truth of the other, cannot be explained by their differing in content, for there is no such difference: both are attitudes toward the same event. So how is it to be understood? It is a difference, if you will, in the modality of containment, but this is less an explanation than what we must explain. While the difference cannot arise from a difference in the content, perhaps it arises from a difference between *what determines* in each case that that event *is* the content of the respective states.

This approach requires us to have some view about the determination of content—about what factors determine that the content (thus the truth or satisfaction conditions) of a mental state, or in general, a representation, is what it is. On this very general question, there is one view (which I am myself inclined to take) which immediately suggests an answer to the present question. The general view is that the content of a mental state is determined by the functional role of a state of that kind, and that this role determines what the causes and the effects of that state would be under ideal conditions (i.e., conditions in which relevant organs and faculties are functioning optimally). Accordingly, to specify a state of affairs as the content of a state of mind is to identify that state of mind in terms of its ideal causes or effects.[4]

Suppose, in this vein, that to specify the content of a belief is to specify, very broadly, its ideal *cause;* and, as a first approximation, that to specify the content of a desire is to specify its ideal *effect.* A particular belief, say, the belief that *p*, is a belief that tends to arise— and thus to be caused—under certain ideal conditions by a state of affairs which is such that *p* is the case. And the desire that it be the case that *p* is a state that tends to result, under certain ideal conditions, in its being the case that *p*. This hypothesis would explain the temporal difference between belief satisfaction and desire satisfaction. My belief that I will win the match is a state the ideal causes of which are such that I will win: its causes are, for instance, states of affairs that comprise *evidence* that that is what will happen. My desire that I win is a state of mind the ideal effect of which is that I win. Since the causes of a state are fixed at the time someone enters into it, a belief is satisfied or not—i.e., true or not—at that time. If the satisfaction of a desire consists in the occurrence of events which are ideally the effects of that desire, then the desire that something be the case will not be satisfied until it comes to be the case, if it is to do so.

Let me review the argument. I questioned whether the functionalist definitions succeed in distinguishing desire from belief. The question arises because both are characterized solely in terms of their effect on action, thus both in terms of their effects, which are, in a way, the same: both states tend to effect the satisfaction of one of them, desire. What is omitted from the way the formulas characterize the causal roles of the two states is any mention of the *causes* of either of them. (Stalnaker comes by a different argument to the same conclusion.) Now, in the general framework of this discussion, what is essential to, and definitive of, a state of mind is taken to be its causal or functional role, the way it works, given certain causes, to produce effects that fulfill the function served by such a state of mind. More specifically, the suggestion is that *kinds* of mental states differ as their causal roles differ. "Causal role," of course, does not begin to be specific enough. We are concerned more specifically just with the causal relation between a state of mind and that state of affairs that comprises its content—that is, the event, or state, or condition, that satisfies it: its truth condition. This delimitation of the notion of functional role, and integration of it with the notion of content, is admirably attempted in Stalnaker's formulations. We deflect an initial suggestion of circularity (i.e., that the definitions depend on an undefined notion of the satisfaction of desire) by insisting that desire satisfaction is merely truth, so that, like truth (presumably), it is a concept intelligible independently from that of desire or belief or indeed from the concept of a mental state. Thus the feature, which both mental states possess, of having a certain content, is exactly the same feature: it is the property of having a truth condition or a satisfaction condition; that is, of being such that there is a certain state of affairs the obtaining of which makes it "true," as we say in the one case, or "satisfied," as we say in the other.

And yet there remains the difference we have tried to explain—that is, that if I will win tomorrow then my belief that I will win is now true, whereas my desire to win is not satisfied, and will not be satisfied until I do win. This, I suggested, is because my belief is ideally *caused by* something that entails its truth, while my desire ideally *results in* something that entails its satisfaction. This explanation has required us to bring in the relevant causes, specifically of the belief, as well as relevant effects. So while the two states may have the same ideal *effect*—viz., the satisfaction of the desire—their ideal causes differ. And there perhaps we have captured what seems to evade the original definitions, the difference between belief and desire. Perhaps.

Nothing has been ventured here about the ideal causes of *desire*, for these have not, so far, seemed relevant to the determination of its content. We may, however, if only for the sake of symmetry, enter a supposition about the proper causes of desires. (I shall go on to argue that this supposition is essential.) Obviously, the desire that *p* is not ideally caused by its *being* the case that *p*. But presumably it would be caused, ideally, by the fact that it would be a good thing if it were the case that *p*.

Now, all these points, regarding the ideal causal and the logical relations among beliefs, desires, and states of affairs present and prospective, can be summarily displayed in the following figure — a sort of "rhombus of the attitudes."

The main points are these:

    (1) Both belief and desire *cause* states of affairs that satisfy *desires*;

    (2) Both belief and desire are *caused by* states of affairs that satisfy *beliefs*.

Thus the desire to escape is ideally caused by the fact that it would be a good thing to escape, a fact that might cause the belief (that it would be a good thing to escape) which it would also satisfy. The desire, and the belief that I will escape if I jump, tend to cause me to jump and therefore to cause the state of affairs (i.e., that in which I do escape) that would satisfy that desire. Normally, of course, a belief does not cause behavior that brings about its own satisfaction, though there are exceptions to that — like the thought, when serving in tennis, that one is going to double-fault. But we take these to be anomalies. Likewise, desires are not caused by states of affairs that also satisfy those desires, though this too is perhaps not impossible. (Maybe there is a kind of conservative whose mind works that way: the fact that it is the case that p makes him want it to be the case that p. That too would be anomalous.)

We have offered a display of differences between desire and belief, in the way the two are related to their idealized causal context and their respective principles of satisfaction, and this consistent with their being joint determinants of rational action, "correlative dispositional states of a rational agent." But the account is still unsatisfactory, for it provides no answer to the question, *Why* should a rational agent act in such a way as to satisfy his desires? That is, why is the fact that he wants what he does *a reason* for him to act accordingly? Certainly this is not explained by the fact that the desire for it disposes him to act in ways that would satisfy that desire. Consider the case of a man who finds himself in a state in which he is disposed to do whatever he thinks would bring it about that he owns a goldfish. The fact that his state of mind comprises a tendency to such behavior in no way reveals the rationality of what he does. Such a man might well regard himself as being in the grip of inclinations that make no sense to him, inclinations that he finds utterly irrational. For indeed the state of mind we have described might not be that of *wanting* to own a goldfish. It is, I suggest, an essential property of a desire that one's having that desire should comprise one's having a reason to act so as to satisfy that desire — it need not necessarily be a good reason, of course, but still it must be a reason of sorts, *something* of a reason.[5] This fact will, I submit, be a corollary of any adequate account of desire. But the functionalist characterization of desire does not, so far, entail this fact. Likewise, it is an essential property of a belief that one's having that belief should comprise a reason for one to believe, or do, what is logically or practically entailed by what one believes. But the fact that a belief is a disposition to believe or do such a thing does not entail that it should have this property.

What does explain this fact in the case of belief? Not its causal tendency to produce action, or desire-satisfying states of affairs, but rather its causal tendency to be produced *by* states of affairs that would entail its own truth. If the belief that p is ideally caused by the very fact which would make that belief true, then, if it is reasonable to suppose the belief to have arisen under ideal conditions, the belief comprises a reason to act as if it is true. The causal profile of belief *rationalizes* such actions. Once again, desires differ: there may well be a reason to suppose, of a particular desire, that one having it will do something that will satisfy that desire: but *this* describes no reason for one to do such a thing. The fact that the *contents* of belief are determined in the way they are — according to the causal view — would explain why it is rational to act on one's beliefs. But suppose the contents of desires are determined in just the same way — *via* the ideal causal relation between the state of mind and the state of affairs that is its truth or satisfaction condition. That is, suppose that the fact that the desire that p tends to cause it to be the case that p is what explains its having p as its content. This explanation does *not* entail that one who has that desire has a reason to act accordingly. The difference between this case and that of belief is clearly that the causal facts about desire relevant to the determination of its content contain no indication that the desire has a *value fully analogous* to that of truth — the value that characterizes belief, and owing to the supposed possession of which it is rational for one to act on a belief. Satisfaction value is disanalogous to truth value, in that the supposition that a desire is, or is to be, satisfied comprises no reason whatever for one to do anything. We can, and should, treat desire satisfaction as a semantic predicate like truth. However, it turns out that there is a difference: the truth of a belief rationalizes actions based on it; the satisfaction of a desire does not. What is needed, to make the cases parallel in this respect, is the identification of such a value as a characteristic of the well-formed desire — well-foundedness, as it might be called.

Earlier, then just for the sake of symmetry, the supposition was introduced that the ideal cause of a desire, e.g., for a drink, is that it would be a good thing to have a drink. It is now apparent that we must take this idea seriously. For this supposition would allow us to explain what makes a desire not merely a tendency to act in a certain way, but a rational tendency to do so. Suppose that one is in a state which one is, under certain ideal conditions, caused to be in by the fact that it would be a good thing if a certain state of affairs p were to obtain. Clearly, that fact would be a reason for one to do whatever would tend to bring it about that p (i.e., in situations in which one's relevant beliefs were true). And, a fortiori, one's being in a state *ideally caused by* that fact (viz., the fact that it would be good if p) would be a reason to do such things as well — certainly to whatever extent it was reasonable to suppose that one's state of mind might have arisen under those ideal conditions. For the state of mind would then be in effect an *indicator* and a source of information as to what it would be good to do, and it would be rational to regard it as such. A desire would be, indeed, epistemically like a *perceptual* state.[6] (One's being in such a state of mind would be sufficient not just for there being a reason to do relevant actions, but sufficient further for one's being in cognitive possession of that reason — that is, for one's "having" a reason to do those acts.)

An augmented characterization of desire may now be drawn up, one which looks forward to the state of affairs that ideally results from it and backward, out of the circle of states of mind, to the state of affairs that ideally causes it.

> To desire that p is to be disposed to act in ways that would tend to result in the obtaining of a state of affairs (i.e., that in which p), which disposition tends, under certain conditions, to be caused by a state of affairs such that it would be good were that desire to be satisfied—that is, *good were it to be the case that p.*

This delivers a plausible answer to an earlier question: why should rational agents be subject to a propositional attitude which makes them tend to do what will bring it about that the propositional objects of that attitude come to be true? (Why should it be that we are subject to desire-like attitudes as well as belief-like ones?) The answer is that these are states that function not just to secure their own satisfaction but also to bring about states of affairs that are actually good ones, e.g., states beneficial to the subject. The account now yields the corollary that a desire is a rational basis for action. That is one thing an adequate account of desire must do.

An adequate account of desire will also provide correct identity conditions for desires—and since desires are distinguished by their objects or contents, this means giving a correct account of the identity of those objects. I wish now to suggest that in such an account, the foregoing suggestion (that the desire that p is ideally caused by the fact that it would be good were p to be the case) plays an indispensable role.

Consider the difficulty, broached at the outset, that besets any causal account of desire: one can want something without wanting the causal consequences of having it. The fundamental strategy of a causal account is to define a mental state by its causal role—what causes it and what it causes—and more specifically to analyze its having the content or object it does in terms of that causal role. We are discussing a treatment of desire that seeks to define the content of desire as the state of affairs tending to result from it (*via* the behavior it tends to result in), thus that would result from it under certain ideal conditions. When it is proposed that a desire that p is a tendency to bring about the state of affairs p, and further that *what* is wanted—the state of affairs one wants to obtain—is *the* state of affairs that tends to result from that desire, the difficulty is plain. For the desire tends to produce not a single state of affairs but a number of them, and some of these may be *un*wanted consequences of the one wanted. Wanting to eat a burrito, one is disposed to do what one thinks will bring that about, but also, ipso facto, to bring about something that one would rather not—heartburn. (Nor is this explained by the fact that one needn't know or consider the consequences, for you may want a burrito, being vividly aware that it will give you heartburn you don't want.)

Anscombe, in a famous sentence, said that "The primitive sign of wanting is *trying to get.*"[7] That may be so (depending on what a "primitive sign" might be) but "trying" involves wanting, so this doesn't further the analysis. The difference between what you're "trying" to get (a suntan) and what you are in fact getting (skin cancer) is that only the former outcome of your actions was wanted. It does not help matters to say that to want a thing is to be *disposed* to do what might result in one's getting it, if one's beliefs are true. To want to smoke is to be disposed to do something which one thinks might result in one's getting cancer, if one's beliefs are true.

One needn't want the consequences of getting what one wants. In the cases cited, the *un*wanted thing is merely a *causal* consequence of the wanted one; there are logically possible worlds in which burritos don't cause heartburn, nor cigarettes cancer. We might try some such formulation as this: for it to be *that p* that one desires, is for one to be disposed to act in ways that would tend to bring it about that *p*, in worlds in which one's beliefs about what actions would do so are true, but in which one's beliefs about the further results of its being the case that *p* are false. (One's knowledge of the bad effects may then inhibit the tendency to action with which the desire is identified, which is now characterized as a tendency that would actually produce action if the world were such that one could get away with it, and/or one thought that one could.) Such a view might serve to identify the thing wanted as a certain ideal effect of the state, separating the relevant from the irrelevant causal implications of the actions. This leaves only the matter of their *logical* implications, and the question whether one who desires that *p* desires everything logically implied thereby. But one can hold that if *p* logically implies *q*, to desire that *p* is to desire that *q*: thus to want to eat a burrito is to want to eat a tortilla; or that the desire to draw a circle is the desire to draw a figure with a center point.[8] This position is controversial, but not untenable.

But it seems in a way wrongheaded to look for the reason the one thing is wanted and not the other in the fact that there is a logically possible world in which the one could be had without the other—a world in which one can eat a burrito without getting indigestion. For it seems the reason one might want to eat a burrito without ipso facto wanting to suffer indigestion is more obvious: the burrito *would be good* while the indigestion would not. It might, indeed, be held that a correct account should somehow deliver just that as the explanation, and that there is something wrong with it if it doesn't do so.

In any case, given our augmented characterization of desire, we can handle the matter in this more obvious way: the state of affairs one wants to obtain is not simply "the" state of affairs that one's consequent actions would tend to bring about; rather, it is the one that would tend to result from those actions where *one's tendency to do such actions in turn results from the goodness of that state of affairs.* One's desire for a burrito is a state that would ideally result from the fact that *it would be good* were one to eat a burrito, and *what is wanted* is the state of affairs in which one eats a burrito, i.e., that particular state of affairs that one's resulting behavior tends to result in, *and* which state of affairs is such that its being a good thing would also ideally *cause* the state of mind from which the behavior ensues. Now, even if eating a burrito causally entails getting heartburn, the fact that it would be good to eat one does not entail that it would be a good thing to get heartburn. It is clear that the "operator" *it is good that* is not closed under causal implication.

Arguably, it is not closed even under logical implication. Thus there is supposed to be a sense in which one can want to draw a circle without wanting to draw a figure with a central point — suppose a prize is offered for this achievement — even though doing the first thing logically implies, or necessarily *is*, doing the second. If this is so, it is because its being a good thing to do the first does not imply that it would be a good thing to do what doing it logically entails. One who denies this kind of opacity to desires, as some do, is also likely to hold that its being a good thing to do the first *does* imply that it is a good thing to do the "second." So whatever view one takes on this issue, it seems to turn on one's view about the logic of *it would be good that*. . ., and this argues for the present suggestion.

Resorting to goodness will make many philosophers uneasy. But it is not sufficiently obvious that we *must* bring in goodness to delimit the contents of desire. We have ignored an attractive possibility. What I want is something I think will result from my disposition to do certain things, but not everything I think will result therefrom is something I want: the freedom is, the broken leg isn't. But one who jumps out the window to escape does so because he believes that the consequences of jumping will include escaping, but while he also believes that they will also include breaking a leg, he does not jump *because* he thinks that that will result, but rather, of course, *despite* that belief. Now suppose our definition requires that one's beliefs about the consequences of the actions the desirer is disposed to do must *cause* that disposition, thus: to desire that p is to be disposed to do what will tend to bring it about that p in a world in which one's beliefs are true, and *to be so disposed BECAUSE one believes that doing those things will tend to bring it about that p.*

This adjustment would serve to eliminate unwanted consequences from our specification of the things wanted.[9] But it raises again a question of rationality. Consider the figure who finds herself disposed to go to the cow market, or to do whatever else would, in her opinion, tend to bring it about that she owns a cow. And, further, her tendency to go to the cow market is (as we now require) the *result* of her belief that going there is sufficient for her to have a cow. But the possibility remains that while she has these tendencies she has no desire for a cow. And that possibility remains if only because it remains a possibility that this disposition, and its causes, as so far specified, do not make this trip to the cow market a rational action. (Whereas, again, one's wanting what one does makes the actions one therein tends to perform rational actions.) To secure that result, we must, I think, fall back on the requirement that the ideal cause of the agent's disposition be the fact that it would be a good thing for her to own a cow.

I suggested above that one might assert that an account of the contents of desire *ought* to yield something like the account I have just been sketching: even if p entails q, one can want it to be that p without wanting it to be that q, because it may be a good thing if p but not a good thing if q. But this assertion should be controversial. For there is a good case for holding that the reason that one can want p without wanting what p entails is the same as the reason that one can believe p without believing what p entails: that is, in either case, that the state is an attitude toward a *proposition*. On this view, Stalnaker's strategy would be correct: find a general view of *propositions* that has the required consequences. The explanation must not be specific to the specific nature of desire; if it is, there is something wrong with it.

I think it should be agreed that the explanation of the intentionality of desire and of that of belief must be fundamentally the same. But I wish to suggest that the treatment *via* goodness, does not, after all, give an objectionably specific account of the intentionality of desire. In both cases the matter has to do with the role of a certain evaluative predicate—a different one in the two cases, but one identical in the relevant logical respects. In the one case, the operative predicate is (something's) *being good: it is good* is not closed under causal implication, nor arguably under logical implication, so it draws precise distinctions between objects of desire and what is necessarily bound up with those objects. In the case of belief, it is supposedly *the fact that p* that is the ideal cause of the mental state. Now, if we had only *this* operator—*it is a fact that*... (i.e., *it is true that*...)—to work with, we could not give the same explanation of the precision of the contents of belief. (For of course this operator is closed under causal or logical implication.) But there is another operator which, like *it is good that*..., is not closed under implication, and it will serve: *it is evident that*....

To believe that p is to be in the defined dispositional state where that is ideally caused by the fact that *it is evident* that p. The fact that p may be evident while what it implies is not. This is obvious where the implication is causal, and arguable where it is logical. Thus it may be evident to someone that a figure is a triangle but not evident that it is a figure the sum of the angles of which is equal to two right angles. Or rather *if* this is so, it is possible to believe the first without believing the second. Some will deny that this *is* really possible; but they, I think, will also deny that the one fact can be evident while the second is not. Without deciding this issue, we have reason to think that the logic of evidentiality is central to it, and this argues for defining the belief that p as a state ideally resulting from its being evident that p.

Now the issue here, parallel to the issue about the relation between goodness and desire, is whether *being evident* can be understood without some *circular* reliance on the notion of belief. We cannot here pursue this question far, but can make one observation. The ideal conditions to which I make reference, in defining the causal role essential to belief, are understood as conditions under which the cognitive mechanisms are functioning optimally—that is, they are conditions such that where they hold, the mechanisms will regularly fulfill their function. Therefore, it is *its being evident* to a subject that would figure as the ideal cause of his belief that p, not just its being a fact that p. For these cognitive mechanisms work in such a way that beliefs are formed only on the basis of evidence, and, arguably, a belief that p formed without such evidence, even if true, and even if it results from the fact that p, is not one formed under ideal conditions in the relevant sense of the phrase. This is so, in any case, if the function of the cognitive mechanism is to achieve cognition—i.e., *knowledge*—and not merely true belief.

Earlier in the discussion, the distinction between self-satisfying states of mind and other-satisfying states of mind was invoked to distinguish desires from beliefs. Desires (which are self-satisfying attitudes) are furthermore distinguished by their being caused, ideally, by the apparent goodness of the state of affairs that would satisfy them, as opposed to its apparently obtaining. But still the account is incomplete. For neither point separates desires from intentions. Just like desires, and unlike beliefs, intentions tend to effect their own satisfaction. Intentions are so far the same as desires: to intend that p (that one do A) is to be disposed to act in ways that would tend to bring it about that p (thus to satisfy that intention) in a world in which one's beliefs are true. Nor does the added clause (requiring a desire that p to be the effect, ideally, of the fact that it would be good if p) seem to help us: for surely the intention that p—that one do something—is likewise the effect, ideally, of that same fact, that it would be good if one did that thing. The problem grows worse when we consider also the *belief that it would be good if p:* for by the present account *this* state too is the effect, ideally, of the same fact as is the intention that *p* and the desire that *p:* the fact that it would be good if *p*.

There are three main tactics whereby one may try to separate these states of mind. *First,* one may look for some phenomenological characteristic of desire not present in beliefs, or in intentions; but this seems contrary to the functionalist framework of our discussion. *Second,* one may try to describe something distinctive about the action-producing potential of the desire, vis-à-vis that of the intention and that of the belief. For example, that of the belief, even this belief, is perhaps contingent on the agent's desires, in a way that the efficacy of the intention is not.

I think the merits of these approaches will accrue equally to a third one, and this is what I shall briefly advocate. One may attribute the differences in the states of mind to an aspect of their etiology that has so far been left out of account. One may attribute them to differences in the underlying internal mechanisms—traditionally, the mental faculties—that generate the respective states of mind. In outline, while the desire that *p* and the belief that it would be good if *p* are ideally effects of the same fact, the former is produced *by* the effect of that fact on one mechanism (the "Appetite") and the latter by its effect on a distinct mechanism (the "Intellect"). To make good this distinction ex machina, we shall have to trace the wires and pulleys. (Plainly the difference between the Appetite and the Intellect cannot be left at this, that the one generates desires and the other beliefs.)

Notice first that while it is true of this particular kind of belief—the belief that it would be good that *p*—that ideally it would be caused by its *being* good that *p*, there is of course no case for supposing that that is generally true of beliefs, regardless of their particular contents, including the belief that snow is white. Thus it is not a fact about *belief* in general, but a fact about these particular beliefs—beliefs to the effect that something or other would be good. On the other hand, there *is* a case for saying that any desire whatever, regardless of its particular content, would ideally be caused by the fact that something (viz., the thing wanted) would be good. Now, we may allow that there are some beliefs that are like all desires, in respect to their *external* ideal causes, these being the states of affairs that define their contents. (Similarly, the external causes of a tactile and of a visual percept, and thus their objects, may be the same.) But the internal or more proximal causes of these beliefs may differ from those of the desires (as do the internal causes—the sensory mechanisms—producing the tactile and the visual percepts): and it is, I suggest, such internal causes that make them mental (or perceptual) states of different *kinds*. We may venture that states of mind of a given kind must be produced by a certain mechanism which is ideally activated *only* by causes of a distinctive kind. Thus, desires arise from a mechanism activated only by the apparent *goodness* of states of affairs; beliefs arise from a mechanism activated only by the apparent *obtaining* of states of affairs.

Thus, again, half the problem, and the suggested solution, is this. A desire is a state of mind caused ideally by the fact that it would be good if *p*, but this is true equally of the belief that it would be good if *p*. So I offer this amendment: a desire is a state of mind caused ideally by the fact that it would be good if *p VIA the effect of that fact on a mechanism which is ideally activated only by the fact that some state of affairs or other would be good.*

This separates the desire that *p* from the belief that it would be good were *p* the case. That was half the problem. The other half is to separate the desire from the intention. To do that, on this same strategy, one must describe a distinct mechanism whereby the facts that cause intentions take effect. (This I take to be the Will: the generator of intentions.) Suppose, for instance, that intentions arise from a mechanism activated not just by the fact that it would be good were *p* to be the case, but further by *the possibility of one's bringing it about that p.* This answers to three important facts about intention. (1) If one intends that it be the case that *p*, one believes that one will, or at least that one can, bring it about that *p*, whereas (2) one may *want* it to be the case that *p* without believing any such thing; one needn't think one's desires are efficacious.[10] Thus the belief that one could bring it about that *p* is a necessary cause of an intention, but not of a desire that *p*, nor of the belief that it would be good if *p*. (3) Given the belief that one could bring it about that *p*, the desire that *p* (which, perhaps like the intention that *p*, is also ideally caused by its being good that *p*) is a normal cause of the intention that *p*; but that intention is not a normal cause of the desire that *p*.[11]

The definitions with which we began emphasize the interlocking character of desire and belief. The discussion has come round to a *complementary* case for what may be called the *autonomy* of the faculties in general, and of the Appetite in particular—in the following sense. It appears that to frame a definition of desire that distinguishes desires from intentions on the one hand and from certain beliefs on the other, we must recognize as an essential feature of a desire that it should be produced by a certain mental mechanism, a mechanism distinguished by the law of its operation: that is, perhaps, by the necessity of its being activated, ideally, by nothing other than the goodness of some state of affairs. This is "its own law," that is, *not* the law governing the mechanism that generates belief, or the mechanism that generates intentions. That the Appetite should be in this sense *autonomous* is consistent with the thesis that belief and desire only jointly determine intention and action.

I have argued here that desire essentially involves a hypothetical causal relation to something's being good, and the definition of desire must reflect this. And I have argued that this proposal is not objectionably specific to desire; it is parallel to an independently well-motivated treatment of belief, as essentially involving a hypothetical causal relation to something's being evident. Finally, I have argued that the distinction between desires and beliefs may be preserved, despite the case in which their causal profile is seemingly identical — the cases of the belief that it would be good if p and the desire that p — provided we recognize the essential role of the underlying mechanisms, mental faculties, in the definition:

> To desire that p is to be disposed to act in ways that would tend to result in the obtaining of a state of affairs (i.e., that in which p), which disposition tends to be caused by a state of affairs such that it would be good were it to be the case that p — and caused *via* a mechanism that is activated, ideally, only by such a state of affairs, i.e., one such that it would be good were something or other to be the case.

To one interested in framing a naturalistic account of desire (or of propositional attitudes in general) the invocation of "goodness" may seem a retrograde step. One reason for being uneasy about this is the old notion that goodness is not an honest "objective" property. A better reason, perhaps, would be that goodness is an "intensional property" — for such properties have dubious citizenship in the natural order.[12]

Now, if we were proposing to employ the predicate (goodness) to allow for, say, the possibility of one's wanting to see the Evening Star but not wanting to see the Morning Star, then this doubt would be justified. And a philosopher might wish to put the predicate to that use: for if it *is* possible to have such a desire as that, then this could be attributed to the possibility of its being a good thing to see the Evening Star but not to see the Morning Star. If one did take that view, then the "fact" or "state of affairs" which might be a good thing while the "other" one is not, is indeed an intensional entity, and its status as a natural thing, and its *causal* efficacy, would be much in doubt. But we have not embraced that view. Nor, I think, is there compelling reason to do so.

There is on the other hand compelling reason to distinguish between what one wants and unwanted causal consequences of the satisfaction of that desire. And it was simply to draw that distinction that goodness was brought into the definition (not for the heroic task of prizing apart logical equivalents). The role here assigned the predicate *it would be good that*... does not depend on its being an intensional operator. For on any plausible view, escaping from a locked room (or eating a burrito) is a distinct state of affairs from breaking one's leg (or getting heartburn). There is therefore no puzzle about how the one may be a good thing and the other a bad thing, not even if they are both effects of the same action or tendency to action. (After all, the effects of being free are quite other than the effects of a broken leg.)

One who is uneasy about goodness may be easier with the notion of need. Since a thing's getting what it needs is a good thing for it, perhaps the present suggestion can be worked out in terms of needs. Of course not everything that would be good, nor everything one wants, is something one needs. But we may nonetheless explore the connections or parallels between the notions. Suppose I *need* to escape — the executioner approaches — and therefore to jump; and if I jump I will necessarily injure myself. But it does not follow that I *need* to injure myself: that is not something I need. Now suppose a certain state of mind is caused, ideally, by a subject's needing it to be the case that p — and that this state of mind ideally causes the subject to act in ways that would bring it about that p: such a state of mind, I suggest, is a desire that p.

It would seem relatively unobjectionable to use the concept of need in pursuit of a naturalistic understanding of desire. Organisms without minds have their needs, and even natural processes, such as combustion, have needs. For a thing to need something is for it to be necessary that it have it, e.g., necessary if it is to continue in existence, as a fire needs oxygen. The relevant necessity is, furthermore, a kind of causal necessity: for the thing's not having what it needs will *result* in its demise. Thus far need seems a legitimate concept. It seems in particular one attractive point of exit from the circuit of mentalistic notions in which our interlocking definitions of desire and belief and intention revolve.

The notion that a desire that p is a state of mind ideally caused by the fact that it would be good were p to be the case, may perhaps be worked out in a satisfactory way in terms of the notion of need. But the project is complex. One aspect of it is the question of the causal efficacy of needs: for there is a question how a need can cause anything to happen at all, and a harder one about how a need might produce a conscious representation of itself. These questions are not altogether easy ones; I have attempted an answer elsewhere.[13]

Another question arises from the fact that the idea of need is not entirely innocent of the idea of what is good — or bad. For A needs B only if A's not having B (at or by the relevant time) will result in something *bad* for A. Not all needs are vital ones, and not everything needed is necessary for existence or survival; and even such requirements qualify as "needs" only because survival is a good thing. But there is, I think, no harm in this. In particular, it does not confound the idea that the efficacy of needs might prove less problematic than that of goodness. For notice that where something is needed, it is the *effect* of not having what is needed that is "bad"; to suppose that the need itself produces some effect (including some mental state) is not to suppose that the value associated with what is needed (its being bad not to get it or good to get it) produces that effect. Value enters into the matter not as a cause, but as an effect — epiphenomenally, if you will.

More speculatively, it is plausible to conjecture that the *function* of desire is principally the representation of needs. This is relevant in the causal-*cum*-functional framework of the present discussion. For the ideal or optimal conditions referred to in the definition of the objects of desire (and of representational states in general) are conditions of well-functioning — conditions, that is, under which the faculty generating the state in question would fulfill its function. It is under such conditions that the "ideal" cause would produce the state or its ideal effect would be produced by it.

Now suppose that the function of the Appetite is to provide conscious representations of our needs. In the discussion so far, we have sought to specify a desire and its object as a state of mind tending (through action) to cause a state of affairs p, which is such that ideally it is the fact that it would be good if p that would tend to cause that state of mind: such a state of mind will be a *desire*, and specifically, a desire *that* p. Under those ideal conditions, the mechanism generating this state of mind would fulfill its function. Now suppose that function to be that of indicating the presence of needs; so under those conditions a desire would be produced by the fact that there is a need that p, and it would produce actions that would satisfy that need.

I wish to address one final point. There being a need that p is sufficient for its being good that p — although it is not necessary. (Thus there are things that would benefit us, make life better — yachts and Lafites — that we don't need to have.) But we can certainly want them. So the treatment of desire in terms of need may seem to constrict the range of desire in an objectionable way. But does it really? Suppose we let the ideal causes of desire be needs, what about the desire for the unnecessary yacht? We might say that this is a *mis*representation of a need. A causal theory of representation could make decent sense of that — if there were a plausible explanation of the desire as arising from a genuine need, through some process of symbolization or confusion or perceptual distortion.[14] But I think it is implausible to hold that every desire is actually a representation of a need. Surely it is implausible if that would mean (as I think it would) that every desire is caused by, and has as its actual object, some need or other.

Nor do I think it necessary to construe the relevance of need in so adventurous a way, in order to read out the clauses of our definition in terms of need. For (on the premise that satisfying a need is a good thing) the definition just implies that under ideal conditions the need that p would produce need-satisfying behavior *via* the state of mind we call the desire that p. The definition does not *require* a need as the causal basis of the well-formed desire, even under ideal conditions. It requires only that the state of mind be formed under conditions such that the need for p *would suffice* to cause it. The definition does not imply that the objects of desires must be needs, even under "ideal conditions"; or that their effects, even under ideal conditions, must be actions that satisfy needs. According to the present conjecture — that it is the function of desire to represent need — the conditions of well-functioning of the mental device generating desires are conditions under which one's needs would be given accurate representation by one's desires. But under those same conditions it may well be that a thing that is not needed but which would nonetheless be good to have would produce exactly the same state of mind, as would the need for it.[15] I am therefore inclined to think the present view does not, after all, imply that the range or scope of the Appetite is confined more narrowly than in fact it is. At least it does not imply that its range is confined, or even that it would ideally be confined, to the production of desires that represent needs. Nonetheless the function of the Appetite may *be* the representation of needs, and it may be this fact that determines the representational character, thus the objects, of desire.[16]

NOTES

1. I will use "desire" simply as the nominal form of the verb "want": if you want something then you have a desire for it, and vice versa. ("Desire" is an awkward verb, but a natural noun, and "want" is a natural verb but a wholly unnatural noun, save in the sense of "want *of*.")

2. The beliefs referred to in the proposed definition of desire must include and be restricted to beliefs about what one could do to get what one wants. Consider the case in which I desire that p but believe there to be nothing I could possibly do that would tend in the slightest way to bring it about that p. In worlds in which *that* belief is true, to desire that p is *not* to be disposed to act in ways that would tend to bring it about that p.

3. Of course there are differences in the proper linguistic expression of the belief and the desire. To construe these states as nonetheless having

the same content, we must construe the differences in their proper linguistic expressions as differences not in the object of the states (that is, not in the state of affairs represented therein), but rather as differences in the modality of its representation, the way it is given representation in the respective states of mind. (The concept of the "content" of a state of mind is the concept of what is contained in it — i.e., "intentionally" *in* it — thus what is *in* the mind of one in that state.) In my opinion, the linguistic differences in the way the two states are expressed and ascribed should be understood in terms of the deeper difference I am trying to bring out. I think it would be getting matters upside down to insist that there cannot be a belief and a desire that have the same content. For if we suppose that a belief and a desire cannot have the same content — because they cannot be expressed in the same language — then the present question will arise in this form: *Why* can they not be expressed in the same language? What is it, about the states, that makes this impossible? Surely in *some* sense, the satisfaction of the desire and the truth of the belief involve one and the same thing — the same event or state of affairs. If this is granted, then *why* is it that the relation between this state of affairs and the respective mental states must be described in these different ways: in the belief, the event is believed to be going to happen (the belief is that *it will happen*); in the desire the event is one desired (the desire is that *it happen*)?

4. I have tried to develop such views elsewhere (see Stampe, 1975, 1977); also relevant is Fodor (1984), and in reply, Stampe (forthcoming-c). A word is required about the relevance of causes to the determination of content. It is agreed in some quarters, now, that the causal relation of the things we talk about, to our linguistic productions, is relevant to the fact that our statements succeed in *being about*, making reference to, those things. And more generally, that our states of mind involve representations of certain things and not others, owing to the causal relations that hold between those things and not the others. If it looks to me as if *Fred* is bored, it is *he* who is looking that way, *he* who occupies my perceptual consciousness and not his twin brother Ted who may look precisely the same way; this is so owing to the way Fred causes my visual state. The matter is of course more complex in the instance of states of mind other than perceptual ones, but my belief may be about Fred, and not Ted, owing to Fred's role in the production of that belief; and likewise any desire I may consequently have, say, to amuse Fred, will be for similar reasons a desire that *he* be amused. Stalnaker brings these causal considerations into his own discussion, with an argument that if they are left out a "fatal relativity of content" results. "The pragmatic analysis," stated above, "tries to explain mental representation entirely in terms of forward-looking propositional relations such as the tendency-to-bring-about relation. The relativity of content that results forces us to recognize that belief is a backward-looking propositional state" (Stalnaker, 1984, p. 18). I shall be arguing in this paper that we must recognize also that *desire* is a backward-looking propositional state, and this fact must figure in its definition. Now, in addition to considerations that argue for a causal theory of *reference*, associated with Kripke's views about names, there is a case for a causal account of satisfaction conditions or truth conditions. I am

speaking here of an account of what determines that the truth conditions of a statement, or belief, or that the satisfaction conditions of a desire, are what they are. We cannot of course say that it is the belief that p and not the belief that q because it is one caused by the fact that p, not the fact that q, because it may not *be* a fact that p. That is, the belief that p may be false. But we may hold that the belief that p is a state of mind that *would* be caused by the fact that p *were certain conditions to hold* that may in fact not hold. Stalnaker and I are evidently in substantial agreement on the merits of this strategy. Now, in addition to these matters of the *semantics* of the desire, which are parallel to the case of belief, I shall be arguing here that the etiology of desire is relevant in still other ways, having to do with its specific character as a desire.

5. In "The Authority of Desire" (Stampe, forthcoming-a), I argue this further and contend that desires differ from beliefs in the way in which, or the conditions under which, they constitute reasons for actions.

6. In the paper cited in the preceding note (Stampe, forthcoming-a), I argue that desire is in fact a form of perception: this thesis explains the peculiar authority of desire.

7. G. E. M. Anscombe (1976), p. 68. This declaration is defended by the statement that "the wanting that interests us . . . is neither wishing nor hoping nor the feeling of desire, and cannot be said to exist in a man who does nothing towards getting what he wants." Surely this is just too strong: the requirement is just that he should be *disposed* to do something toward getting what he wants. There is no sense or kind of wanting that requires actually trying, and we do not get to confine our interests just to the cases that conform to our account. There is no justification for dismissing the prima facie counterexample to her claim, namely, wanting as the term is applied (as she puts it on p. 67) "to the prick of desire at the thought or sight of an object, even though a man then does nothing towards getting the object." This *is* wanting, however momentary, and even if it is behaviorally idle. Here the notion that there is a substantive distinction between desiring and wanting is working as an ad hoc protection for an account that needs correcting.

8. If, with Stalnaker, one construes the content of desires to be defined by their propositional character, and understands propositions as he proposes — as functions from possible worlds to truth values — then the following problem arises. If "p" and "q" are necessarily equivalent — if there is no possible world in which one is true and the other false — then they express the same proposition. So to believe that p is to believe that q — and to want it to be the case that p is to want it to be the case that q. As Stalnaker points out, this imposes implausible identity conditions on propositions and therefore on propositional attitudes: the fact that it is impossible that p be true without q's being true means that to believe that p *is* to believe that q, or to want p to be true is to want q to be true. That is indeed implausible, and perhaps worse. But it is not my aim to tax Stalnaker with this difficulty or to judge the adequacy of his attempt to meet it.

9. It leaves untouched the problem of "unwanted causes" of the things we

want: the necessary means to our ends. I can escape only by jumping out the window, and I know it. But I don't want to jump. If because I want to escape I *am* inclined to jump, then do I want to jump? One may "will" the necessary means to the end—be willing to do what it takes: but one need not *want* to do what it takes.

10. By the same token, it needn't be the case that the desire *is* efficacious. We may continue to say, with Stalnaker, that "to desire that *p* is to be disposed to act" in certain ways, only with reference to a possible belief that some possible action will tend to bring it about that *p*. (I am indebted here to a comment of Joel Marks.) And more generally this characterization is accurate only with respect to beings assumed to have the full normal complement of mental and physical powers. Could there not exist a being equipped with Appetite but neither Intellect nor Will, who feels desire but believes nothing, and intends to do nothing? It is not ruled out by anything in the present essay. In the end, the *kernel* of our definition may accordingly consist in the specification just of the necessary and ideal *causes* of a desire.

11. This is apparently denied by Frankfurt (1984), as is the more general notion that desires are affective states, analogous (as I suggest) to perceptions. Frankfurt asserts: "Many of a person's desires are...voluntary, since they derive simply from his own decisions. Someone typically acquires the desire to see a certain movie, for example, just by making up his mind what movie to see. Desires of this sort are not aroused in us; they are formed or constructed by acts of will that we ourselves perform, often quite apart from any emotional or affective state" (p. 4). I find this altogether unpersuasive. It may be that one just wants to see a movie, and decides upon this one: in that case one may have no "particular desire to see *this* one," this one in particular. So that case doesn't prove the point. In another case, having picked this movie to see, one does then want to see this one in particular, and will be disappointed if it is sold out, even if there is another one to go to. But this case doesn't prove the point either, for the possibility of the former case shows that he does not come by this desire "just by making up his mind what movie to see." It must arise in part from some additional factor: and this may well be the anticipation of the particular pleasures aroused in one's mind by the decision and consequent expectation that one will be seeing this particular movie. So no persuasive case is provided here for the existence of Frankfurt's "voluntary desires," or against the traditional view that all desires are in the nature of passions. (Of course, since the intention to do something gives rise to the belief that one will, or probably will, do it, and all that that entails—and because one may have a general desire to do what one has decided to do—the Will provides "input" to the Appetite. But nothing more than that.)

12. By an "intensional property" I mean a property belonging to entities individuated as finely as are "intensions," or distinguished with the "precision" of distinctions of meaning: as the meaning of the phrase "morning star" differs from that of "evening star," and the desire to see the Evening Star differs, arguably, from the desire to see the Morning Star. I have used another example—the desire to draw a circle without drawing a figure with a center point—of a kind which would suggest that the objects of desire may be distinguished even more finely than

that, for the meaning of "circle" includes that of "figure with a center." But one might not know this, so a person might *mean by* "circle" something other than what the term properly means, so the term's *intension in that ideolect* might *not* include that of "figure with a center." And *if*, therefore, it might be good to draw a circle but not good to draw a figure with a center, this *goodness* would be an "intensional property" of this remarkable intensional entity, a circle without a center. (I have no wish myself to *endorse* any of this apparatus for characterizing the individuation, etc., of mental states.)

13. In a paper called "Need" (Stampe, forthcoming-b), which supports certain other claims I am making about needs.

14. In a first effort to treat desires as representations of needs, I tried to make out such a view in Stampe (1978).

15. To see more fully how this might be, we should have to consider the ways the Appetite might receive information regarding needs, and whether these processes won't inevitably provoke the production of desires even where there is no need at the causal source.

16. I profited from remarks of and discussion with Berent Enç, Martha Gibson, Joel Marks, and Robert Wicks.

> *The natural position to be opposed is this: since all motivated action must result from the operation of some motivating factor within the agent, and since belief cannot by itself produce action, it follows that a desire of the agent must always be operative if the action is to be genuinely his.*
>
> —THOMAS NAGEL

Wanting, Desiring, and Valuing: The Case against Conativism

Mitchell Staude

Abstract. The concept of desire that is most consistent with ordinary ways of talking about desires and their conflicts with duties is isolated by distinguishing several senses of "wanting" found in paradigm situations where a person denies that he wanted to do what he intentionally did. The results undercut the plausibility of the view that cognitive states are incapable by themselves of motivating a person to act (conativism) and suggest that some form of cognitivism (the denial of conativism) *may* be more helpful in capturing the distinctions embedded in ordinary ways of talking about wants and desires.

One central disagreement among philosophical examinations of motivation, especially those occurring in ethical theories, concerns the relationship between cognitive states (reasons, beliefs) and conative states (desires, passions, volitions) in the generation of action. *Cognitivism*, in the context of theories of motivation, claims that reason is capable of motivating a person to act—in other words, that some cognitive states have conative power.[1] *Conativism*, on the other hand, is the general theory of human nature claiming that actions can be generated only by nonrational, noncognitive influences (e.g., instinct, impulse, volition, desire).[2] Conativism is dominant in the writing of Anglo-American analytic philosophers, although the notions of impulse, instinct, volition, and will are practically anathema. Passions, appetites, and aversions, along with those phenomena that nonanalytic philosophers call volitions, are usually either analyzed in terms of desires or simply reclassified as such—as one philosopher puts it: "In old-fashioned language, the Will is not a separate faculty from Desire."[3]

Philosophers on both sides of the debate between cognitivism and conativism seem to agree that "want," or "desire," has wider and narrower senses and that there is a widest sense such that, whatever a person intentionally does, (1) he can be said to have wanted to do it and (2) it can be given a want-explanation.[4] In most discussions of the relation between wanting and acting, especially those by conativists, the focus has been on this widest sense.[5] But understanding the concept of want or desire in this widest sense provides very little insight into what is being said when a person denies that he wanted to do what he intentionally did do or when he claims that there was something other than what he intentionally did that he had wanted to do *more;* it is almost useless for understanding the way agents talk about desires and conflicts between desires and duties. To account adequately for these ways of talking, narrower senses of "wanting" must be articulated.

In this paper, the concept of desire that is most consistent with ordinary ways of talking about desires and their conflicts with duties is isolated. The procedure involves distinguishing several senses of "wanting" found in paradigm situations where a person denies that he wanted to do what he intentionally did do. The results are that three different factors can determine what ends a person is motivated to pursue — pain, pleasure, and value — and that desires are essentially connected with pleasure and logically distinct from values. The conclusion is that these results undercut the plausibility of conativism and that some form of cognitivism *may* be more helpful in capturing the distinctions embedded in ordinary ways of talking about wants and desires.

1. CONATIVISM AND DIFFERENT SENSES OF "WANTING"

The widest sense of "wanting" is that sense in which a person can be said to have wanted to do anything he did intentionally — for if he hadn't wanted to do it, he would not have done it. Using just this widest sense, a person cannot claim that he didn't want to do what he did intentionally, for to do something intentionally is to want to do it. Consequently, whenever a person does make that claim he must either be denying that some aspect of his behavior was intentional or be using some narrower sense of "wanting."

In examinations of the widest sense of "wanting," most writers fail to realize that "wanting" in this sense refers not to what is motivating a person to act but rather to his being motivated to act:[6] the widest sense of "wanting" is the motivated sense.[7] A central feature of wants, in this motivated sense, is the transference of motivational influence.[8] When a person who is motivated to do something, A, acquires a belief that doing B will bring about or contribute to doing A, he may become motivated to do B—and thus be said to want to do B. What motivates this person to do B, however, is not a want to do B but the belief that doing B is a means to doing A; his wanting to do B is his being motivated by this belief.

Conativists recognize that beliefs concerning the means to goals gain motivational influence. They distinguish between two narrower senses of "wanting." To *extrinsically want* to do something is to be motivated to do it *as a means* to something else one wants; to *intrinsically want* to do something is to be motivated to it *as an end in itself.* The debate between cognitivism and conativism now centers on whether cognitive states are capable of motivating a person to pursue something as an end. Cognitive states, according to conativism, have only the power of modifying motivational direction, not of initiating it. Desires are the source of the motivational influence that gets transferred to such beliefs. But "desire" here is no longer being used in the widest sense, but in a narrower one such that only things pursued or done as ends in themselves are objects of desire. According to conativism, a person can deny that he wanted to do what he intentionally did. In so doing, he is denying that what he did was wanted as an end in itself: to intentionally do what one doesn't want to do is to do what one is doing *only* as a means to something one intrinsically wants; it is not something one would do if it weren't believed to be such a means.

In addition to the distinction between extrinsic and intrinsic wants, conativism recognizes a different distinction. Consider the following example.

Case One: The Disappointed Applicant

Robert wants to become a good philosopher and make some contribution to his field. He believes that the best way to achieve his goal is by being part of a philosophy faculty at a college or university. He wants very much to go to the University of Texas at Austin because he believes he would learn much through working with several members of that philosophy department, whose work he finds stimulating. But he accepts a job at a local community college, for it was the only one offered. Robert does not want to work at this community college, but this is what he will do.

Since both what Robert is said to want (to teach at Austin) and what he does but claims not to want are means to an end, the distinction between intrinsic and extrinsic wanting is inapplicable to this contrast. Usually, the distinction between *really* wanting and *wanting all-things-considered* is introduced to explicate this kind of contrast. (The notion of wanting all-things-considered is the motivated sense applied to actions: at the time of acting one always performs that act one is most effectively motivated to do.) This distinction indicates that some factor in the agent's situation, as he sees it, has interfered with the effectiveness of one of his wants. The interfering factor in this case is Robert's (correct) belief that he did not have (since he was not given) the opportunity to teach at Austin. Both the *all-things-considered* qualification and the contrast with *really wanting* serve to point out that (1) until something interfered, one had been more strongly motivated to do something other than what one did, and (2) if that interfering factor had not appeared, the agent would not have acted as he did but would have done what he is said to have really wanted to do.

Thus, according to the conativist, there are two different things a person could be claiming when he denies that he wanted to do what he intentionally did, depending on the context: (1) he could be claiming that he didn't intrinsically want to do it, but only did it as a means to something else, *or* (2) he could be claiming that he would have done something else if he had been able to do so. But there are other types of situations in which a person intentionally does what he says he doesn't want to do, cases for which both the distinction between extrinsic and intrinsic wants and that between really wanting and wanting all-things-considered fail to do justice.

2. CONATIVISM AND AVERSIONS

Case Two: The Rape

On the night of August 21, 1974, Anne Tonglet and Araceli Castellano were camping in a pine forest on the Mediterranean shore near Marseilles. About 1 a.m. they were awakened when three men entered their tent, brandishing stones, and began to beat them. After being beaten and threatened with death, the women agreed to engage in sexual activities with these men. What followed was described, on the one hand, by the women as a "five-hour nightmare," while, on the other hand, by the men as "five hours of joyous group sex . . . since in the end the girls agreed." The women, fearing death, intentionally engaged in various activities and pretended to be very friendly as the men left, afraid that they would not leave or that they would kill them before leaving. The intentional behavior of the women throughout that morning was later used by the men's lawyer as refuting the women's charge of rape: "a non-consenting woman cannot be forced to practice certain caresses."[9]

The Tonglet-Castellano case can be used not only to illustrate a case in which it makes sense to deny that one wanted to do what one did do but also to show how the widest sense of "wanting" can be used to make very misleading statements. In the widest sense of "wanting," they wanted to do what they did, for they intentionally did it; and yet the position taken by the men's attorney that the women wanted to have sex with them because they actively participated is surely mistaken. Nor is the distinction between wanting all-things-considered and really wanting helpful. What the women would be said to really want to do is to go back to sleep unmolested; but they were much more strongly motivated to do what they didn't want to do than they were to simply go back to sleep unmolested.

Even though the women intentionally engaged in sexual activity, rather than continuing to struggle or even simply remaining passive (for both would have been seen by the men as resistance), they were forced to do so; they had no choice.[10] They were not simply forced to *act*, they were forced to *want* to act. By denying that they wanted to do what they did, by charging the men with rape, the women are pointing out that their being motivated to do what they did was forced upon them by the threat of death.

One way in which the notion of intrinsic wanting might be applied to this case is to point out that Mss. Tonglet and Castellano wanted to avoid being further harmed and did what they did in order to avoid that; thus the end they were pursuing, the object of their desire, is said to be "the avoidance of further harm." But explaining someone's behavior by saying that the purpose of it was "the avoidance of Y" places that behavior into an avoidance, not a pursuit, pattern; it does not identify as a goal of pursuit behavior something called "the avoidance of Y." "Avoidances," whatever they are, are not something a person pursues; states of affairs, actions, and activities, on the other hand, are the kinds of things a person will sometimes pursue and sometimes avoid.[11]

The transference of motivational influence may, and often does, generate avoidance motivation. If John wants to invite his friends to his house to watch the game on TV and believes that if he does anything to irritate Mary he won't be able to have his friends over, he will be motivated to avoid doing anything he believes might irritate Mary. But the avoidance motivation in the Rape case is not generated by pursuit motivation. What Mss. Tonglet and Castellano were motivated to avoid was not something they believed to be incompatible with achieving some goal they were motivated to pursue. Painful things, harmful things, and deadly things are not things a person avoids because they are believed to be hindrances to the achieving of some goal; they are things that are avoided simply because of what they are, i.e., they are avoided as "ends in themselves."

There are a class of actions and a class of wants that are explained in terms of an end one is motivated to avoid — an end one is repelled by — rather than in terms of an end one is motivated to pursue — an end one is attracted to, as it were. There are purposive patterns of behavior that have as their goal the avoidance of such a repellent end.[12] The Rape case illustrates that there is one class of repellents in some way associated with pain and avoided *because* they are so associated. In order to keep this form of motivation distinct from both pursuit motivation and any other forms of avoidance motivation there may be, motivational states of avoiding repellents associated with pain can be called *aversions*.

Neither the separation of aversions from other wants nor the distinction needed to fully appreciate the Rape case poses any serious problem for conativism. Although some conativist theories may be incompatible with the recognition that aversions are a distinct class of motivational states, conativism can incorporate aversions into its framework without much difficulty. The result will be a view of motivation that claims there are *two* different kinds of sources of motivational influences, both of which are noncognitive states: desires and aversions.[13]

The force of the Rape case lies in its implicit reliance on the moral difference between engaging in sexual activities because one is threatened with violence if one doesn't and engaging in sexual activities because one wants to. This difference, one might argue, does hint at a narrower sense of "wanting," for surely when one is said to be engaging in sexual activities because one wants to, something more is being said than simply that one is motivated to do so — and this something more is that one desires to. But all "because one wants to" excludes when it is contrasted with "because one was forced to" or "because one was threatened" is precisely that one wasn't forced to or threatened. That Janet's having sex with Bill was not an instance of rape but was done because she wanted to gives no clues to Janet's motivation for doing it *except* that it wasn't done out of fear: all that it indicates is that the goal she is pursuing by acting is not one forced upon her by the will of another. One does not know whether she is acting out of desire, curiosity, pity, or gratitude, or whether she is seeking revenge against her husband or paying an old debt. Thus, using the notion of engaging in sexual activity because one wants to, and not because one is being forced to, does not utilize the narrower sense of "wanting" that applies only to ends.

But this notion of engaging in sexual activity because one wants to *does* suggest a narrower sense of "wanting," once it is realized that the question "As opposed to what?" can have different answers. Instead of contrasting doing something because one wants to with doing something because one is forced to, one can contrast it with other kinds of motivational influences. If Bill is curious as to why Jill has consented to having sex with him, she may try to reassure him that she is doing it neither because she is curious about what it's like to do it with someone other than her husband, nor because she feels sorry for him, nor because she's angry with her husband, etc., but because she really wants to do it. The same notion of wanting is working when Jill tells her friend that she doesn't really want to have sex with her husband anymore, but that she does so anyway because she thinks it's her duty, or she doesn't want to hurt him, or she doesn't want him to walk out, etc. The narrower sense of "wanting" implicit here can be made explicit by examining a clearer case of motivational conflict.

3. ON NOT WANTING TO DO WHAT ONE INTRINSICALLY WANTS TO DO: PLEASURE MOTIVATION

Case Three: The Depressed Friend

William has been looking forward all week long to attending a Sherlock Holmes film festival on Saturday, which will feature two films with Arthur Wontner that are rarely shown and that he has never seen. So that spending all day at this festival would not conflict with his job responsibilities, for the past week everything else has been sacrificed in order to get all of his work done by Friday. On Saturday morning, as he is getting ready to leave for the festival, he receives a phone call from a close friend. This friend suffers from occasional fits of depression during which she loses touch with reality and becomes a danger to herself; she is in one of those now and asks if he would keep her company during the day. Having done it before, William knows what it will be like if he goes — a protracted, tedious, and exasperating attempt to convince her of her own worth and to dissuade her from suicide, an experience that will leave him so psychologically exhausted that he will have great difficulty concentrating for days. He has a choice as to how he'll spend his day, a choice he doesn't like to make, a choice he wishes he didn't have to make. Realizing, however, that at the present time he is probably the only one to whom she can turn, he agrees to come over. But although William chooses to spend the day with his friend, he doesn't want to. He doesn't want to do his duty; he wants to attend the Sherlock Holmes festival.[14]

When William claims that he didn't want to do what he did he cannot, of course, be using the widest sense; but neither is he using the narrower sense that indicates intrinsic wanting. For in denying that he wanted to spend the day with his friend, that he wanted to do his duty, he is not simply saying that he was motivated to do so as a means rather than as an end in itself: there was nothing further that he wanted to accomplish by doing his duty. Keeping his friend company and from committing suicide were not things he hoped to accomplish by doing his duty: accomplishing them *was* his duty. And whether one describes what he intrinsically wants as doing his duty or as keeping his friend from harming herself, William could intelligibly and sincerely claim both that he doesn't want *to have to* do it today *and* that he doesn't want to do it *at all* today.

The distinction between wanting all-things-considered and really wanting also fails to capture the contrast being made in this case. To say that going to see the films is what William really wanted to do is not simply to say that that is what he would have done if his friend hadn't called, although it *is* what he would have done. One can imagine a situation in which he was going to spend the entire day drawing up a proposal, which he doesn't like to do very much. In one sense, he really wants to get that proposal out of the way—in the sense that he was strongly motivated to do so. In both cases, he would rather spend the day doing what he had planned on doing before he had received the call; in both cases, the original motivating influence is overridden by the call of duty.

And yet, William's wanting to see the Sherlock Holmes films is very different from his wanting to spend the day writing a proposal. When William claims he really wants to go to see the films or that he wants to see the films more than he wants to visit his friend, something more is being said than simply that his motivation to do so was overridden by the call of duty. And when he denies that he wants to do his duty, he is not denying that he is motivated to do so as an end; this again suggests that something is missing. His being motivated (wanting) to see the films has some features that are not present either in his being motivated (wanting) to visit his friend or in his being motivated (wanting) to complete a proposal.

There are many indications of William's wanting to see the films: he was willing to do without other things he enjoys so that he would be able to go see them; he had been looking forward to seeing them all week; he had been excited when he first heard about them; he has mentioned several times the rare thrill it was to see Holmes come alive before one's eyes, something that only happened in Wontner's films. After he had decided to spend the day with his friend, there were indications that he didn't really want to do so: he certainly wasn't looking forward to it, and he thought it would be a joyless, difficult time. Clearly, the central factor involved in this case is *pleasure*.

Pleasure seems to be connected with seeing the films in *two* ways: first, William is pleased and excited about seeing them—he is looking forward to it—and second, he seems to believe that seeing them will be enjoyable. And in just these ways, pleasure is absent from visiting his friend: he is not looking forward to it *and* he believes that it will not be enjoyable. But pleasure is not a mere *additional* factor to William's being motivated to see the films, it is an integral part of his wanting, it makes his wanting what it is—he would not want to do it if that factor were missing.

It would seem, then, that the connection a proposed action has with pleasure can be a relevant factor in an agent's being motivated to perform that action. In the sense that William wanted to see those films, in the sense that is connected to looking forward to something, being excited about it, believing that it will be pleasurable, he certainly did not want to go visit his friend, although in the motivated sense, visiting his friend is what he wanted to do "most," since that is what he did do.

4. ON NOT WANTING TO DO WHAT ONE INTRINSICALLY WANTS TO DO: VALUE MOTIVATION

Case Four: The Philandering Artist

> Pierre wants very much to become a good artist and believes he can make some contribution to the advancement of art. Although he is conscientious in completing works specifically commissioned, during the past two years he has produced very little original work. At present there is a painting he wants to do, and he feels strongly about completing it. But although he believes the painting will be quite important, he spends his time chasing women instead of creating. He doesn't understand his behavior and, in moments of reflection, he despises himself for it. He wants very much to be an artist and to excel at it; he thinks that his project is not only interesting but also has the potential of being noticed. He wants to complete the project and doesn't want to chase women, but this is what he does every chance he gets.

In the history of philosophy, there has been much discussion of situations similar to Pierre's, although these situations were differently described. For some philosophers the issue was whether, and if so, how, *akrasia* was possible: roughly, *akrasia* occurs when a person does not do what he believes to be the right thing to do. The classical formulation of the denial of the possibility of *akrasia* is that of Socrates, reported and defended by Plato;[15] the classical formulation of the anti-Socratic position can be found in the plays of Euripides.[16] Christian thinkers, however, were either concerned with a different phenomenon or described it differently; the issue was weakness of the will: How is it possible to want to do that which one knows is good and yet not do it? The classical formulation of this problem is presented by St. Paul: "I do not do the good I want, but the evil I do not want is what I do."[17] Pierre's situation seems to be one of weakness of the will.

How does Pierre view the two activities in question? Creating art, and doing it well, has been his ambition for years; for him, it is the most worthwhile activity in which to be engaged. When asked what he does or is interested in, he begins to talk about art; whenever he is in a less than frivolous conversation, he introduces issues involving art. Of the historical and contemporary figures he admires most, the majority are either artists or persons known for their appreciation and support of art. He is pleased with those artistic abilities he has so far developed and is proud of those achievements he has made. Chasing women, however, is not something he likes to talk about, nor is it something he admires in the behavior of others. He doesn't consider it a worthwhile or meaningful endeavor, no matter how successful. He is ashamed when he hears his colleagues making jokes about him and "his women," and in moments of reflection, he despises himself for his behavior. All of the various attitudes have something in common: value judgments. What distinguishes his being motivated to create from his being motivated to chase women is that the former is connected to his values, while the latter is incompatible with them. But Pierre's values are not simply an additional factor to his being motivated to create — as if he wants, in the widest sense, to create *and*, in addition, values it as well. His values are an integral part of his wanting; they make his wanting what it is — for if his values were not involved in the way that they are, he would not have the wants that he has.[18] Apparently, the connection that an activity or action has with the agent's values can be a factor in the agent's being motivated to engage in that activity.

5. DESIRING AND VALUING

The Depressed Friend and the Philandering Artist cases are illustrations of that perennial paradigm of motivational conflict, alternatively characterized as "pleasure versus the good," "inclination versus duty," "desire versus reason," and "the flesh versus the spirit" — a motivational conflict that goes straight to the heart of the debate between cognitivism and conativism.

In the Depressed Friend case, William's being motivated to see the film is explained in terms of the characteristics he believes that activity has in itself, rather than in terms of any relation it has to some other act, activity, or state of affairs. His account of why he wants to see the films is likely to be couched in terms of how enjoyable, exciting, thrilling they are, i.e., in terms of the pleasurableness of experiencing them. Seeing the films is, for William, an end in itself. In the Philandering Artist case, Pierre's chasing women isn't seen by him to further his advance on some goals, but as an exciting and enjoyable activity. On the conscious level, Pierre is motivated to pursue sexual activity with a particular woman as an end, and it is an end because he enjoys such activity. It should be clear from these two cases that there are patterns of purposive behavior whose ends are actions, activities, or states of affairs that are believed to be in some way associated with pleasure and are pursued as an end because they are so associated.

William is motivated to visit his friend because he believes that it is his duty to do so. Doing his duty, for William, is not seen as being a means to something else, nor is it in any way associated with pleasure. In fact, he believes the experience will be unpleasant and have unpleasant consequences for him. Pierre is motivated to engage in artistic creation because he believes it to be a noble and worthy endeavor. Creating art is not seen by him as simply being a means of livelihood. Pierre's case illustrates that the values involved in value motivation need not be *moral* values; they may be aesthetic values, political values, religious values, intellectual values, etc. But what these cases do show is that there are purposive patterns of behavior whose ends are in some way deemed valuable in themselves and are pursued as ends because they are so esteemed.[19]

From one's own experience, it should be obvious that pleasure motivation and value motivation can come into conflict. Some things a person enjoys doing or that give him pleasure are not things he values; some may even be incompatible with his values, as in Pierre's case. Some things a person does because he values them are not necessarily pleasant; some may even be unpleasant to do. And while one value motivation may at times conflict with another value motivation, these conflicts will either be resolved by, or cause a change in, the internal structure of a person's system of values. But value-pleasure conflicts are different in kind, in that their resolution does not depend upon what the agent's value system is; for it is precisely that value system that is being opposed from without. The resolution depends not upon *what* the agent's values are, but on how strong, motivationally, they are. It seems reasonable to conclude that pleasure motivation and value motivation are different, distinct kinds; pursuing and doing that which is (believed) good is not always pleasurable, nor believed to be, while pursuing and doing that which is pleasurable is not always valued.

The way in which "want" is used in the Philandering Artist case is different from the way in which it is used in the Depressed Friend case. But in both cases, the use of "want" is different from the narrower sense of "wanting" that indicates intrinsic wants; for although what the agent is said to want to do, in both cases, is wanted as an end, so too is what he is said not to want. In the Philandering Artist case, the end Pierre is said to want, but which he does not pursue, is thought to be in some way pleasurable; while the end he is said not to want, but which he does pursue, is something not associated with pleasure. "Wanting," 'in this case, is being used to apply only to those ends associated with pleasure; consequently, it is a *different* narrower use of "wanting" than that found in the Philandering Artist case.

There is historical precedent for calling the concept corresponding to the sense of "wanting" applicable to pleasure motivation the concept of desire: traditionally (1) pleasure has been associated with desires whenever values were associated with reason, and (2) desires have been most often cited as that which is responsible for pleasure-value conflicts. The concept of desire, then, will be that concept of wanting governing pleasure motivation; both William's and Pierre's situations are ones in which desire and values are in conflict.

6. REALLY WANTING AND WANTING ONE THING MORE THAN ANOTHER

If conativism is to resist the separation of value motivation from pleasure motivation, it must provide an account of the contrasts embedded in the Depressed Friend case and the Philandering Artist case, an account using the three distinctions it can accommodate. In neither case is the distinction between intrinsic wanting and extrinsic wanting adequate for the contrasts being made. Nor is the distinction, made in discussing the Rape case, between coerced wanting and uncoerced wanting useful. Perhaps, then, the distinction between *really wanting* and *wanting all-things-considered* will be sufficient to handle these two cases.

When a person is described as having really wanted to do other than he did, the most plausible interpretation of the function of "really" is that it is augmentative: what a person is said to *really* want among alternatives is that which he wants *more* and *most*. Using the widest sense of "wanting," to want something more than something else is to be more strongly motivated to do it. Consequently, it does not make sense to say, using the widest sense of "wanting," that an agent wanted to do something *more* than what he did do. What, then, is being claimed when a person is described as wanting to do one thing more than another?

In the Disappointed Applicant case, really wanting, or wanting to do something else more than the thing one did, indicates not only a motivational influence frustrated by one's situation or overridden by a stronger want, but also a want that is strongly felt. The strength of a motivational influence can be exhibited in *two* ways: (1) the degree to which it affects the agent's behavior and (2) the degree to which it affects the agent's consciousness—his feelings, thoughts, etc.[20] One indication that a person is very strongly motivated to do something is that doing it is what occupies his thoughts and is what he is said to feel strongly about. This criterion for strength in a motivational influence applies to all forms of motivation. This kind of motivational strength is frequently manifested when the motivating force is frustrated. And although the turbulence present in consciousness is likely to be different for value motivation than for desires, when frustrated there can be turbulence nonetheless. The frustration of a desire (e.g., in the Depressed Friend case) frequently takes the form of disappointment—the stronger the desire, the more the person is disappointed. The frustration of a value motivation by some other (nonvalue) motivational influence (e.g., in the Philandering Artist case) may reveal itself to consciousness in the form of guilt or of dissatisfaction with one's self: the more value the person places on acting in such a way, the more he feels dissatisfaction. In some contexts, then, to talk about wanting one thing more than another is to talk about that concerning which one is more strongly affected.

When someone who must make a choice is advised to do what he wants to do most, what is he being told to do? If the widest sense of "wanting" is being used, he is being told to do that which he is most strongly motivated to do. But when John's wife presents him with the ultimatum to decide which he wants more, his family or his promotion, she is not asking him to conduct an introspective inquiry into which he is more strongly motivated at the present time to pursue; she apparently believes she already knows the answer to *that* question, which is why she is giving the ultimatum. In many cases, "Which do you want more?" can be used, as it is here, to say: consider your priorities; which is more important to you, valued by you? On the other hand, when Robert is asked which he wants to do most on his birthday, see *Star Wars*, hear *Das Rheingold* at Wolf Trap, or explore some secondhand bookstores, he is not being asked about priorities, about his system of values; he is being asked which activity he would enjoy more.

The meaning of the question "Which does an agent want to do most?" depends upon which sense of "wanting" is being used: is the agent being asked which option he would enjoy most, or which does he consider most worthy, most important? In situations where both pleasure and value are factors, it becomes even more crucial to be clear about which question is being asked. Conflicts between pleasure motivation and value motivation cannot always be arbitrated by the realization that doing what one values won't be any fun or by the judgment that enjoying oneself is not all that important. Since values and desires are separate and often conflict, what one is said to want most, or more than something else, will in many situations depend upon from what perspective one is judging—from the point of view of possible pleasure or from that of value.[21]

"Agent S wants to do A more than he wants to do B" can be used to make several different claims: (1) the agent believes that doing A has more value than doing B, (2) he believes doing A will be more pleasurable than doing B, or (3) he is more strongly motivated to do A than he is to do B. "Agent S really wanted to do other than he did" is usually used to indicate that the agent's consciousness was more affected by what he is said to really want than was his behavior. This can be accounted for either by the blocking of the behavioral effectiveness of that want by some inhibiting factor or by the want's being "overridden" by a motivational influence that was stronger, but not felt to be stronger. The meaning of "really wanting" is context-dependent; it leads to the question "As opposed to what?" In some contexts what it is opposed to is "being forced," in others it is "out of duty," "guilt," etc., and in still others, it is "in order to. . . ."

7. SENSES OF "WANTING" VERSUS REASONS FOR WANTING

It might be argued that one need not postulate two narrower senses of "wanting," one applying to pleasure motivation, the other to value motivation, in order to deal adequately with the cases of the Depressed Friend and the Philandering Artist. What these two cases illustrate, it could be said, is not two different senses of "want," but two different reasons for wanting. Limiting the discussion to pursuit motivation, there are three kinds of reasons for wanting to do something: (1) it is a means to something else one wants, (2) it is pleasurable, and (3) it is good (has value).[22] Explaining an action or a want in terms of the first kind of reason shows that the behavior was performed as a means and the want was generated by another want; explaining an action or a want in terms of the second or third kind of reason shows that the behavior was performed as, and the want directed to, an end. Reasons as inducements operate in a similar way. Given that a person wants to do A, then if he was to be convinced that doing B is a means to doing A, he may (by transference of motivational influence) come to want to do B. Similarly, given a person who is usually motivated to do pleasurable things or to do worthwhile things, to convince him that doing A will be pleasurable or will be worthwhile is likely to result in his becoming motivated to do A.

Relying on the notion of a reason for wanting, however, rather than distinguishing between two narrower senses of "wanting," will not be enough to render intelligible the conflicts involved in the two cases. In the first place, William and Pierre are both motivated toward two different ends, one of which is wanted because it is associated with pleasure, the other because it is valued: even using just the notion of a reason for wanting, there is a distinction between value motivation and pleasure motivation. But the crux is that these two motivational influences conflict in each case. Even if one were to know what can count as a reason for wanting, how those reasons can conflict, and what it is for one reason to be stronger than another, the descriptions of the agents as not wanting to do what they did and of wanting to do what they didn't will remain unintelligible if only the intrinsic sense of "wanting" is used. Clearly, these cases do indicate different reasons for being motivated, but it is equally clear that these cases cannot be adequately understood *unless* "want," in each case, is used to mean something more than "is motivated to as an end"—for in each case, "want" is used in such a way that the reason for being motivated is involved in its *meaning*.

8. CONATIVISM AND VALUE MOTIVATION

The separation of value motivation from pleasure motivation strikes at the core of all forms of conativism. For when value motivation stands alone, it is not only plausible to restrict the use of "desire" to pleasure motivation, but it is also plausible to identify the source of value motivation as one's value *judgments* or value *beliefs*, i.e., as *cognitive* states. The conativist, it seems, cannot deny that both the Depressed Friend and the Philandering Artist cases reveal a fundamental kind of motivational conflict; what he must do is argue that this kind of motivational conflict—one between pleasure and value—can be accounted for without contributing to the plausibility of cognitivism.

One is forgetting, the conativist argues, that the recognition that something is one's duty will be motivationally effective only if one *wants* to do one's duty; unless one wants to act in accordance with some values, value beliefs will be powerless. Thus, whenever a person pursues the Good (in whatever sphere: morals, religion, politics, etc.), he is motivated not by value beliefs alone, but by his *desire* for the Good. And when one rejects hedonism by separating pleasure motivation from value motivation, one is recognizing that there are different kinds of desires. Restricting the usage of "desire" to pleasure motivation is misleading in implying that something other than desire moves a person to pursue the Good. The two cases under discussion reveal conflicts between two foundational desires: the desire for pleasure and the desire to do one's duty.

This argument requires careful consideration. But first, a preliminary point: there is an important difference between the pursuit of a pleasurable end and the pursuit of pleasure as an end, although the difference is somewhat difficult to articulate. The hedonist, sensualist, and thrill seeker do things *in order to* enjoy themselves. William, Pierre, and most others, while doing things because they are enjoyable, do not see the pleasure as a result to be achieved. Although pleasure can be taken as an end in itself, being pleasurable in these cases, and in most cases, is a property of one class of ends, not an end in itself. The object of desire, then, is usually not pleasure, but that thing (object, action, activity) that is thought to be pleasurable.

Now to the conativist's argument. On the surface, this argument seems to miss the point. As pointed out above (sec. 5), William's being motivated to visit his friend is neither separate nor separable from his valuings: he does not value doing his duty *and in addition* want to do it. It is unnecessary to posit an additional want in order to explain his action. But the conativist can agree with this point by claiming that values or valuings *contain* wants. According to this view, a valuing is a compound "act": a judgment to the effect that doing it has (value) property P *and* a want to do things that have property P.[23] This response is motivated by the conativist's belief that there *must* be some noncognitive motivating element that accounts for value motivation. To show why this need not be the case requires some reflection on the way "want" is used in the explanations of actions.

The widest sense of "wanting" is a *motivated* sense; it indicates the fact that the agent is motivated to act, but it does *not* indicate what it is that is motivating him to act. The distinction between intrinsic and extrinsic wantings merely divides the territory of the widest sense between these two types of wanting: but both are still "motivated wants." To say that S intrinsically wants to do A is to say that S is motivated to pursue doing A as an end in itself; it does not indicate what it is that is motivating S to so pursue doing A. William does intrinsically want to do his duty. But this leaves open the question as to what is motivating him to do his duty.

To say that William would not have done his duty if he had not wanted to do so is a truism because it is using a motivated sense of "wanting": he would not have done it if he had not been motivated to do it. If motive determines whether one does one's duty, it can even be said that he would not have done it if he had not been motivated to do it *as an end in itself.* If all that is meant by a desire to do one's duty is that one is motivated to do one's duty as an end in itself, this is not incompatible with the falsity of conativism.

A person who pursues something as an end is pursuing it not because of some external relationship it has to something else, but because it is what it is, because it has certain properties. Pursuing something as an end *can* be explained in terms of its having certain properties, as when William is said to want to see the films because they are enjoyable and to want to visit his friend because it is his duty; but the property that determines something as an end is not something *else* being pursued as an end; it is not the *real* end of that pursuit. When it is noticed, however, that over a period of time there are patterns in a person's behavior, that many of the ends he pursues have some property in common, which is often cited as explaining the pursuit, a disposition to pursue ends having that property is attributed to the agent. Explanations of particular pursuits are given in terms of his wanting or desiring things with that property: a person who regularly pursues things connected with glory is said to desire glory, a person who collects things because they are beautiful is said to have a desire for beauty, a person who pursues goals because they are moral is said to desire to be moral, and so on. Explaining a person's purposive behavior by citing such a want or desire places it within a pattern of similar behavior. Significantly, many such patterns are called *character traits*, for in explaining an action in terms of such a pattern, we are explaining it by referring to the kind of person the agent is.

To say that William visited his friend because it was his duty is to explain his behavior in terms of a disposition to do or to pursue things that are his duty. To talk of a desire or want to do his duty is to talk of just such a disposition, just such a trait in his character—it is to use "desire," or "want," in the motivated sense. His desire, or want, is not what is motivating him to pursue that kind of end, but is simply his disposition, his tendency, to be motivated *by* considerations of duty. Although recognizing that William's moral act is explained in terms of a long-term dispositional want to do the moral thing, the conativist is misled by the motivated sense of "wanting"; particular moral actions can be explained in terms of dispositional wants, i.e., character traits, but these wants are *patterns* of motivation, not something that *accounts* for such patterns.

If the foregoing story of what is meant by "wanting to do one's duty" is plausible,[24] the conativist's objection to separating value motivation from desire loses much of its force. Instead of viewing William's valuings, for example, as containing a want, an equally plausible account would claim that his valuing, his value judgment, *is* his want. In fact, on this latter view, "want" *is* being used to refer to *motivating* states: William's value judgment is his want because it is what is motivating him.

9. CONCLUSION

What is being claimed when a person denies that he wanted to do what he did intentionally depends upon what sense of "wanting" he is using. In this paper, it has been argued that the senses of "wanting" acknowledged by conativism do not do justice to the distinction between pleasure motivation and value motivation. It has been argued not that conativism is false, but rather that the separation of value motivation from pleasure motivation provides some plausibility for cognitivism, in that some form of the latter *may* be more helpful in capturing the distinctions embedded in ordinary ways of talking about motivational conflicts. To the extent that the argument of this paper contributes to the plausibility of cognitivism, it detracts from the plausibility of conativism.[25]

NOTES

1. Plato is considered the paradigm cognitivist. His characterizations of the "types of souls," ranging from the tyrant to the philosopher, provide illustrations of the different ways in which reason can be related to the passions, appetites, and desires (*Republic*, bk. 10, 543a-592b). For Plato, unhappiness, immorality, and civil injustice are the results of an improper relationship between reason (the cognitive) and the nonrational conative aspects of human nature. Kant's distinction between motivation by duty and motivation by inclination can also be cited as an instance of cognitivism (see his *Foundations of the Metaphysics of Morals*). For Kant genuine moral behavior is only possible when one is motivated by reason, rather than by some noncognitive influence.

2. Hume is the paradigm conativist. He sees all human action, including moral action, as springing from what he calls the passions, and he presents the clearest articulation of the conativist position on the relation between the cognitive and the conative: "Reason is, and ought only to be the slave of the passions, and can never pretend to any other office than to serve and obey them" (Hume, 1978 [1739], p. 415). One consequence of conativism, since reason has no function in determining ends, is that neither desire nor passion nor goals pursued are rational or irrational. Certain goals may well be imprudent, i.e., the achieving of that goal would involve or result in the frustration of many other desires, but wanting that goal is in itself not irrational. But since no end pursued is either rational or irrational, and since ends, goals, are simply the objects of desire or passion (etc.), it follows that the value an end has is not something recognized, discovered, or determined by reason but is merely a function of whether it satisfies some motivating influence. And if the value an end has is solely determined by its being an object of a motivating influence, the question of whether the end is good or bad *in itself*, i.e., independently of its being desired or willed, is meaningless. Spinoza is the classic proponent of

this view: "We neither strive for, wish, seek, nor desire anything because we think it to be good, but on the contrary, we adjudge a thing to be good because we strive for, wish, seek, or desire it" (Spinoza, 1949 [1677], pp. 135-136).

Richard Taylor labels these two competing views of human motivation *rationalism* and *voluntarism*, instead of *cognitivism* and *conativism* (see Taylor, 1964, 1970). For some purposes Taylor's terminology would be preferable, e.g., if one were discussing the connection between certain voluntaristic views of ethics or religious beliefs and conativist theories of motivation. In a way, the label "conativism" is misleading; for if cognitivism is correct, then there are cognitive states that are *also* conative states. Although "noncognitivism" would probably be a better label than either "conativism" or "voluntarism," there are reasons for using "conativism," e.g., it is used in Joel Marks's essay in this volume.

3. Armstrong (1968), p. 152.

4. See Alston (1967b), Audi (1973a), Brandt and Kim (1963), Hare (1963), and Locke (1974, 1982). Alan R. White, however, in comments on an earlier draft of this paper, writes concerning this purported agreement about a widest sense of "wanting": "if they do [agree], they are mistaken."

5. For a rare exception, see Brandt and Kim (1963), p. 426.

6. I examined the widest sense of "wanting" and argued for this claim in Staude (1982).

7. This point is made, although stated somewhat differently, by Nagel (1970), pp. 29-30.

8. See Nagel (1970), p. 33.

9. The description of this case is based upon, and the direct quotations are taken from, Claude Servan-Schreiber, "The Rape Case That Is Shaking Up France," *Ms.* 5:4 (October 1976): 124, 126-127.

10. When it is claimed that they had no choice, the intentionality of their behavior is not being denied. What is being claimed is that what they did—or even, if you insist, what they *chose* to do—was the *only* rational alternative open to them; for the only other alternative they had was to continue to be beaten, perhaps to their deaths. Aristotle, however, believes that in some coerced situations in which you are given the choice between being killed and doing something horrible, death is the rational thing to choose (*Nicomachean Ethics*, bk. 3, sec. 1).

11. In comments on an earlier draft of this paper, Robert Audi suggested that perhaps "seeking to avoid" could be used to avoid separating avoidance motivation from pursuit motivation. I am unsure how to respond, but my intuition is that this would not be helpful. "Seeking" usually is used to mean "trying to find"; "seeking" itself seems to suggest a pursuit of some kind. It also is usually followed by a noun (e.g., "seeking happiness," "seeking a new job"), rather than an infinitive.

12. It seems odd to continue calling these states of affairs or experiences that *repel* "ends"; for lack of a better word, I shall call them "repellents," not "ends."

13. Thomas Hobbes is a good example of a conativist who recognizes the

difference between pursuit motivation and avoidance motivation. For Hobbes, all human action and feeling are generated by *desire* and *aversion*, by the *pursuit* of pleasure and the *avoidance* of pain. See *Leviathan* (Hobbes, 1972, pt. 1, chap. 6).

14. A case similar to this one is discussed, for a similar reason, by Gosling (1967, pp. 87-90).

15. See *Meno*, 776-786; *Protagoras*, 352b-358d; *Gorgias*, 466-481b.

16. See *Medea*, lines 1075-1080; *Hippolytus*, lines 375-378.

17. Romans, 7:19 (RSV).

18. In section 8, I consider the objection that values contain wants.

19. Although pursuing a goal and avoiding a repellent are different kinds of motivation, value motivation involves both. Values are two-sided; a *value* consists of both a positive value, a *good*, and a negative (dis)-value, an *evil*. (A disvalue or evil is not simply the absence of its corresponding good, but a *positive* opposite.) Part of what it is to value something (e.g., a property of actions or activities) is to disvalue its opposite. Value motivation is such that a person is motivated not only to pursue as ends those things that have the positively valued property, but also to avoid as evils those things that have the negatively valued property. For example, a person who values honesty will not only be motivated to pursue honesty, but will also find himself in situations in which he will be motivated to avoid being dishonest; a person who values supererogatory behavior will not only, at times, be motivated to do more than his duty requires, he will also be motivated to avoid doing less than his duty (or, perhaps, doing only his duty). Value motivation involves both the pursuit of goods and the avoidance of evils, and each pattern of motivation can involve, by the transference of motivational influence, both pursuit behavior and avoidance behavior. And since values are agent-dependent, not only are the pairs of opposed properties, taken as values, agent-dependent, but so, too, is the matter of which of the opposed pair is to have the positive or negative value. A person may take perversion, dishonesty, and infidelity as his positive values, pursuing things that have those values and avoiding things that are socially acceptable, honest, and loyal. For example, Jean Genet presents a character who sees his path to sainthood, to moral perfection, in becoming the most perfect pervert, thief, and traitor that he can (Genet, 1964).

20. See Armstrong (1968), p. 153.

21. This separation of pleasure motivation from value motivation would not occur for a hedonist.

22. That there are these reasons is implicit in Aristotle's discussion (*Nicomachean Ethics*, bk. 3, secs. 1-5) and in Anscombe (1976, secs. 34-35).

23. This was suggested by Robert Audi. It also seems to be the view of Donald Davidson (1963). Davidson does *not* speak of *wanting* to do actions that have the property in question, but of "a pro-attitude of the agent towards actions with a certain property" (p. 68). The point is that the conative power of a reason is a function of this noncognitive *pro-attitude*. A view similar to Davidson's is given in Hempel (1962), where *motivating reasons* are composites of beliefs *and* goals

(objectives).

24. For a very different kind of argument against the idea that there is a desire to do one's duty that is the source of moral motivation, see Ladd (1958).

25. This paper is a revision of Staude (1979, chap. 2). Earlier drafts were read at the University of Maryland (1980), Agnes Scott College (1981), and a National Endowment for the Humanities Seminar on Reasons, Justification, and Knowledge (1983). Many people have been generous with their time and comments on earlier versions of this paper. I would like to thank the following: faculty at the University of Maryland: Samuel Gorovitz, Jerrold Levinson, Raymond Martin, Alan Pasch, Moreland Perkins, Steven Stich, and Frederick Suppe; visitors at the University of Maryland: Richard Brandt and Alan R. White; faculty at Agnes Scott College: David Behan; at the NEH Seminar: Robert Audi and all of the participants in the seminar; at Otterbein College: Paul Redditt.

Akrasia and the Object of Desire

Michael Stocker

Abstract. Akrasia involves acting against one's better judgment because of contrary desire. It thus poses severe difficulties for accounts of desire and the relations between desire and action, rationality, and evaluation — but it also affords an opportunity for a rich understanding of these notions and relations. I shall here investigate whether akrasia requires that there be multiple objects of desire. In doing this we will get clearer about the nature and individuation of objects of desire — as well as about some features of hedonism and maximization, also important for an understanding of desire.

Weakness of will involves acting against one's better judgment. It thus poses severe difficulties for accounts of evaluation, rationality, action, and desire, and their interrelations. *Akrasia* (often translated by "weakness of will"), as discussed by Aristotle in Book Seven of the *Nicomachean Ethics*, involves acting against one's better judgment because of contrary desire. It thus poses even more severe difficulties for understanding those notions and relations. But for just the reasons it poses these difficulties, it offers an opportunity to gain a rich understanding of those notions and relations. In this paper, I shall make use of this opportunity by considering a particular problem it poses for desire — viz., how to individuate objects of desire.

The problem is this: If the better act will (so far as the agent believes) achieve whatever the akratic act will and something else in addition, it seems that it would be incoherent, or simply ridiculous, to act akratically. But whatever else akrasia is, it is neither incoherent nor simply ridiculous. Thus, it might be concluded that for there to be coherent akrasia, the desired object of the akratic act — i.e., the goal one has in doing the act — must be different from the object of the forgone, better act. This is to say that coherent akrasia requires a multiplicity of objects of desire.

I shall not be concerned to discuss whether there are multiple objects of desire or, on the contrary, whether all our desires are aimed at one thing, such as satisfaction. For, as I shall be concerned to argue, it is unclear what it is for there to be multiple objects of desire or for there to be but one object of desire. It is unclear, that is, how to individuate objects of desire. I shall argue for this — and try to alleviate some of this obscurity — by criticizing the argument that coherent akrasia requires multiple objects of desire. I shall show that this argument relies on a notion of an object of desire, or of *one* object of desire, which few if any objects of desire could satisfy. Showing this will help us understand what it is to be an object of desire — or at least what it is to be one, rather than another, object of desire. In doing this, I shall touch upon some issues about the commensurability and the comparability of desires and values, and on some issues about hedonism and maximization — issues which are important in their own right and also for a general understanding of desire.

This paper, thus, traverses many difficult and tangled issues. But no easier route is available if we are to gain an understanding of either akrasia or desire.

1. THE PROTAGOREAN PREDICAMENT

Some have thought that all akratic acts are *internally incoherent* in that the agent's goal is *contradicted* by what the agent believes. The paradigmatic example of such internal incoherence is presented in the *Protagoras* where it is said of akratic agents that they perform akratic acts in order to maximize pleasure even though they believe or know that another act open to them would produce even more pleasure.

The structure of such internal incoherence is that the akratic agent believes at once that the akratic act will not secure the goal that the act is, supposedly, done to secure — e.g., maximize pleasure — and also that another possible act would secure that goal. Many would undoubtedly agree with David Wiggins's claim that *if* akratic acts fit that description, agents can have no reason at all, much less any good reason, to do them.[1] After all, securing that goal is the reason for acting and, as the agent believes, the other act will do that while the akratic act will not. If an agent has no reason at all, much less any good reason, to do these acts, they might well seem incoherent. Indeed, they might well seem so incoherent that they do not even qualify as acts. I shall call this set of worries about akrasia the *Protagorean Predicament.*

This paper discusses Wiggins's attempt to show that coherent akrasia — i.e., akrasia which escapes the Protagorean Predicament — requires that there be plural goals which are incommensurable. Wiggins is joined by many in this view.[2] His argument develops from what seems to be a perfectly acceptable understanding of what it is to be a goal, or more particularly *one* goal. As I shall be concerned to argue, when we have correctly understood the nature and individuation of goals, we shall see that coherent akrasia does not require a plurality of goals, much less incommensurable ones.[3]

In the argument I am concerned to examine, Wiggins claims that the attack on akrasia in the *Nicomachean Ethics* is importantly different from the attack on akrasia in the *Protagoras*. For the goods of Aristotle's eudaimonia are incommensurable, and thus allow for coherent akrasia. Aristotle does not exploit this. But, Wiggins suggests, had he done so, his would have been a better account, and perhaps even a more Aristotelian account, of akrasia.

I shall not discuss whether this is the correct interpretation of Aristotle on akrasia. So, too, I shall not discuss, but shall merely accept, Wiggins's interpretation of the *Protagoras*. I am here concerned to discuss the nature of goals and the bearing of this on akrasia, rather than the interpretation of classical texts.

2. COMMENSURABILITY AND THE PROTAGOREAN PREDICAMENT

To make out his case that, and how, the *Protagoras* treats akrasia differently from the *Nicomachean Ethics*, Wiggins focuses on 354d-355d, especially where Socrates claims it is "ridiculous nonsense" to suggest that an akratic agent might "do evil knowing it to be evil because he is overcome by good.... By being overcome you must mean taking evil in exchange for greater good..." (Wiggins, 1978-79, p. 267). So understood, the akratic hedonist must be understood as knowingly taking a lesser pleasure in exchange for a greater one, which from the hedonist's own point of view is ridiculous nonsense. Wiggins's gloss on this passage is worth quoting at length:

> Let F be the universal or all-purpose predicate of favorable assessment. A man will only be incontinent if he knows or believes the thing he doesn't do is the thing with most F to it. But if that is the alternative that has most F to it, and if nothing else besides F-ness counts positively for anything, there is nothing to commend any other course of action over the one that is most F. He could have had no reason, *however bad*, for choosing the other. The choice of a smaller amount of pleasure now against a larger amount of pleasure later is explicitly described as a form of ignorance in the supposedly single dimension F.... If everything with any relevance to choice is comprehended in the question how F a given course of action is, and how F its competitors are, then no rational sense can be made of weakness of will. This is the *Protagoras* argument. (Wiggins, 1978-79, p. 267)

It might seem that in order to avoid the Protagorean Predicament all we need are plural goals which in Wiggins's terms may be commensurable or incommensurable. So, it might seem that an akratic hedonist can avoid that predicament by going for a piquant pleasure, even though as seen by that person, a languorous pleasure which is also available is more pleasurable. For here, the akratic hedonist would be going for a piquant pleasure and away from a languorous one. And this is not, incoherently, going for and away from the very same thing at the same time.

The reason for requiring that the goals be incommensurable, not merely plural, is this: Suppose that for the hedonist "everything with any relevance to choice is comprehended in the question" of how pleasurable a course of action is. Thus, the hedonist desires (or values) the piquant pleasure and the languorous pleasure simply as instances of pleasure. But then the Protagorean Predicament is not avoided. For even though there are differences between piquant and languorous pleasures, those differences do not figure in the attraction. They are not grounds or reasons for that. Rather, only pleasure—taken generally as we might say—figures in the attraction. Thus, here the hedonist would indeed be at once going for and away from the same thing.

This is to say, then, that avoiding the Protagorean Predicament requires that the goal of what is akratically desired and sought is not the same goal as is forgone. Not only this, the goals must be incommensurable.

Exactly what such commensurability and incommensurability come to will be developed below. But it is, I trust, clear enough that in order to understand Wiggins's claim we must give central importance to what is covered by "everything with any relevance to choice." Socrates, as presented by Wiggins, took those he attacked in the *Protagoras* to hold that hedonism, indeed maximizing hedonism, gives the proper desiderative and evaluative understanding of that everything.[4]

3. COMMENSURABILITY AND COMPARABILITY

Aristotle claims that the elements that make up human good—eudaimonia—are not one: "But of honor, wisdom, and pleasure, just in respect of their goodness, the accounts are distinct and diverse" (*Nicomachean Ethics*, bk. 1, chap. 6, 1097a24). Many have taken him therefore—and in any case, also—to hold that eudaimonia is not one thing. After all, the very next sentence reads, "The good, therefore, is not some common element answering to one Idea." We, however, need not enter into the well-known disputes about the nature of eudaimonia and its relations to its elements.[5] For even if eudaimonia admits of the sort of unity Wiggins denies, the various elements of eudaimonia are irreducible to each other or to eudaimonia. As noted above, they are mutually irreducible. And they are goals and goods—

as we might say, in themselves—even if or when they do not help conduce to eudaimonia: "for if nothing resulted from them, we should still choose each of them" (*Nicomachean Ethics*, bk. 1, chap. 7, 1097b2 ff.).

Wiggins concludes that if eudaimonia is not one thing, it cannot play the role of one goal which, on the Protagorean model, the akratic agent must at once go toward and away from. The Aristotelian agent can, thus, act akratically without falling into the Protagorean Predicament.

Whether or not *coherent* akrasia requires incommensurable values, coherent *akrasia* requires that these values be comparable. For in doing the akratic act, the agent does the lesser over the better act. And to make sense of talk of the lesser and the better, evaluative comparisons must make sense. So, we are told that goals and values can be comparable without being commensurable and that coherent akrasia requires that they be comparable without being commensurable.

4. COMPARABILITY, AFFECTIVITY, AND FRAGMENTATION

If commensurable goals preclude coherent akrasia, how do do incommensurable goals allow for it? To follow Wiggins's account of this, we must introduce the important, if difficult, distinction between the *cognitive* and the *affective*—as we might say as a beginning, between the way something is seen and is felt. Wiggins says that the lesser act may have "some peculiar or distinctive charm [which the better act lacks] that the incontinent man is susceptible to" (Wiggins, 1978-79, p. 269). Charmed by the lesser act, the agent akratically does it.

Wiggins conjoins the distinction between the affective and the cognitive and the distinction between commensurability and comparability to show akrasia coherent.[6] For, he holds, were the acts commensurable, then what the agent found attractive in the lesser act would also be in the greater act. Thus, if the lesser act were attractive, so would be the better act to at least the same degree as the lesser. But if they are only comparable, they can come apart so far as attraction is concerned. If faced with incommensurables, the akratic agent is not in the position of at once going toward and away from the same thing. For, as guaranteed by their being incommensurable, what is attractive about the akratic act is not found in the better act.

As Wiggins says, "Incommensurability was introduced . . . in order to suggest the heterogeneity of the psychic sources of desire satisfaction and evaluation" and these have "a certain liability to fragmentation" (Wiggins, 1978-79, p. 262). In short, what is incommensurable is, as such, liable to fragmentation. Where there is fragmentation, there is room for the affective to diverge from the cognitive. This divergence shows how akrasia can be coherent and possible — how akrasia can avoid the Protagorean Predicament.

How this divergence can show akrasia coherent was seen in Stocker (1979, 1983a). (They also showed that akrasia can be coherent in other ways, too.) Here it is important to repeat what was said there to help make clear what is meant by saying that the lesser act attracts — charms, fascinates, etc. — the akratic agent more than the better act. I do not mean, as those words might suggest, that the agent has so focused on the lesser act or on its attractive feature as no longer even to be aware of the better act or its values. This would explain how an agent goes for the lesser act. But it would do so by invoking ignorance, thereby precluding akrasia. It would do this by saying that the better act and its values have left, or have been forced out of, the akratic agent's cognitive range of attention.

Nor do I mean that, for instance, because of its affective features, that item is now valued more than it was. This, too, is not to talk of the affective range of attention.

By saying that a feature of the lesser act charmed the agent, I here mean something at least partially affective, not entirely cognitive. Here we would be speaking of that feature's having a special luster, of its being more attractive, more compelling, and the like. The better act is still in the agent's cognitive range of attention and is still seen as better. But now the demandingness and the allure of the act which is seen to be better is either not felt at all or not felt with any considerable strength. Either it has entirely left the agent's *affective* range of attention; or if it is still there, it is there less vividly than the lesser act. I call this an affective range of attention to emphasize that its conditions of membership are importantly affective, even if they are also in part cognitive.

This distinction between the affective and the cognitive is hardly neutral in the dispute over whether akrasia is possible, and if possible whether it is coherent. By allowing that the lesser can charm, fascinate, attract us more, we are clearly well on our way to making akratic action coherent. For allowing this is to allow for what is or comes close to being an akrasia of *attention* and of *attraction* — being attracted more by the lesser than by the better.[7]

Those who think all cases of akrasia in general, or akratic action in particular, incoherent are, thus, presented with a problem. They should reject either the possibility of an affective range of attention or the possibility of its independence from the cognitive range of attention. Rejection of either, however, flies in the face of clear phenomenological facts. As argued in various works, I see no plausible way to deny that there is an affective range of attention and that it is importantly independent of the cognitive range of attention.[8]

5. HEDONISM ALLOWS FOR AKRASIA

The argument so far has been that (1) the sort of akrasia depicted in the *Protagoras* is incoherent, since it involves commensurable goals — indeed, only one goal. (2) The sort of akrasia depicted in the *Nicomachean Ethics* is coherent, since it involves incommensurable goods. (3) We can show akrasia coherent if, but only if, there are incommensurable goals. For the fragmentation that is revealed or generated by incommensurability allows one to act akratically without falling into the Protagorean Predicament. This is shown, for instance, by the room made for divergences between cognitive and affective features of acts.

I think that (2) and (3) are correct. But for the very reasons they seem correct, we must reexamine (1). In particular, we must ask whether there is room for the distinctions central to (3) even within a single goal, such as that allowed by hedonism, or within a wholly commensurable group of goals. If even in such contexts there is room for these distinctions and such fragmentation, the distinction between commensurability and comparability, and also the issue of whether there are multiple objects of desire, will be seen not to be relevant to the issue of whether akrasia is possible.

As I think we can easily see, there is room for such distinctions and fragmentation within such contexts, including hedonism. Let us reconsider the *Protagoras* argument which concludes that the combination of hedonism and akrasia is incoherent.

Let us consider an akratic agent — called, henceforth, Akrat — whose attention is restricted to two possible acts, drinking wine laced with pepper and drinking unadulterated wine. Akrat knows or believes that the latter would be more pleasurable. But the former has a certain feature that fascinates Akrat. Let us suppose that this feature is the unusual origin of the former's pleasurableness: wine laced with pepper. It is not that Akrat expects to find drinking the peppered wine more pleasurable than drinking the pure wine. It is, rather, that Akrat is fascinated by pleasure coming from that unusual concoction. The wine qua laced with pepper occupies the center of Akrat's affective range of attention. Thus, Akrat desires it and indeed drinks it, even though Akrat sees that drinking the pure wine would be more pleasurable.

Here it must be kept in mind that we are taking it that the cognitive and the affective can diverge. So we must guard against taking the above story as showing that a monistic hedonism, so to speak, is inadequate to Akrat's cognitively held or appreciated values. As noted above, we are *not* interested in a story in which novelty as such, or novel pleasures, are now among Akrat's goals. Rather, our story has it that Akrat maintains the same sort of hedonism as before. But now, there is an important divergence—an akratic divergence—between what Akrat *sees* as most pleasurable and therefore best and what *attracts* most.

If this sort of story is coherent, then, even within hedonism, fascinated action is possible. Thus, even within hedonism, akratic acts can avoid the Protagorean Predicament—if, that is, such affective considerations show that Aristotelian akratic acts can avoid the Predicament. And if hedonism can escape the Predicament, so can at least many of the more complex sets of commensurable values.

It might be objected that while the above story is, itself, coherent, it is not hedonistically coherent. For it might be held that hedonism would not allow that such features of a pleasure as its origin, as such, can be relevant for hedonistic evaluation or motivation. These and all other features can be relevant if, but only if, they affect or are believed to affect the pleasurableness of the pleasure.

The problem here is to give an indication of what such *pleasurableness* is. We need to know what features of pleasure are *proper* to pleasure. But for two reasons, we need not pursue this difficult issue. First, this is a problem not only for a hedonist, but also for anyone concerned with the nature of pleasure. Second, we can use features that are clearly proper to pleasure to show that hedonism can allow for akrasia without falling into the Protagorean Predicament.

The *intensity* of a pleasure would certainly seem to be a feature proper to pleasure. And indeed, it is central to at least many hedonisms to insist that, other pleasurable features being equal, one pleasure is to be preferred, is better as a pleasure, if it is more intense. Using intensity, we can retell our story to show that hedonism can allow for akrasia without falling into the Protagorean Predicament.

Suppose Akrat is considering which of two pleasurable acts to do. One act is believed more pleasurable—perhaps simply because it has a greater intensity of pleasure. But Akrat has never before come across an act with just the intensity of pleasure that the other act has. Fascinated by just that intensity, Akrat acts akratically and does the less, rather than the more, pleasurable act.

Intensity is clearly not the only dimension of pleasure which is proper to pleasure. There are the dimensions discussed by Bentham. As well, there are all the more purely phenomenological modalities— e.g., piquancy, sharpness, languorousness.

All of these allow for a distinction between pleasures. They allow for different objects of attraction, charm, fascination. And more importantly, they allow for the degree of such *affectively felt* attraction, charm, and fascination to diverge from the degree of *cognitively seen* pleasure. It is possible to be so charmed by the particular piquancy, say, of an act's pleasure that one desires and does that act even though another and even more pleasurable act is seen to be possible. Pain, too, allows for such divergences.

To preclude such divergences, the theory would have to hold that people could be attracted only by *pleasure* and not by any *features* pleasure might have, not even by any *pleasurable features*. On this view pleasure would be like a *metaphysical point* — proof against fragmentation — so far as attractiveness is concerned. While it might well have, and be seen as having, distinct features, it would have no features, other than itself in its entirety, that attracted. There would be no room in any of the aspects of pleasure for attraction to gain a foothold. This is to hold that pleasures attract only in virtue of their being pleasures — not also in virtue of the distinct sorts of pleasures they are. Further, they attract either in proportion to their pleasurableness or simply if they are maximally pleasurable.

Perhaps this is the view Socrates attributes to those under attack in the *Protagoras*. Perhaps they took the claim that the only object of attraction is maximum pleasure to mean that maximum pleasure and only maximum pleasure can attract. Perhaps all *pure* or *true* hedonisms are committed to this view. If so, the position I suggested above, though close in spirit to the hedonism of the *Protagoras*, is not a Socratic hedonism or is not a hedonism at all, but only a quasi-hedonism.

However this last issue is to be settled, we have, I think, constructed a hedonism or quasi-hedonism that parallels, with sufficient closeness, Wiggins's understanding of eudaimonia and its role in akrasia. But then, we now have a hedonism or quasi-hedonism that can allow for coherent akrasia. This should make us wonder whether Wiggins's distinction between commensurability and comparability is relevant for understanding akrasia. For it now looks as if that distinction depends on an implausible account of commensurability or of hedonism or of both.[9]

6. HEDONISTIC INCOMMENSURABILITY RECONSIDERED

To help sustain these last claims, I want now to consider a worry about the parallel between the hedonism developed above and eudaimonia. As noted earlier, perhaps the hedonism in the *Protagoras*, and perhaps all true or pure hedonisms, take maximum pleasure considered indissolubly to be the only object of attraction. But the hedonism or quasi-hedonism used to generate coherent hedonistic akrasia depended on taking particular sorts of pleasures as objects of attraction. So, for example, it was allowed that a languorous pleasure qua languorous pleasure — not simply qua pleasure, which as it happens is languorous — can attract. And it can attract even if another sort of available pleasure, a piquant one, say, is seen as even more pleasurable.

The worry is that I have introduced incommensurable pleasures into my hedonism. For a languorous pleasure qua languorous pleasure is incommensurable with a piquant pleasure qua piquant pleasure. Using Wiggins's terms, there is no evaluative, or other sort of, notion F such that "nothing else besides F-ness counts positively for anything"; there is no F such that "everything with any relevance to choice is comprehended in the question how F a given course of action is, and how F its competitors are." Insofar as the general category of *pleasurableness* counts for both acts, they are commensurable in regard to generalized pleasure. But such pleasurableness is not the only feature that I say counts. Being *languorously* pleasurable counts in favor of one act, while being *piquantly* pleasurable counts in favor of the other act.

The worry is that my argument claiming to show that even with a field of commensurable values such as pleasure there can be coherent akrasia works or seems to work only because it, albeit covertly, relies on incommensurability — between languorous pleasures as such and piquant pleasures as such. Thus, it would be held that my argument sustains, rather than confutes, the claim that the distinction between commensurability and comparability is important for coherent akrasia.

7. PLAUSIBLE HEDONISMS AND INCOMMENSURABILITY

However, this worry is importantly self-refuting. For, as I shall now argue, it depends on a notion of commensurability that cannot be used for understanding akrasia or, indeed, for much of anything.[10] It should be recalled that the reason for allowing for divergences between pleasurableness and attractiveness in my hedonism was to parallel the account of coherent akrasia in regard to eudaimonia, which was said to be a realm of incommensurable, but comparable, goals. In regard to both eudaimonia and my hedonism, the divergence between value and attraction was said to show how akrasia could there be coherent.

For in both cases, what is seen as lesser is nonetheless more attractive and is done because it is more attractive. Such akratic acts have some sort or some degree of attraction the better act lacks. Thus, in such cases of akrasia, the agent does not find everything relevant for choosing the akratic act in the forgone, better act. And in this sense, the acts are incommensurable.

It might seem, therefore, that akratic acts are indeed incommensurable with the forgone act. This is true. But *not* for reasons specific to akrasia. Rather, this is true because of perfectly general features of choice. Even in *non*-akratic action — when, e.g., the better act is chosen over the lesser act — the acts are incommensurable in the presently relevant sense.

Indeed, with one exception, it is a perfectly general feature of choices of any act over another. That exception, irrelevant for our purposes, is a choice of complete indifference. We need not pursue the issue of how to understand the choice involved in choosing one act rather than another where so far as the agent is concerned there are no features relevant for choice distinguishing the acts: a choice made and suitable to be made by a coin toss, say. For akratic acts — at least the ones considered here — are not like this. Rather, they are acts which attract the agent more than the better act. In these akratic acts and in at least many *non*-akratic acts, the choice depends on finding in the chosen act something the forgone act lacks. In this sense, the chosen act and the forgone act must involve incommensurable reasons.

But this sense of incommensurability is extremely weak. It can be satisfied if an act is chosen because it has a given feature to a certain degree where the forgone act has that very feature but to a different degree. And this is so even if the degrees involved are wholly commensurable in a different, but perfectly straightforward, understanding of commensurability — e.g., where the feature is money and the degree is amount of money — and where the chosen act has less of that feature than the forgone act. For all that is needed is that the complex of the feature and its degree attracts more. And, as I think should now be clear, this is and must be a feature of all nonindifferent choices. It is not a feature peculiar to, or explanatory of, akratic choices.

Thus, it can be no objection to my hedonism that it involves such incommensurability. For finding such incommensurability in akrasia is simply finding that the akratic act has some feature relevant for choice that the better act lacks. But, once again, this is a perfectly general feature of choices.

Thus, if the hedonism in my argument involves incommensurability, it does this because differential attraction for all acts — not simply akratic acts — involves such incommensurability. Commensurability, in the presently relevant sense, could be had only if the akratic act has *no* attractive feature relevant for choice that the better act lacks. But if there is absolutely no feature the chosen act has which is not also had by the forgone act, and if it is not a case of indifference, it is difficult to understand how the agent could, or could be said to, choose it.

My conclusion, then, is that commensurability in this sense does not help show how akrasia is possible.[11]

8. ARE THERE ANY COMMENSURABLE GOALS?

It is important to draw out some further implications of this notion of commensurability. Consider the following question that we can take the *Protagoras* to be asking: What can a person who is committed to maximal pleasure find attractive in an act seen not to be — or not seen to be — maximally pleasurable? On the understanding of commensurability that figures in the worry about my argument, that question can be appropriately answered by citing some feature of the akratic act, such as its being pleasurable, albeit nonmaximally so. But this is no answer to what I take the question to be asking: How could a maximizing hedonist, a person committed to maximal pleasure, be sufficiently attracted by what is seen to be nonmaximally pleasurable to go for that instead of what is seen as maximally pleasurable?

To be sure, these questions can come very close to each other — e.g., if hedonism is understood as concerned with maximum pleasure taken indissolubly. If one goes for something other than maximum pleasure, one is not then and there such a hedonist. And if, contrary to what was thought, one is not such a hedonist and does not have maximum pleasure as one's goal, it is important to ask what the goal of one's action is. This is even more to the point if such hedonism is thought of as the only viable account of motivation.

I am here not concerned to discuss whether Socrates did have that view of hedonism — or whether he held a similar view about seeking other values or valuable things. (Below, I offer some reasons which might have inclined him to hold such a view or which might incline us to attribute such a view to him.) If he did have such a view, then what I suggested was implausible as an answer to the question about akrasia — telling *what* was sought rather than *how* it could be sought — is at least close to an answer to his question. If so, the considerations which I took to show that that was an implausible answer now show that such a theory of motivation is implausible precisely because it holds that goals are metaphysical points, not subject to fragmentation.

But goals need not be understood as such metaphysical points. They present an array — often a disturbing array — of different features. It is in regard to goals so understood that at least many problems of akrasia arise, including the Protagorean Predicament or similar worries about coherence.

9. VALUE FINALITY

If I am right that the present distinction between commensurability and comparability is unimportant for understanding akrasia, it must be explained what was going on in the *Protagoras* argument. Did Socrates think—mistakenly, as we now see—that issues of commensurability and incommensurability settled the matter? Or was something else in play?

The dialogue does not provide an answer to this. Whether other dialogues do is not a question I shall canvass here. Rather, what I shall do to conclude this paper is draw attention to two features of the *Protagoras* argument that can at once explain why Socrates might well have taken the argument to be conclusive and also why it might be thought that that argument turns on issues of commensurability. These features are what I shall call *value finality* and *value maximization*.

Value finality is—roughly, but adequately for our purposes—the view that only what gives good reasons for acting can attract. Put briefly, only the good can attract. So, I can be attracted to this pleasure only if I believe that this pleasure will conduce to what is good or is itself an instance of what is good. (Here, of course, "good" is understood as what the agent believes good.) Value finality is, thus, a claim about what people find as reasons for acting. It is, in short, a descriptive claim about acting or a descriptive, or perhaps better a conceptual, claim about good reasons.

It was in order not to assume *value* finality that akrasia was described in terms of doing an act because it had feature F even though it had less than maximal F. This allows, but does not require, that F is goodness or some other value. It is important to allow for akrasia which is not cast explicitly in terms of value, and which may well not involve value. "How can a maximizing hedonist go for a less than maximally pleasant act?" poses many, even if not all, the same problems and questions as "How can a person not go for what is best?"

The relations between value finality and problems with akrasia may seem direct, but they are not. To be sure, there is this direct connection: The agent does not believe that the akratic act is the best available act; and thus cannot, in doing that act, be acting in order to do what is best. So, for example, the akratic evaluative hedonist cannot think that going for the peppered wine is as pleasurable or as good as going for the pure wine would be.

The lack of direct connection can now be seen: if value finality is to be used to show akrasia incoherent, it must be supplemented with claims about commensurability and maximization. If it were shown that drinking the pure wine would achieve the very same good as would drinking the peppered wine and some more relevant good in addition, then, on the assumption of value finality, it would be shown that drinking the latter and forgoing the former is incoherent. But if the goals involved are incommensurable, this cannot be shown. Further, unless it is incoherent to go for less than maximal obtainable value, value finality allows for coherent akrasia.

As argued in Stocker (1979, 1983a), value finality is not acceptable as part of a plausible and realistic theory of motivation. Often enough, what we find attractive does not stand to our values the way descriptive value finality claims.

Before turning to maximization, it is important to point to a less objectionable use of value finality — a regulative use, rather than either of the descriptive ones. The divergence between values and sources of attraction can, and often enough does, point to a moral defect or problem.[12] Here we might note the probative force of asking someone who claims to value F, and F maximized, e.g., a maximizing hedonist, "How could you, who claim to value maximal pleasure, knowingly go for this lesser pleasure?" So, too, consider the probative force of "How could you not live up to your values? How could you do what you think less than maximally good?" Both questions can function as a reproof and as an invitation for the agent to rethink and to choose differently.

10. VALUE MAXIMIZATION

Let us now turn to maximization, first maximization in general and then value maximization. Many, I think, endorse some such schema as the following: If, in order to achieve F, agent B does act c, rather than d, then B must believe c to conduce to more F than d does. With little ado, this can be turned into a claim about maximization: If B does act c in order to get F, B must believe c to conduce to the most F available. (For our purposes it is irrelevant whether it is c alone or c in conjunction with other acts that B thinks will maximize F. So, too, it is irrelevant whether these claims are put forward because it is held that if, to achieve F, B does c rather than d, then B must believe that c conduces more to F than does d.)

If some such maximization principle is correct, then whenever a person does an act which is seen or felt to conduce to less F than another act, F cannot be the feature which constitutes the person's reason for acting. The person cannot there be acting in order to maximize F or acting because F is the most attractive feature. Correlatively, there must be some other feature — perhaps simply the conjunction of F and something else — that is such a feature. Since this feature is a different feature from F, these features are incommensurable.

Principles asserting the maximization of *value* — e.g., maximization plus value finality — have been used in arguments to show that akrasia is impossible. On such an assumption, whatever feature the agent acts to get must be believed by the agent to be best. Thus, what looks like acting for a lesser amount of a value is really acting for a greater amount of *another* value. Presumably the claim is also that the value of the "akratic" act is incommensurable with the value of the other act relative to which it is less good.

If this argument is correct, then, maximization requires incommensurability for akrasia — if, indeed, it allows for akrasia. This is one strand of my argument about the connections between maximization and commensurability.

The other strand is that if we accept maximization, we shall have problems in seeing how akrasia is possible even in regard to comparable but incommensurable values and attractions. For, if the present claim about maximization holds, what is seen as better must attract more. The better must be chosen over the lesser.

In regard to Wiggins's argument, it is particularly to the point that Aristotelian agents are committed to seeking and being most attracted by maximum eudaimonia. This in no way requires that eudaimonia is seen or felt as one value, or that eudaimonic elements are seen or felt as commensurable. Rather, all that is required is that these elements be comparable in regard to their contribution or otherwise to eudaimonia and that the agent be committed to seeking the element that will most conduce to eudaimonia. Thus, given a suitable maximization requirement, it is difficult to see how a lesser eudaimonic element can be sought by an Aristotelian agent. It is as difficult to see this as it is to see how a lesser pleasure can be sought by a Protagorean maximizing hedonist.

My argument has not been that it is impossible to maintain a principle of maximization. I have, rather, been concerned to point out the extremely high cost of maintaining this principle. For our purposes, we can simply remind ourselves of the difficulties it puts in the way of understanding akrasia and of understanding commensurability. These, I think, are sufficient to warrant giving it up.

To advocate giving up maximization is not, we might note, to advocate slackness or immorality, to advocate a policy of "second best" — if even that — or of "falling short." Not to go for the maximum of what one goes for, e.g., not to do what one thinks best, need involve none of these moral failings.[13] Perhaps we always *may* do what is best, but it is not true that we always *must* do what is best. So, I may think that although I could make my life or a portion of it better, it is good enough. As I might say, it is not worth the effort to make it better. Some take this to suggest that I think that were the supposedly better state discounted by the effort, the resultant would actually be no better than what I now have. But this is mistaken. Even though the resultant would be better, the effort can still not be worth it. If my life is good enough, it would not be immoral or irrational to leave things as they are and not make the effort and gain what on balance is a benefit.

But, although it is false that morally we always must—on pain of irrationality or immorality—do what is or what we think best, my present argument is not so much with that claim. Rather, it is with the descriptive claim that we always do try to maximize what we go for. And it is also with the conceptual claim that for an act to be seen as coherent—i.e., for something to be counted as an act—it must be seen as aiming at the maximization of some goal. These claims are both false and pernicious. To mention only what has been discussed here, they make understanding akrasia and commensurability impossible. They have no place in any adequate moral psychology.

To argue for their exclusion—or rather, since one or both are so widely accepted, their extirpation—from moral psychologies, it is useful to point to the troubles they, singly and jointly, engender. But it may also be necessary to try to understand and defuse their appeal. One source of this appeal is the great simplicity they allow. Such simplicity is obvious enough—and overcoming it requires overcoming the appeal for simplicity, which is no easy matter.

Another source of this appeal is the seeming neutrality—or perhaps it should be called the seeming transparency—of the descriptive and also the conceptual maximizing claims. This neutrality or transparency comes out in a natural interpretation of Wiggins's gloss on the *Protagoras* argument, especially of "if nothing else besides F-ness counts positively for anything, there is nothing to commend any other course of action over the one that is most." This certainly seems to say that simply by caring for F—i.e., desiring and valuing F—one cares more for more F than less F.

So, for example, many hold that to be a hedonist is really to be a maximizing hedonist. Even more generally, many hold that the "logic" of caring for F involves caring more for more F and most for most F. Claims of such maximization, it would be said, add nothing to the claims about the caring. They are already implicit in them.

But, on the contrary, the transition from caring for F to caring more for more F is problematic. Such a transition is not necessary. Indeed, it can be unjustified. Where it is justified, that it is justified must be shown. Maximization, then, is neither neutral nor transparent.

As noted earlier, there is nothing incoherent about a person caring only that there be some F, where as that person sees or feels, additional F would not be an improvement. So, too, there is nothing incoherent about a person caring for some F, but also caring that there not be more than a certain amount of F. This person could even be repelled by more F than a given amount.

Nonetheless, in their different ways, these two sorts of people may evaluate things by how F they are, and by nothing but how F they are. So, too, F may be the only source of attraction for them.

Even where caring for F involves caring more for more F and most for most F, there are complexities. Some maximizers see value in, and feel attraction by, what is F even if it is less than maximally F. But other maximizers see value in, or are attracted by, only maximal F taken indissolubly. They find nothing of value or attractive in what is less than maximally F.

It might, of course, be thought misleading to say that these are all cases of valuing F and nothing but F. In all of these cases, it might be denied that *just* F is cared for. Someone who wants some F but is indifferent whether there is more or less F might be said to care for *some* F. Someone who wants some F but finds more than a certain amount of F repellent might be said to care for *a moderate amount* of F. Someone who cares about only maximal F taken indissolubly might be said to care for *maximal* F.

Such modifications or interpretations of F and what the agent finds attractive in it may sometimes be attributed to that person's particular psychology. But sometimes they are due to the nature and role of F. A philosopher who wants to know about Kant is not committed thereby to welcome just one insignificant fact or to attend a five-year, full-time course on every known fact about Kant.

This is to say that at least often we can explain why an agent who cares or seems to care for F does not care more for more F or does not care at all for less F than a given amount. Indeed, it might be urged that we see a need to explain such cases. This, it might be further urged, is in contrast to the natural cases, which need no explanation, where the person who cares for F cares more for more F and cares at least somewhat for less F.

Perhaps this is the natural, possibly even the correct, way to think of *some* goals, attractions, and values — perhaps even some *basic* or *important* ones. But, we require distinctions and arguments to show which goals, attractions, and values are like this.

Further — and this is my main and concluding point — we have to realize that in adopting or discovering whatever maximization principles we do adopt or discover, they are substantial principles. We are not engaged in a perfectly neutral or transparent, and universally acceptable, activity — even if we are there justified in that activity.

In all cases, it must be made clear what sort of maximization is involved and why it is thought proper that it should be involved. Even where some form of maximization holds, it is a weighty and substantial doctrine that makes a significant impact. It must be noted, investigated, and treated with all care—which we can hardly do if it is thought of as neutral or worse if, because of its seeming transparency, it remains unnoticed.

11. CONCLUSION

Many difficult questions remain about identity and individuation conditions for objects of desire. Indeed, we still have to see how they are individuated. What we have seen is one important way they are not to be individuated. On the way to this, we also saw that coherent akrasia does not require multiple objects of desire. As well, we also reached some significant results about hedonism and maximization. All these—and, of course, far more—are needed for an adequate understanding of akrasia or desire.[14]

NOTES

1. Wiggins (1978-79), p. 267. See too, Burnyeat (1980), p. 87. Wiggins and Burnyeat argue against that description of akrasia and for the possibility of akratic acts having reasons.

2. See, among others, Burnyeat (1980), Davidson (1969), and Nussbaum (1984). Part of my argument that coherent akrasia does not require plural values was given in Stocker (1984). Another argument that coherent akrasia does not require plural values is given by Jackson (1984).

3. My argument, it should be noted, is directed against only this one argument in Wiggins's paper. It is not directed against the separable, even if not separated, argument that at least many moral psychologies deny the possibility of akrasia because of oversimple views of moral psychology. Once the real complexity of moral psychology is recognized, we can see any number of ways a person can act akratically without falling into the Protagorean Predicament. Complementary arguments are given in Rorty (1980, 1983) and in Stocker (1979, 1983a).

4. Socrates does not attack this view itself but rather the conjunction of it and the claim that akrasia is possible. See Santas (1966).

5. See Ackrill (1974), Hardie (1965), and Wiggins (1978-79), sec. 6.

6. In Stocker (1984), the distinction between the affective and the cognitive, as well as the distinction between guiding concerns and goals—developed in Stocker (1981)—was used to explain how akrasia is possible. In parts of Stocker (1984) not incorporated in this present work, the latter distinction was used to account for the distinction between commensurability and comparability. It now seems to me that these last two distinctions have little, if anything, to do with each other in regard to akrasia.

7. On this and other varieties of akrasia, see Rorty (1980, 1983).

8. See Stocker (1979, 1981, 1983a, 1984).

9. The above sections revise Stocker (1984).

10. Although I shall not try to show this, these arguments also bear, decisively I think, against the claim of Charles Taylor (1977) and others that hedonism allows only for shallow, and not also deep, evaluation.

11. My thanks are owed to Richard Sorabji for discussing this, and much else in this work, with me.

12. This is discussed in Stocker (1976, 1979, 1981, 1983a, 1983b).

13. For instance, see Wolf (1982).

14. My thanks are owed to Graeme Marshall for many discussions of the issues in this paper. My thanks are also owed to Graham Nerlich, Peter Railton, and the Philosophy Departments of the University of Melbourne and the Australian National University for their comments on drafts of this work.

Emotions and Wants

C. C. W. Taylor

Abstract. This paper explores the various ways in which emotions involve desires. Emotions are classified as (1) appetitive, involving desires for a state of affairs not realized, and (2) possessive, where the emotion is a reaction to the satisfaction of a desire. Further, in some emotions the element of desire is the desire to dwell on an object in thought. The existence of these emotions, which are forms of enjoyment, suggests that physiological changes, etc., are not necessary features of emotion.

A common feature of much discussion of the emotions at different periods of philosophy has been the insistence that emotion is closely bound up with desire. This association goes back at least as far as Aristotle, whose treatment of emotion in the *Nicomachean Ethics* shows the intimacy of the connection between that concept and that of desire. Emotions such as fear, anger, envy, and hatred are listed (1105b21-b23) under the heading of *pathē*, i.e., short-term states of the *appetitive* soul (1102b30-1103a3), and the first item on the list is *epithumia*, desire. Excellence of character is determined by actions and *pathē* (1109b30). Hence, emotions are a subject of central interest to ethical enquiry insofar as they are motivational states, a characterization which links them intimately with desire, since in Aristotle's view motivation is impossible without desire (*De Anima*, 433a21-a29).

This Aristotelian conception of emotion as involving desire has remained influential in medieval, postmedieval, and modern philosophy. Thus we find Aquinas (*Summa Theologica*, I-II, 22, 3) placing the emotions in the functioning of the sensory appetite and citing with approval the definition of St. John of Damascus: "Emotion [*passio*] is the movement of the sensory appetitive faculty caused by the imagination of good or evil." Hobbes (*Leviathan*, pt. 1, chap. 6) classifies the various emotions as elaborations of the basic impulses to pursue some objects (appetite, desire) and to shun others (aversion). Spinoza classifies them as modifications of the basic impulses of desire, pleasure, and pain (*Ethics*, pt. 3, prop. 10n; prop. 57), while apparently counting the latter two as themselves forms of desire (prop. 9n; prop. 57). For Aquinas and Hobbes, then, and perhaps also for Spinoza, emotions are forms of desire; for Descartes, on the other hand, they are primarily causes of desire. He writes (*Passions of the Soul*, pt. 1, art. 40):

> The principal effect of all the passions in men is that they incite and dispose their soul to desire those things for which they prepare their body, so that the feeling of fear incites it to desire to fly, that of courage to desire to fight, and so on. (Descartes, 1977b [1649])

Contemporary writers, too, while also differing from one another in detail, mostly agree in emphasizing the central place of desire in an account of the emotions.[1] Typical expressions are the following quotations from Kenny and Lyons:

> Desire in the sense of wanting. . . is hardly an emotion: nevertheless, an account of it is essential to any treatment of the emotions. For the connection between emotions and behavior is made by desire: one emotion differs from another because of the different sort of things it makes one want to do. Fear involves wanting to avoid or avert what is feared; anger is connected with the desire to punish or take vengeance on its object. Love, of one kind, is linked with the desire to fondle and caress the loved one, and shame with the desire to conceal whatever it is that makes one ashamed. (Kenny, 1963, p. 100)

And:

> Most, though not all, emotions contain desires as part of their occurrent states, and. . . with some emotions, this appetitive aspect is part of their very concept. It is this aspect which explains how emotions can be cited as motives, and how behavior can reveal the nature of emotions, for the desires generated by the evaluative aspects of emotions are the causes of the behavior associated with emotion. (Lyons 1980, p. 209)

In this paper I shall assume the truth of this consensus. Taking it as my starting point I shall seek to make progress by examining in somewhat greater detail than has hitherto been attempted the various ways in which reference to desire enters into our talk of the emotions. My aim will be to consider whether any general account of the relation between the two concepts is possible, or whether we must settle for a number of different relations, each applying to a specific range of emotions.

The most obvious way in which desire enters into descriptions of the emotions is the fact that such paradigm cases as fear, joy, and anger characteristically involve the desire to act from or out of the emotion. (See the quotation from Kenny above.) Acting from or out of an emotion covers two sorts of activity, which shade into one another but which provide sufficiently distinct cases to be worth separating from each other. These are, first, activity which is directed toward a goal the desire for which is (at least typically, and perhaps necessarily) part of the emotion, and, second, activity which is not (at least, not primarily) goal-directed, but primarily expressive of the emotion. A clear example of the first kind is fleeing from some danger out of fear, and of the second, jumping for joy. A case where the two shade into one another is shouting abuse at someone out of anger, which satisfies the desires both to give expression to one's anger and to try to hurt the person with whom one is angry. Some brief discussion of these kinds of activity is appropriate.

Let us consider the second kind first. The qualification "primarily" is necessary because some expressive behavior may itself be goal-directed. The most obvious cases such as jumping for joy and rolling on the floor in grief have indeed no goal, i.e., they are not cases of trying to do something. But in some cases one can express or evince an emotion by trying to do something, which may even be something quite difficult; in C. P. Snow's novel *The New Men* a character expresses his delight at winning some academic success by trying time and again to throw an india rubber eraser up onto a picture rail. It might be suggested that such behavior cannot properly be termed "expressive," since it lacks the essential characteristic of spontaneity. But that criticism is unfounded; such behavior is indeed less purely instinctive than the more obvious cases, but it may be nonetheless spontaneous, in that the explanation of the eraser-throwing might be simply that the agent was so delighted that he felt he had to do just that. I call such goal-directed behavior primarily expressive on the ground that the only, or at least the main, point of trying to attain that particular goal is just that trying to attain that goal is what one is impelled by one's emotion to do.

With regard to the first kind of activity, it will hardly be disputed that at least some emotions characteristically involve the desire to act in such a way as to attain a goal. A problem which presents itself is whether this involvement is necessary rather than merely character-istic, but I doubt if any clear answer to that question is possible. Anger might seem to be a particularly clear case. Typically, the angry person believes that he or someone or something whose interests he cares about has been injured, slighted, frustrated, or otherwise badly treated by another person or persons, and he desires in some measure to retaliate against that person or persons.[2] It might be claimed that every case of anger necessarily involves some form of that desire, but consideration of various cases, none of them particularly fanciful, gives grounds for doubt.

Consider: (1) anger with or at an inanimate object (typically a tool or machine which does not work); (2) anger at some act of injustice or other wickedness in the remote past, e.g., the persecution of the Albigensians; (3) anger at oneself for some failure; (4) anger at some occurrence for which no one is even thought responsible, e.g., baffled fury when bad weather spoils a long-awaited outing. These cases diverge in various ways from the simple model. In the first case, apart from the extreme instance when one is driven to make a physical assault on the recalcitrant object, one does not actually want to damage it, but one acts as if one did, going through a kind of ritual of treating it as if it were an agent opposing its will to one's own (commonly swearing at it), and acting toward it in ways which would be damaging or hurtful if it were an agent. In the second case I am certainly angry at the persecution, but it does not make sense to talk of wanting to retaliate against *that*. If I am angry at the persecution it follows that I must be angry with or at the persecutors, but while it makes sense to describe me as wanting to retaliate against *them*, I cannot in fact want to do so in a situation where I am aware that nothing I might do could conceivably hurt them. At best I might wish that I were in a position to hurt them. It seems possible, however, that I merely wish that they might suffer, or might have suffered, for what they did, without having any desire, even a mere wish, that *I* should cause, or should have caused, them to suffer. Being angry with oneself does not imply any real desire to punish oneself, though once again one may go through a performance as of self-castigation, as in the case of being angry with a tool. In the case of anger at the weather, not only is one not in fact able to take it out on the weather, but also one cannot want to or even wish to, since there is nothing one can even imagine doing which could count as taking it out on the weather. One might perhaps wish that there was something that one could do to get one's own back on that bloody weather, but that hardly seems necessary. What does seem necessary is that one should have some impulse to regard the weather as somehow personally motivated toward spoiling one's enjoyment or otherwise doing one down, and that one should feel aggrieved in consequence.

It is clear from these examples that it is impossible to maintain a strong version of the necessity thesis, viz., that on every occasion when someone is angry that person has the desire to retaliate against the agent whom he believes to have injured him (or persons or things he cares about). For, as we have seen, the angry person need not believe that any agent has injured him or persons or things he cares about, and even when he does believe that he need not desire to retaliate. What is less clear is whether some weaker version of that thesis can be established, e.g., that the cases where that desire is present are necessarily central, such that all other cases have to be understood as departures from them. All the above cases were indeed described on the model of a basic situation where one agent is angry with another and wants him to suffer for what he has done; it therefore seems plausible, failing counterarguments, that that may be a conceptually central case.

But even there, it is problematic how far wanting someone to suffer implies wanting to bring it about that that person suffers. It is certainly possible to want someone to suffer some harm without wanting to bring that about, even in a case where one has the opportunity; one might have so strong a natural revulsion to violence as to be incapable of wanting to harm someone or have him harmed by someone else, coupled with sufficient malice to welcome his falling victim to some misfortune such as a painful disease. That seems an odd case, since it involves an unusual degree of disassociation between desire for an end and acceptance of means readily available to bring that end about, but the oddity does not amount to conceptual incoherence. Here our original question arises again, viz., is this merely an unusual form of anger, or is it necessarily a deviant form? As I do not know how to answer that question I shall not pursue it, but shall turn instead to some general consideration of this peculiar kind of desire, viz., the desire that some state of affairs should obtain, without any desire to act in such a way as to bring it about.

At first sight, examples of this kind of desire seem plentiful, being apparently provided by those emotions which are concerned with an unwelcome state which one knows to be incapable of change for the better. Examples are grief and shame: in the former case one longs for something irrevocably lost, typically the presence of a dead person, and in the latter one longs for it to be the case that one had not committed the shameful act, but in neither case is one impelled by the emotion to do anything with a view to bringing the desired state about. Grief may rather produce a condition of total apathy, in which one has no impulse to do anything, and where one is moved to do something by grief or shame the behavior will more normally be of the expressive than the goal-directed sort. The reason is obvious, that the desired state is known to be altogether beyond the reach of the person who has the emotion, not merely in the particular case, but always in cases of this kind. Thus though a frightened man may attempt evasive action in a case where he knows such action to be useless, nevertheless there is a characteristic pattern of evasive action in frightening situations because such action has some chance of success in some cases. But since it is known that nothing could ever bring someone back from the dead or undo the past we find that grief and shame do not exhibit any analogous pattern of goal-directed behavior. It is, however, misleading to describe such cases in general as involving a desire that some state of affairs should obtain, without *any* desire to act in such a way as to bring that state about. For since the desired state is known to be impossible of attainment, the desire for that state must be a wish that it obtained, not a want that it should.[3]

This fits ordinary usage: one wishes that one's father had not died, or that one had not made such a fool of oneself, but one cannot be said to want those things. Now to the extent that one desires the end, viz., that of wishing that it were realized, one will normally desire to act in such a way as to realize it, in that one will naturally, though not necessarily, wish that one could act in that way. (The qualification "normally . . . though not necessarily" is required to allow for the possibility of disassociation between desire for the end and desire for the means noted in connection with the example of the medieval persecutors. I might wish that they had been roasted over a slow fire without wishing that I had been able to lend a hand.) "If only I could undo what I have done" is as natural an expression of shame as "If only I had not done that," while "I should do anything to bring him back" is a characteristic expression of grief. In the cases of grief and shame, then, we find that the desire to act from or out of the emotion, where it exists at all, is secondary, the primary desire being the wish that an unwelcome situation did not obtain. In contrast to the forward-looking desire to act (in one way or another) this type of primary desire is backward-looking. Anger, too, as we saw from our example, may involve mere wishes instead of full-blooded wants; the major difference is that whereas that is best understood as a peripheral case of anger, wishing rather than wanting is typical of grief and shame.

This requires us to abandon our original and natural assumption that wanting figures in emotions primarily in the form of a desire to act from the emotion, either toward a goal or in an expressive manner. Our examples have revealed a range of emotions where the desire to act from the emotion, if present at all, is secondary to a backward-looking desire which is not itself a desire to act. We might, then, be tempted by a simple classification of emotions into those where the primary desire is forward-looking and those where it is backward-looking. But that leaves too many loose ends. In the range of emotions typified by pride (in some achievement) the forward-looking desire for expressive behavior seems, as in the cases of grief and shame, to be secondary to a backward-looking attitude; but while in grief and shame that attitude is itself a desire, in pride and its relatives the attitude is rather consciousness of the satisfaction of a previous desire.

And while that previous desire was itself forward-looking, it need not have been a desire to act, but may just have been the desire that some state of affairs should obtain.

These complications, which elude capture by a simple classification in terms of forward- and backward-looking desires, are, I believe, dealt with by another classification in terms of desires, itself suggested by the examples we have considered, as follows. Some emotions involve the thought of some state as desired but not, or not yet, attained, and hence of that state as something to be attained by action, either actually or, as it were, *per impossibile*. Where the desired state is of a kind that might sometimes be achieved by action, we find a characteristic pattern of such action and at least the impulse to undertake it. Where, on the other hand, the desired state could not conceivably be attained by any action, we find no pattern of activity and consequently no impulse to undertake any, but at most a mere wish that one could do something to bring about the desired state.

Contrasted with these are emotions where a desired state is thought of as attained; the most obvious examples are the various kinds of joy, such as elation. Here, since that state is conceived of as already attained, there is no room for activity directed toward it as a goal, nor for the wish that such activity might be undertaken. Our basic distinction, then, is between what we may call appetitive emotions on the one hand and possessive emotions on the other, the former being subdivided into forward-looking "wanting" emotions with their characteristic patterns of goal-directed behavior and backward-looking "wishing" emotions where such patterns are lacking. The desire to indulge in purely expressive behavior is common to both basic kinds of emotion, being characteristic of possessive emotions and "wishing" appetitive emotions, but occurring also in cases of "wanting" appetitive emotions, especially in circumstances where satisfaction of the primary want is known to be impossible.

This provisional classification presents some of the usual borderline problems. Thus tenderness has some of the features of an appetitive and some of a possessive emotion. One aspect of tenderness is joy in the physical proximity of a beloved person, as instanced by a mother's tender feelings as she peeps round the nursery door at her sleeping baby. Thus far it seems to be possessive, but it may also manifest itself in the desire to kiss, caress, etc., which can reach the intensity of a craving if satisfaction is delayed; to that extent it seems rather appetitive. The explanation is perhaps that the desired state is possession of the beloved person, and that what constitutes possession may vary from time to time, even over very short intervals. At one time being near the beloved, or even being able to think of the beloved as near, is enough; at others physical contact is necessary. I cite this merely as an example, and turn now to consider whether there are emotions which involve no element of desire at all. Since both appetitive and possessive emotions are defined by reference to a desired state of affairs, it will be clear that any emotions involving no element of desire fall outside our classification altogether.

What we are looking for are examples of emotions where (1) one does not want to do anything expressive of the emotion, (2) one does not, in virtue of one's experiencing the emotion, want any state of affairs other than a state of one's own behavior to obtain, and (3) ascription of the emotion to a subject does not require the ascription of some antecedent desire to that subject. We have seen that the joy range of emotions satisfies requirement 2: being pleased, delighted, etc., that the Raiders have won the Superbowl does not require one to want anything other than a state of one's own behavior to be the case; in particular, one cannot be said to want or wish them to have won it. Requirements 1 and 3 are not, however, satisfied. One's present elation has to be understood as resulting from an antecedent desire that the Raiders should win the Superbowl (requirement 3); further, we saw that elation and similar reactions involve the desire for expressive behavior (requirement 1). There are, however, other attitudes in the joy range which are less excitable, being rather kinds of contentment. Here there may be no urge to do anything expressive of the emotion, no requirement of an antecedent desire and, prima facie, no desire for any state of affairs not a state of one's own behavior to obtain. Here, if anywhere, is where we should look for emotions without desires.

An objection might be made straight off to counting any kind of contentment as an emotion, on the ground that "emotion" implies an element of disturbance or excitement lacking from contentment;[4] the latter should be classed rather with such unemotional attitudes as feeling fit or feeling lethargic. I am not able to settle that question by offering any general account of what an emotion is; I shall, however, produce some cases which strike me as clear cases of emotion where the element of disturbance is minimal, if present at all, and where the dominant attitude is one of contentment, calm, and peace. Consider for instance the following:

> As we listened (say to the slow movement of Bach's Double Violin Concerto) I was filled with a sense of joy and serenity such as I had never experienced. All desire and longing were stilled, and I felt that I had an inkling of the happiness that the blessed are said to enjoy in Heaven. When the music stopped, neither of us spoke or moved for some moments. Then we smiled quietly to one another, each aware of what it had meant to the other.

That certainly strikes me as a description of a shared emotional experience, and was intended by me to convey just that impression.

Had I added a description of our being moved to tears, then no one, I believe, would hesitate over counting it as such. Yet I find it hard to believe that the absence of tears or even of the impulse to weep is sufficient to disqualify the case as described from counting as an instance of emotion. In either case the reaction to the music, as manifested in the thoughts which it arouses, is identical; tears might merely indicate a level of response more superficial than the profound serenity which I have tried to convey. I shall take it, then, that I have succeeded in depicting an emotion. If that is so, it is, prima facie, one which does not require (1) that one wants to do anything expressive of the emotion, (2) that one wants anything else (i.e., wants the obtaining of any state of affairs not a state of one's behavior), or (3) that one should antecedently have wanted to be the case anything which was not then the case.

A possible objection is that there is indeed something expressive of the emotion which one wants to do, viz., sit still and be quiet; there is no ground, other than a prejudice in favor of movement, for refusal to describe sitting perfectly still as expressive behavior. Now it is true that in the imagined case I am still because I am so full of joy, and that my stillness expresses my joy, but it is not clear that I want to be still. Rather, it may be that I am so full of joy that I have simply no thought of doing anything, and hence remain perfectly still. This seems parallel to being apathetic from grief; a bereaved person is correctly described, not as wanting to sit in a chair all day from grief, but as being so grief-stricken that she does not want to do anything at all. It might be urged that we ought rather to say that she is so grief-stricken that she does not want to do anything *else*, which implies that she does want to sit in the chair. That, however, counts as a case of wanting only on the assumption that whenever one ϕs voluntarily one wants to ϕ; but that assumption is shown to be false by cases of apathy such as we are now considering. A totally apathetic person may ϕ voluntarily, in that nothing compels him to ϕ, without wanting to ϕ, since there is literally nothing which he wants to do; he ϕs, not because he wants to ϕ, but because, given the situation he is in, ϕing (or continuing to ϕ) is something he can do without a reason, whereas he would have to have some positive reason to do something else, and ex hypothesi he sees no reason for doing anything.

Stillness from joy is like apathetic grief to this extent, that in either case the effect of the emotion is to make any activity seem pointless, or even to drive all thought of activity out of one's head. Both emotions are characterized by "inwardness"; while anger, elation, etc., are "outgoing," in that they demand outward expression, whose inhibition is itself a source of frustration, the essence of the kinds of joy and grief which I have been discussing is that the person experiencing them is turned in on his or her own thoughts and feelings to the exclusion of any interest in outward activity. The natural manifestation of these emotions is therefore an inner dwelling on certain thoughts and experiences, whose only outward sign is passivity.

Since in joy one dwells on the experience as rewarding, one is likely to feel frustration, not at inhibition of the impulse to expressive behavior, since there is none to be inhibited, but at any distraction from total absorption in the experience itself. Even here, then, we have to conclude that there is an element of desire, in that one wants to dwell on the source of one's joy and is therefore disposed to feel frustration at distraction from dwelling on it. The "indwelling" of apathetic grief lacks those features, since the source of grief is dwelt on as something unpleasant, and distraction is therefore welcomed (though we are familiar with the phenomenon of grief itself becoming a pleasure); here, however, the element of desire is supplied by the wish that the beloved person had not died.

This account applies to some other emotions. Thus nostalgia consists in dwelling with a kind of pleasurable sadness on agreeable memories, though presumably in so far as it contains an element of regret that happy days are no more it also involves the wish that they might be again. Awe is a matter of having one's attention held by some majestic object, such as a landscape or work of art, in a way which combines pleasure, fear, and reverence (or, in Berkeley's vivid phrase *[Second Dialogue]*, "a pleasing horror"). As in the case of serene joy, though there need be nothing which one wants to do to express one's awe, one wants to dwell on the object of one's awe. An interesting case is that of being "moved" by something, which from the etymology one might expect to be a very paradigm of emotion. This emotion is characteristically felt in pathetic or solemn contexts; for instance, one might be moved by the sight of a child's grave, by an account of unavailing heroism, or by a solemn artistic performance. Some cases are close to pity and regret (see below), which involve at least the wish that someone had not suffered some misfortune, but that will not cover all cases of being moved by doings and sufferings, and is obviously inappropriate to many of the artistic examples. It is tempting to say that in every case one wants to indulge in some expressive behavior, generally weeping, but that suggestion is no more plausible for these cases than for the case of calm joy (see above). Here, as in that case, what seems central is the concentration of attention on an object seen as in some way worth concentrating on, in that it provides an enriching or ennobling or merely pleasurable experience. Being moved is therefore very close to that kind of calm joy, and in some cases, such as one's response to a piece of solemn music, it would appear to be indifferent whether one designated the emotion by one term or the other.

I conclude, then, that rather than having discovered a class of emotions which contain no element of desire, and therefore fall outside our provisional classification of emotions into appetitive and possessive, we have rather extended the range of possessive emotions. Those emotions which looked as if they might contain no desire turn out on examination to contain the desire to possess a valued object, in the sense of dwelling on it in thought. That desire need not be an antecedent desire, since I may, for instance, be moved by something which I had in no way anticipated; nor is it the desire for anything further to be attained via the enjoyment of the desired object. Rather, it is the sort of desire which is constitutive of enjoyment itself, viz., the desire to have the thing enjoyed for the appropriate time, and to be free of distraction from it.[5]

This contrasts with attitudes such as elation, which we saw to imply an antecedent desire for the occurrence which is the object of the emotion. The ground for the distinction is, I think, this. Attitudes such as elation have to be grounded in reasons, which in turn are constituted by beliefs and desires. Thus if I am elated that an event of some kind has occurred, I must have wanted the occurrence of an event of that kind either for its own sake or for the sake of some further end which that occurrence promotes. There are no reasons for enjoyment in the same way, though there are reasons in the senses *(a)* of specific features of the thing enjoyed and *(b)* of causal explanations of one's enjoyment. Some elation-type reactions are themselves sorts of enjoyment, rather than elation that anything is the case; being ecstatic about Mahler is not a case of being ecstatic that or because anything has occurred, but is simply a way of responding to Mahler's music. In those cases, as in the other cases of enjoyment, there need be no underlying desire.

Consideration of the relation between emotion and desire has now led us to the topic of pleasure. That there is a close connection between pleasure and displeasure on the one hand and emotion on the other is another commonplace.[6] Thus some emotions, such as elation and disgust, are just particularly intense ways of being pleased or displeased that something is the case, while the range which includes fear, anger, and jealousy involves finding something in various ways unwelcome or distressing. We might attempt to systematize this relation in terms of the possessive-appetitive distinction as follows. (1) Emotions which are both possessive and "expressive" (i.e., which include the urge to outward expression) are forms of being pleased that something is the case. These include elation and pride. (2) Many appetitive emotions involve finding a situation in various ways unpleasant, the appetitive element being in part the desire (want or wish) to change the unpleasant situation for the better. Our present discussion has suggested a third thesis which is, perhaps, something less of a commonplace, viz., that some kinds of possessive emotion are not forms of being pleased that something is the case, but rather forms of enjoyment.[7] They are delight, joy, etc., in or at something, rather than delight that anything is the case. That is most clearly seen from the case of what I have called "calm joy," but it also, I suggest, gives the best account of awe and the range of feelings which we indicate by such phrases as "being moved" and "being touched."

The ground for regarding these emotions as forms of enjoyment is that the attempt to describe them reveals as their essential features *(a)* concentration of thought or attention on an experience, *(b)* evaluation of that experience as something worthwhile in itself, and *(c)* reluctance to be distracted from that experience, features which are at least sufficient for enjoyment. The possessive aspect of the emotion of love and of tenderness may perhaps come under this head. Certainly, being filled with love or tenderness for a person is hard to distinguish from a certain way of enjoying being with or thinking about that person.

An objection might be made to the suggestion that being moved is a form of enjoyment, to the effect that while it would be quite normal to be moved, e.g., by a harrowing television film of famine in Africa, only a bizarre sort of sadist could enjoy such a thing. The reply to this objection is in two stages. First we should concede that not every case of being moved is an instance of enjoyment. In the example we have a case of pity, an emotion closely related to that of being moved (hence the appropriateness of the description "I was very moved"), but distinguished from it by the absence of the element of quasi-aesthetic appreciation; the contrast becomes clearer if we place the harrowing account in the context of a work of art such as a tragedy,[8] or add to it elements (such as heroism in adversity) evoking the aesthetic response of admiration. The second stage of the reply consists in insisting on the distinction, familiar by now from the work of Grice (1961) and Searle (1966), between conversational nuance and philosophical analysis. It will often be odd to *say* of an experience which one found deeply moving, exalting, or sublime that one enjoyed it, because saying that suggests a rather shallower response appropriate to the lighter forms of entertainment. Yet consideration of such experiences shows them to exhibit the conceptually central features of enjoyment. I conclude that the objection to calling the emotion of being moved a form of enjoyment is to be rejected.

Some emotions, then, are forms of enjoyment. This conclusion raises the question of what distinguishes those forms of enjoyment which are emotions from those which are not. It is tempting to look for some feature characterizing all or at least an important class of emotions and distinctive of those enjoyments which we should recognize as emotions. One might be attracted by the view of emotions as disturbances, leading one to the suggestion that exciting or upsetting enjoyments are emotions, as opposed to more placid enjoyments such as the enjoyment of gardening. But the emotional enjoyments which we have considered are precisely the cases which present counter-examples to the thesis that all emotions involve disturbance, being essentially cases of calm enjoyment. Nor does it seem more plausible to rely on the prominence of bodily sensation or of overt physiological changes such as sweating or blushing as a criterion to distinguish emotional from nonemotional enjoyments. In our examples neither bodily sensation nor overt physiological change is in any way prominent, while on the other hand either or both might be very prominent in some cases of nonemotional enjoyment, such as the enjoyment of a warm bath. The nearest I can come to suggesting a criterion is to point out that, while we have both excitable and calm emotions, it is natural to describe the latter by such spatial metaphors as "uplifting" and "exalting," which imply some sort of change from a uniform state.[9]

The suggestion amounts to this, that while one's equilibrium is not upset by calm joy, as it is by fear or elation, nevertheless that kind of emotion lifts one out of one's ordinary mental state in a way which enjoying a hamburger does not. The former makes a difference, even if only temporarily, to one's way of looking at things, to one's sense of what really matters; the latter leaves one's sense of the significance of things unchanged. In this type of emotional enjoyment, I suggest, the desired object is seen as worth attending to not just as pleasant, but as significant in the light of some higher value. If this is right it appears that the account of emotions as disturbances consequent upon evaluation, favored by Alston and others (see note 4), needs to be extended; while retaining the connection with evaluation, we should, instead of concentrating on disturbances, investigate different kinds of change of consciousness, of which disturbance is one, a prominent kind indeed, but only one. The working out of this suggestion belongs to a general account of emotion, which it is not the business of this paper to provide.

There is, then, no simple general account of the relation between emotion and desire. All that can be said in general is that every emotion is a type of complex psychophysical state, one element of which is some desire-type. But, like many philosophical theses, that achieves its uncontroversial status by dint of lack of content. We approach an informative account of the relations between emotions and desires only when we attempt, as in this paper, to consider the different kinds of emotion and the different kinds of desire appropriate to each. First, desire itself provides a principle of classification of emotions into appetitive and possessive, according as a desired state of affairs is conceived of as attained or as not (or not yet) attained. Then emotion of either kind may involve desires for behavior, expressive in the case of possessive emotions, expressive and/or goal-directed in the case of appetitive. Finally, some possessive emotions involve only the desire to possess their object in thought, i.e., they are forms of enjoyment. The interest of the latter is twofold. First, while it is a familiar thesis that emotions are intimately bound up with pleasure and distress, that connection is generally elucidated (as above) via the notions of being pleased (e.g., overjoyed) or distressed (e.g., angry or ashamed) that *p*, not via the notion of enjoyment. It is therefore interesting to be able to supplement the established view by pointing to a class of emotions which are forms of enjoyment. Second, in providing a counterexample to a widely held theory of emotion (i.e., the "disturbance" theory), that same class of emotions emphasizes not merely the complexity of the relations between emotions and wants, but the irreducible complexity of the phenomenon of emotion itself.[10]

NOTES

1. Marks (1982) identifies emotions as "belief/desire sets...characterized by strong desire," while Shaffer (1983) assumes an analysis of an emotion as "a complex of physiological processes and sensations caused by certain beliefs and desires." Solomon (1977), in upholding a judgmental theory of emotion, is emphatic that these sets of judgments are "laden with *intention to act*" (his italics). "Every emotion," he continues, "...is also a personal ideology, a projection into the future, and a system of hopes and desires, expectations and commitments, intentions and strategies for changing our world" (p. 212).
    A recent study which places special weight on the role of desire in emotion is that by Robinson (1983). While stressing the importance of cognitive assessments in emotions she argues that such assessments are (1) caused and (2) "colored" by desires, concluding that a desire-determined conception of an object is always necessary and in certain cases sufficient for the occurrence of an emotion.

2. Cf. Aristotle's "formal" definition of anger as desire for retaliation (*De Anima*, 403a30-b2; *Rhetoric*, 1378a31-a33).

3. I take wishes to be a sort of desires, viz., desires for what the desirer believes to be unattainable. Normally, the belief that the object of one's desire is unobtainable is sufficient to ensure that one does not try to obtain it, and in the case of some wishes, e.g., the wish that the past had been different in some way, nothing could count as trying to obtain it. Hence ordinarily wishes do not prompt to action. But there is a borderline area between wishing and wanting (see Anscombe,

1976, p. 67), where it is unclear whether the agent should be described as (1) prompted to action by a mere wish, or (2) trying to do what he believes impossible, or (3) not really believing that what he is trying to do is impossible (perhaps hoping against hope). The description given above of a frightened man attempting evasive action "in a case where he knows such action to be useless" falls within this area.

4. That disturbance or excitement is an essential feature of emotion is maintained by Shaffer (1983) and Alston (1967a). The latter writes that we "arrive at a definition of an emotional state as a more or less disturbed state of the organism, together with the bodily sensations produced by this state, arising from a perceptual evaluation of something. . . . It seems impossible to envisage a clear case of an emotional state which does not involve such a disturbance, along with sensations of it." This claim is supported by such data as the fact that the description of someone as an emotional person implies that that person is excitable. For reasons for rejecting the claim see the text to which this note refers.

5. See Warner (1980).

6. Cf. Aristotle's description of *pathē* as "in general what are accompanied by pleasure and distress" (*Nicomachean Ethics*, 1105b23; *Rhetoric*, 1378a21-a22) and Locke's classification of emotions as modes of the simple ideas of pleasure and pain (*Essay*, bk. 2, chap. 20).

7. For the distinction see Taylor (1963).

8. Where pity itself becomes part, as Aristotle saw, of the appropriate aesthetic response (*Poetics*, 1449b27-b28).

9. This terminology goes back to the Stoics, some of whom described *pathē* as "elevations and depressions of the soul." See Gosling and Taylor (1982, p. 419).

10. An earlier version of this paper was written for a class on the emotions which I gave jointly with Rosalind Hursthouse in Oxford some years ago. I am most grateful to Dr. Hursthouse and to the editor of this volume for their comments.

Contributors

ROBERT AUDI is Professor of Philosophy at the University of Nebraska. He received his B.A. from Colgate University in 1963 and his Ph.D. from the University of Michigan in 1967. His main research interests are in the theory of knowledge, the philosophy of mind (especially action theory), ethics, and the philosophy of the social sciences, particularly psychology. His principal publications have been in these fields, and he is currently writing books in the theory of knowledge and the philosophy of action.

ANNETTE C. BAIER teaches philosophy at the University of Pittsburgh, and earlier taught at Carnegie-Mellon University, the University of Sydney, and the University of Auckland. She is the author of *Postures of the Mind: Essays on Mind and Morals* (University of Minnesota Press, 1985), and is working on a book about the unity of Hume's *Treatise.*

WAYNE A. DAVIS studied philosophy and psychology at the University of Michigan (B.A., 1973), and did his graduate work in the History and Philosophy of Science Program at Princeton University (Ph.D., 1977). He has taught at the University of California at Los Angeles, Rice University, and Washington University, and is currently Associate Professor of Philosophy at Georgetown University in Washington, D.C. He has published articles on happiness, pleasure, intention, and other concepts related to desire, articles on conditionals and causation, and an introductory logic textbook.

RONALD B. DE SOUSA was educated in Switzerland, Britain (B.A., Oxon), and the United States (Ph.D., Princeton). He teaches at the University of Toronto, and has visited at the University of California at Berkeley and at Santa Barbara, and at the University of British Columbia. His book, *The Rationality of Emotion*, will be published in 1987 by MIT Press — Bradford Books.

ROBERT M. GORDON is an Associate Professor of Philosophy and a Research Fellow in Metropolitan Studies at the University of Missouri — St. Louis. He is the author of *The Structure of Emotions: Investigations in Cognitive Philosophy* (forthcoming from Cambridge

University Press), as well as numerous scholarly articles concerning the emotions.

O. H. Green received the D.Phil. from Oxford University and has taught at the University of North Carolina at Chapel Hill and at Tulane University, where he is currently Associate Professor of Philosophy. He is the author of a number of scholarly articles on topics in philosophy of mind and ethics. He is presently completing a philosophical study of emotions, *Emotions and Rational Representation.*

Joel Marks received the B.A. in psychology from Cornell University and the Ph.D. in philosophy from the University of Connecticut. His areas of special interest are ethics, philosophy of mind, comparative philosophy, and philosophical methodology, and he has published on emotion, moral psychology, and the teaching of philosophy. He has taught perception and psychology of art at the Portland School of Art, and philosophy at the University of Connecticut, St. John Fisher College, and the University of Rochester; he is currently Assistant Professor of Philosophy at the University of New Haven.

Dennis Stampe was an undergraduate at Indiana University, did a D.Phil. at Oxford (1965), and has been teaching philosophy at the University of Wisconsin–Madison since then. He has published papers on various topics in the philosophy of language and regarding the theory of representation, and has for some years been engaged in extending a causal account of meaning and of the nature and typology of speech acts to questions about the nature and typology of mental acts, or states, and their contents. The essay in the present volume is a part of this work.

Mitchell Staude received his Ph.D. from the University of Maryland (1979), writing his dissertation on the concept of desire. His research interests are in philosophical psychology, philosophy of religion, and existential philosophy. He is currently Assistant Professor in Philosophy at Otterbein College in Ohio.

Michael Stocker studied at Columbia College (B.A., 1961) and Harvard University (Ph.D., 1966). He is now a Reader in Philosophy at La Trobe University (Melbourne, Australia), and has taught at various universities in the United States and Australia. He works mainly in ethics, moral psychology, and the history of these topics. One of his main concerns is detailing the complexities of morality and moral psychology—thus his interest in akrasia and desire.

C. C. W. Taylor is a Fellow of Corpus Christi College, Oxford. He has published a translation and commentary for Plato's *Protagoras*, is coauthor (with J. C. B. Gosling) of *The Greeks on Pleasure*, and has published papers on Greek philosophy, the Empiricists, ethics, and topics in philosophy of mind. His current research includes studies on the theme of the intellect in Plato and Aristotle.

Bibliography

This bibliography contains full citations for the sources referred to in this book, as well as some additional sources that are especially relevant to theory of desire but happened to escape mention in the essays. Historical sources have been included only where a particular edition or translation has been cited in the text; other references to such sources can be located using the index. Names of authors which appear in brackets at the ends of entries refer to the essays by those authors in this volume, exclusive of the Introduction, in which reference is made to the source cited.

Abel, Donald (1983). *Freud as Moral Philosopher: His Implicit Theory and an Aristotelian Alternative.* Ph.D. dissertation, Northwestern University. Ann Arbor: University Microfilms No. DA8400644.

Abelson, R. (1965). "'Because I Want to'." *Mind* 74: 540–553.

Ackrill, J. L. (1974). "Aristotle on Eudaimonia." *Proceedings of the British Academy* 60: 339–359. [Stocker]

Adams, Robert M. (1980). "Pure Love." *Journal of Religious Ethics* 8: 83–99.

Alston, William P. (1967a). "Emotion and Feeling." In Paul Edwards (Ed.), *The Encyclopedia of Philosophy*, vol. 2. New York: Collier Macmillan. [Taylor]

Alston, William P. (1967b). "Motives and Motivation." In Paul Edwards (Ed.), *The Encyclopedia of Philosophy*, vol. 5. New York: Collier Macmillan. [Davis] [Marks] [Staude]

Alston, William P. (1977). "Self-Intervention and the Structure of Motivation." In T. Mischel (Ed.), *The Self: Philosophical and Psychological Issues.* Oxford: Basil Blackwell.

Alt, Wayne (1980). "There Is No Paradox of Desire in Buddhism." *Philosophy East and West* 30: 52–59.

Anscombe, G. E. M. (1976). *Intention* (2nd ed.). Ithaca, NY: Cornell University Press. [Davis] [Stampe] [Staude] [Taylor]

Armstrong, D. M. (1968). *A Materialist Theory of the Mind.* London: Routledge & Kegan Paul. [Staude]

Audi, Robert (1972). "On the Conception and Measurement of Attitudes in Contemporary Anglo-American Psychology." *Journal for the Theory of Social Behaviour* 2: 179–203. [Audi]

Audi, Robert (1973a). "The Concept of Wanting." *Philosophical Studies* 24: 1–21. [Audi] [Davis] [Staude]

Audi, Robert (1973b). "Intending." *The Journal of Philosophy* 70: 387–403.

[Audi] [Davis] [Marks]

Audi, Robert (1979). "Weakness of Will and Practical Judgment." *Nous* 13: 173–196. [Audi]

Audi, Robert (1980a). "The Structure of Motivation." *Pacific Philosophical Quarterly* 61: 258–275.

Audi, Robert (1980b). "Wants and Intentions in the Explanation of Action." *Journal for the Theory of Social Behaviour* 9: 227–249. [Audi]

Audi, Robert (1982). "A Theory of Practical Reasoning." *American Philosophical Quarterly* 19: 25–39. [Audi]

Baier, Annette C. (1970). "Act and Intent." *The Journal of Philosophy* 67: 648–658. [Davis]

Baier, Annette C. (1982). "Caring About Caring: A Reply to Frankfurt." *Synthese* 53: 273–290. [Baier]

Baier, Annette C. (1985). "Mixing Memory and Desire." In *Postures of the Mind: Essays on Mind and Morals*. Minneapolis: University of Minnesota Press. [de Sousa]

Barnes, Gerald (1977). "Some Remarks on Belief and Desire." *The Philosophical Review* 86: 340–349.

Bedford, E. (1966). "Intention and Law." *The Journal of Philosophy* 63: 654–656. [Davis]

Bennett, Jonathan (1983). "Teleology and Spinoza's Conatus." In Peter A. French, Theodore E. Uehling, Jr., & Howard K. Wettstein (Eds.), *Contemporary Perspectives on the History of Philosophy*. Midwest Studies in Philosophy, vol. 8. Minneapolis: University of Minnesota Press.

Bennett, Jonathan (1984). *A Study of Spinoza's Ethics*. Indianapolis: Hackett Publishing. [Baier]

Bentham, Jeremy (1983). *A Table of the Springs of Action*. In *Deontology*, edited by Amnon Goldworth. Oxford: Clarendon Press (originally published, 1817).

Birck, L. V. (1922). *The Theory of Marginal Value*. London: Routledge & Kegan Paul. [Davis]

Blum, Lawrence A. (1980). *Friendship, Altruism, and Morality*. London: Routledge & Kegan Paul.

Bond, Edward J. (1974). "Reasons, Wants, and Values." *Canadian Journal of Philosophy* 3: 333–347. [Davis]

Bond, Edward J. (1983). *Reason and Value*. Cambridge: Cambridge University Press.

Brand, Myles (1970). "Causes of Action." *The Journal of Philosophy* 67: 932–947. [Davis]

Brand, Myles (1984). *Intending and Acting: Toward a Naturalized Action Theory*. Cambridge, MA: MIT Press. [Audi]

Brandt, Richard B. (1979). *A Theory of the Good and the Right*. Oxford: Clarendon Press.

Brandt, Richard B., & Kim, Jaegwon (1963). "Wants as Explanations of Actions." *The Journal of Philosophy* 60: 425–435. [Davis] [Staude]

Bratman, Michael (Forthcoming). "Two Faces of Intention." *The Philosophical Review*. [Audi]

Bricker, Phillip (1980). "Prudence." *The Journal of Philosophy* 77: 381–401.

Broad, C. D. (1952). "Egoism as a Theory of Human Motives." In *Ethics and the History of Philosophy*. London: Routledge & Kegan Paul.

Burnyeat, M. F. (1980). "Aristotle on Learning to Be Good." In Amélie Oksenberg Rorty (Ed.), *Essays on Aristotle's Ethics*. Berkeley and Los Angeles: University of California Press. [Stocker]

Butler, Joseph (1897). *Fifteen Sermons Preached at the Rolls Chapel*. In *The Works of Joseph Butler*, 2 vols., edited by W. E. Gladstone. Oxford: Clarendon Press (originally published, 1726).

Casey, Edward S., & Woody, J. Melvin (1983). "Hegel, Heidegger, Lacan: The Dialectic of Desire." In Joseph H. Smith & William Kerrigan (Eds.), *Interpreting Lacan*, vol. 6. New Haven: Yale University Press.

Chisholm, Roderick M. (1970). "The Structure of Intention." *The Journal of Philosophy* 67: 633–647. [Davis]

Chisholm, Roderick M. (1981). *The First Person: An Essay on Reference and Intentionality*. Minneapolis: University of Minnesota Press.

Churchland, Paul M. (1970). "The Logical Character of Action Explanations." *The Philosophical Review* 79: 214–236. [Davis]

Churchland, Paul M. (1984). *Matter and Consciousness*. Cambridge, MA: MIT Press.

Conee, Earl (1984). "Prudence and Preference." Paper presented at the Pacific Division Meeting of the American Philosophical Association, Long Beach, California, March 22–24.

Cooper, John M. (1984). "Plato's Theory of Human Motivation." *History of Philosophy Quarterly* 1: 3–21.

Danto, Arthur C. (1972). *Mysticism and Morality*. New York: Harper & Row.

Danto, Arthur C. (1973). *Analytical Philosophy of Action*. Cambridge: Cambridge University Press. [Green]

Darwall, Stephen L. (1983). *Impartial Reason*. Ithaca, NY: Cornell University Press. [Audi]

Daveney, T. F. (1961). "Wanting." *Philosophical Quarterly* 11: 135–144. [Davis]

Davidson, Donald (1963). "Actions, Reasons, and Causes." *The Journal of Philosophy* 60: 685–700. Reprinted in Davidson (1980). [Staude]

Davidson, Donald (1970). "How Is Weakness of the Will Possible?" In Joel Feinberg (Ed.), *Moral Concepts*. Oxford: Oxford University Press. Reprinted in Davidson (1980). [Audi] [Davis] [Stocker]

Davidson, Donald (1978). "Intending." In Yirmiahu Yovel (Ed.), *Philosophy of History and Action*. Boston/Dordrecht: D. Reidel. Reprinted in Davidson (1980). [Audi] [Davis]

Davidson, Donald (1980). *Essays on Actions and Events*. Oxford: Clarendon Press.

Davis, Wayne (1981a). "Pleasure and Happiness." *Philosophical Studies* 39: 305–317. [Davis]

Davis, Wayne (1981b). "A Theory of Happiness." *American Philosophical Quarterly* 18: 111–120. [Davis] [Marks]

Davis, Wayne (1982). "A Causal Theory of Enjoyment." *Mind* 91: 240–256. [Davis]

Davis, Wayne (1984a). "A Causal Theory of Intending." *American Philosophical Quarterly* 21: 43–54. [Audi] [Davis]

Davis, Wayne (1984b). "The Two Senses of Desire." *Philosophical Studies* 45: 181–195. Reprinted, with additions, in this volume. [Marks]

Deleuze, Gilles, & Guattari, Felix (1983). *Anti-Oedipus: Capitalism and Schizophrenia.* Minneapolis: University of Minnesota Press.

Dennett, Daniel C. (1978). *Brainstorms.* Cambridge, MA: MIT Press. [Green]

Descartes, René (1977a). *Meditations.* In *The Philosophical Works of Descartes*, translated by E. S. Haldane & G. R. T. Ross. Cambridge: Cambridge University Press (originally published, 1642).

Descartes, René (1977b). *The Passions of the Soul.* In *The Philosophical Works of Descartes*, translated by E. S. Haldane & G. R. T. Ross. Cambridge: Cambridge University Press (originally published, 1649). [Baier] [Taylor]

de Sousa, Ronald B. (1974). "The Good and the True." *Mind* 83: 534–551.

de Sousa, Ronald B. (1980). "The Rationality of Emotions." In Amélie Oksenberg Rorty (Ed.), *Explaining Emotions.* Berkeley and Los Angeles: University of California Press. [de Sousa]

Donagan, Alan (1981–82). "Philosophical Progress and the Theory of Action." *Proceedings and Addresses of the American Philosophical Association* 55: 25–52. [Audi]

Duncker, Karl (1940). "On Pleasure, Emotion, and Striving." *Philosophy and Phenomenological Research* 1: 391–430.

Elster, Jon (1982). "Sour Grapes: Utilitarianism and the Genesis of Wants." In Amartya Sen & Bernard Williams (Eds.), *Utilitarianism and Beyond.* Cambridge: Cambridge University Press.

Ezorsky, G. (1960). "Wishing Won't — But Wanting Will." In S. Hook (Ed.), *Dimensions of Mind.* New York: Collier Macmillan. [Davis]

Fleming, B. N. (1964). "On Intention." *The Philosophical Review* 73: 301–320. [Davis]

Fleming, B. N. (1981). "Autonomy of the Will." *Mind* 90: 201–223.

Fodor, Jerry A. (1983). *The Modularity of Mind: An Essay on Faculty Psychology.* Cambridge, MA: MIT Press. [Gordon]

Fodor, Jerry A. (1984). "Semantics, Wisconsin Style." *Synthese* 59. [Stampe]

Foot, Philippa (1972). "Reasons for Action and Desires." *Proceedings of the Aristotelian Society* supp. vol. 46: 203–210. Reprinted in Foot (1978). [Davis]

Foot, Philippa (1978). *Virtues and Vices and Other Essays in Moral Philosophy.* Berkeley and Los Angeles: University of California Press.

Frankena, William K. (1958). "Obligation and Motivation in Recent Moral Philosophy." In A. I. Melden (Ed.), *Essays in Moral Philosophy.* Seattle: University of Washington Press. [Audi] [Davis]

Frankfurt, Harry G. (1971). "Freedom of the Will and the Concept of a Person." *The Journal of Philosophy* 68: 5–20. [Davis] [de Sousa] [Gordon] [Green]

Frankfurt, Harry G. (1982). "The Importance of What We Care About."

Synthese 53: 257–273. [Baier]

Frankfurt, Harry G. (1984). "Necessity and Desire." *Philosophy and Phenomenological Research* 45: 1–13. [Stampe]

Freud, Sigmund (1895). *Project for a Scientific Psychology*. In *The Standard Edition of the Complete Psychological Works*, vol. 1, translated and edited by James Strachey. London: The Hogarth Press, 1961. [de Sousa]

Freud, Sigmund (1905). *Three Essays on the Theory of Sexuality*. In *The Standard Edition of the Complete Psychological Works*, vol. 7, translated and edited by James Strachey. London: The Hogarth Press, 1961. [de Sousa]

Freud, Sigmund (1920). *Beyond the Pleasure Principle*. In *The Standard Edition of the Complete Psychological Works*, vol. 18, translated and edited by James Strachey. London: The Hogarth Press, 1961. [de Sousa]

Gardiner, H. M., Metcalf, R. C., & Beebe-Center, J. G. (1970) *Feeling and Emotion: A History of Theories*. Westport, CT: Greenwood Press (originally published, 1937).

Gauthier, D. P. (1963). *Practical Reasoning*. Oxford: Oxford University Press. [Davis]

Geach, Peter (1957). *Mental Acts*. London: Routledge & Kegan Paul. [Stampe]

Genet, J. (1964). *The Thief's Journal*. Translated by B. Frechtman. New York: Grove Press.

Goldman, Alvin I. (1970). *A Theory of Human Action*. Englewood Cliffs, NJ: Prentice-Hall. [Audi] [Davis]

Goldstein, I. (1973). "Happiness: The Role of Non-Hedonistic Criteria in Its Evaluation." *International Philosophical Quarterly* 13: 523–534. [Davis]

Gordon, Robert M. (1969). "Emotions and Knowledge." *The Journal of Philosophy* 66: 408–413. [Davis]

Gordon, Robert M. (1973). "Judgmental Emotions." *Analysis* 34: 40–48. [Davis]

Gordon, Robert M. (1974). "The Aboutness of Emotions." *American Philosophical Quarterly* 11: 27–36. [Davis]

Gordon, Robert M. (1980). "Fear." *The Philosophical Review* 89: 560–578. [Davis]

Gordon, Robert M. (1986a). "Desire and Self-Intervention." *Nous* 20(2). [Gordon] [Green]

Gordon, Robert M. (1986b). "The Passivity of Emotions." *The Philosophical Review* 95: 339–360. [Green]

Gordon, Robert M. (Forthcoming). *The Structure of Emotions: Investigations in Cognitive Philosophy*. Cambridge: Cambridge University Press.

Gosling, J. C. B. (1969). *Pleasure and Desire: The Case for Hedonism Reviewed*. Oxford: Clarendon Press. [Davis] [Staude]

Gosling, J. C. B., & Taylor, C. C. W. (1982). *The Greeks on Pleasure*. Oxford: Clarendon Press. [Taylor]

Grandy, Richard E., & Darwall, Stephen L. (1979). "On Schiffer's Desires." *Southern Journal of Philosophy* 17: 193–198.

Green, O. H. (1979). "Wittgenstein and the Possibility of a Philosophical

Theory of Emotion." *Metaphilosophy* 10: 256–264. [Marks]

Green, O. H. (In preparation). *Emotions and Rational Representation.* [Green] [Marks]

Greenspan, Patricia S. (1980). "Emotions, Reasons, and 'Self-Involvement'." *Philosophical Studies* 38: 161–168.

Grice, H. P. (1961). "The Causal Theory of Perception." *Proceedings of the Aristotelian Society* supp. vol. 35: 121–168. [Taylor]

Grice, H. P. (1971). "Intention and Uncertainty." *Proceedings of the Aristotelian Society* 57: 263–279. [Audi]

Hampshire, Stuart (1975). *Freedom of the Individual.* Princeton: Princeton University Press. [Davis]

Hardie, W. F. R. (1965). "The Final Good in Aristotle's Ethics." *Philosophy* 40: 277–295. [Stocker]

Hare, R. M. (1952). *The Language of Morals.* Oxford: Oxford University Press. [Davis]

Hare, R. M. (1963). *Freedom and Reason.* Oxford: Oxford University Press. [Audi] [Staude]

Hare, R. M. (1971). "Wanting: Some Pitfalls." In *Practical Inferences.* New York: Macmillan.

Hare, R. M. (1981). *Moral Thinking: Its Levels, Methods, and Point.* Oxford: Clarendon Press.

Hare, W. F. (1970). "Trying." *Kinesis* 3: 43–58. [Davis]

Harman, Gilbert (1976). "Practical Reasoning." *Review of Metaphysics* 29: 431–463. [Davis]

Harman, Gilbert (1983). "Rational Action and the Extent of Intentions." Paper presented at a Conference on Rationality, Evidence, and Human Limits, University of Rochester, April 8–9.

Hempel, Carl G. (1962). "Rational Action." *Proceedings and Addresses of the American Philosophical Association* 35: 5–23. [Staude]

Hempel, Carl G. (1965). "Aspects of Scientific Explanation." In *Aspects of Scientific Explanation and Other Essays in the Philosophy of Science.* New York: The Free Press.

Herman, A. L. (1979). "A Solution to the Paradox of Desire in Buddhism." *Philosophy East and West* 29: 91–94.

Herman, A. L. (1980). "Ah, But There Is a Paradox of Desire in Buddhism: A Reply to Wayne Alt." *Philosophy East and West* 30: 60–63.

Hobbes, Thomas (1972). *Leviathan,* edited by C. B. MacPherson. New York: Penguin Books (originally published, 1651). [Baier] [Taylor]

Hospers, John (1967). *An Introduction to Philosophical Analysis* (2nd ed.). Englewood Cliffs, NJ: Prentice-Hall. [Marks]

Hume, David (1975). *Enquiry Concerning the Principles of Morals.* In *Enquiries Concerning Human Understanding and Concerning the Principles of Morals,* edited by L. A. Selby-Bigge & P. H. Nidditch. Oxford: Clarendon Press (originally published, 1751). [Marks]

Hume, David (1978). *A Treatise of Human Nature,* edited by L. A. Selby-Bigge & P. H. Nidditch. Oxford: Clarendon Press (originally published, 1739). [Baier] [Gordon]

Jackson, Frank (1984). "Davidson on Moral Conflict." Paper presented at the Conference on the Philosophy of Donald Davidson, Rutgers University, April 28 – May 1. [Stocker]

Jackson, Frank (1985). "Internal Conflicts in Desires and Morals." *American Philosophical Quarterly* 22: 105–114.

Jeffrey, Richard C. (1965). *The Logic of Decision*. New York: McGraw-Hill.

Jeffrey, Richard C. (1974). "Preference Among Preferences." *The Journal of Philosophy* 71: 377–391.

Jenkins, J. (1965). "Motive and Intention." *Philosophical Quarterly* 15: 155–164. [Davis]

Keller, Evelyn Fox, & Grontkowski, Christine R. (1983). "The Mind's Eye." In Sandra Harding & Merrill B. Hintikka (Eds.), *Discovering Reality: Feminist Perspectives on Epistemology, Metaphysics, Methodology, and Philosophy of Science*. Boston/Dordrecht: D. Reidel.

Kenny, Anthony (1963). *Action, Emotion and Will*. London: Routledge & Kegan Paul. [Taylor]

Kraut, Robert (1985). "Individualism and the Emotions." Paper presented at a Colloquium on the Concept of Emotion, University of Cincinnati, March 8–9.

Ladd, John (1958). "On the Desire to Do One's Duty for Its Own Sake." In A. I. Melden (Ed.), *Essays in Moral Philosophy*. Seattle: University of Washington Press. [Staude]

Lawrence, R. (1972). *Motive and Intention*. Evanston, IL: Northwestern University Press. [Davis]

Lewis, C. I. (1946). *An Analysis of Knowledge and Valuation*. LaSalle, IL: Open Court. [Davis]

Lichtman, Richard (1982). *The Production of Desire: The Integration of Psychoanalysis into Marxist Theory*. New York: The Free Press.

Locke, Don (1974). "Reasons, Wants, and Causes." *American Philosophical Quarterly* 11: 169–179. [Davis] [Marks] [Staude]

Locke, Don (1982). "Beliefs, Desires and Reasons for Actions." *American Philosophical Quarterly* 19: 241–249. [Marks] [Staude]

Lyons, William (1980). *Emotion*. Cambridge: Cambridge University Press. [Marks] [Taylor]

Marks, Joel (1982). "A Theory of Emotion." *Philosophical Studies* 42: 227–242. [Marks] [Taylor]

Marks, Joel (1983). "The Rationality of Dispassion, or Why Richard Brandt Should Be a Buddhist." In K. D. Irani & G. E. Myers (Eds.), *Emotions: Philosophical Studies*. New York: Haven Publications.

McCann, Hugh J. (Forthcoming). "Rationality and the Range of Intention." *Midwest Studies in Philosophy*. [Audi]

McGinn, Colin (1979). "Action and Its Explanation." In N. Bolton (Ed.), *Philosophical Problems in Psychology*. London: Methuen.

McGuinness, B. F. (1956–57). "'I Know What I Want'." *Proceedings of the Aristotelian Society* n.s. 57: 305–320.

Meiland, J. W. (1970). *The Nature of Intention*. New York: Barnes & Noble. [Davis]

Mele, Alfred R. (Forthcoming). "Intending and the Balance of Motivation." *Pacific Philosophical Quarterly*. [Audi]

Menger, C. (1871). *Principles of Economics.* New York: The Free Press, 1950. [Davis]

Miller, A. R. (1980). "Wanting, Intending, and Knowing What One Is Doing." *Philosophy and Phenomenological Research* 40: 334–343. [Davis]

Montmarquet, James (1982). "Nagel on Motivation." *The Australasian Journal of Philosophy* 60: 20–28.

Moore, F. C. T. (1978). *The Psychological Basis of Morality: An Essay on Value and Desire.* New York: Barnes & Noble.

Moore, Michael S. (1975). "Some Myths About 'Mental Illness'." *Inquiry* 18: 233–265.

Morton, Adam (1980). *Frames of Mind: Constraints on the Common-Sense Conception of the Mental.* Oxford: Clarendon Press.

Moulton, Janice (1977). "Comments on Shaffer." Paper presented at a meeting of the Society for the Philosophy of Sex and Love, Washington, D.C., December 28.

Myers, G. E. (1964). "Motives and Wants." *Mind* 73: 173–185.

Nagel, Thomas (1970). *The Possibility of Altruism.* Oxford: Clarendon Press. [Davis] [de Sousa] [Marks] [Staude]

Nagel, Thomas (1979). *Mortal Questions.* Cambridge: Cambridge University Press. [Baier]

Narveson, J. (1967). *Morality and Utility.* Baltimore: The Johns Hopkins University Press. [Davis]

Neely, Wright (1974). "Freedom and Desire." *The Philosophical Review* 83: 32–54. [Davis] [Green]

Neu, Jerome (1977). *Emotion, Thought and Therapy.* Berkeley and Los Angeles: University of California Press. [Marks]

Norman, R. (1971). *Reasons for Action.* New York: Barnes & Noble. [Davis]

Nussbaum, Martha C. (1984). "Plato on Commensurability and Desire." *Proceedings of the Aristotelian Society* supp. vol. 58: 55–80. [Stocker]

O'Shaughnessy, Brian (1980). *The Will: A Dual Aspect Theory,* vol. 2. Cambridge: Cambridge University Press.

Page, Alfred N. (Ed.) (1968). *Utility Theory: A Book of Readings.* New York: John Wiley & Sons.

Parfit, Derek (1984). *Reasons and Persons.* Oxford: Clarendon Press. [de Sousa]

Pears, David (1975). *Questions in the Philosophy of Mind.* New York: Barnes & Noble.

Penelhum, Terence (1979). "Human Nature and External Desires." *The Monist* 62: 304–319.

Penner, T. (1971). "Thought and Desire in Plato." In Gregory Vlastos (Ed.), *Plato Two: Ethics, Politics, and Philosophy of Art and Religion: A Collection of Critical Essays.* Garden City, New York: Anchor Books. [de Sousa]

Perry, Ralph B. (1926). *General Theory of Value.* Cambridge, MA: Harvard University Press.

Peters, R. S. (1969). *The Concept of Motivation* (2nd ed.). Atlantic Highlands, NJ: Humanities Press.

Platts, Mark (1980). "Moral Reality and the End of Desire." In Platts (Ed.), *Reference, Truth and Reality: Essays in the Philosophy of Language.* London: Routledge & Kegan Paul.

Prichard, H. A. (1940). "The Object of a Desire." Reprinted in *Moral Obligation and Duty and Interest.* Oxford: Oxford University Press, 1968.

Prichard, H. A. (1945). "Acting, Willing, Desiring." Reprinted in *Moral Obligation and Duty and Interest.* Oxford: Oxford University Press, 1968.

Principe, Michael A. (1982). "Restraint of Desire in the *Gorgias.*" *Southern Journal of Philosophy* 20: 121–132.

Rachels, James (1969). "Wanting and Willing." *Philosophical Studies* 20: 9–13. [Davis]

Radford, C. (1970). "Hoping and Wishing." *Proceedings of the Aristotelian Society* supp. vol. 44: 51–70. [Davis]

Ramsey, Frank P. (1931). "Truth and Probability." In *The Foundations of Mathematics and Other Logical Essays.* London: Kegan Paul.

Regan, Tom (1982). "Frey on Why Animals Cannot Have Simple Desires." *Mind* 91: 277–280.

Rey, Georges (1980). "Functionalism and the Emotions." In Amélie Oksenberg Rorty (Ed.), *Explaining Emotions.* Berkeley and Los Angeles: University of California Press.

Robins, Michael H. (1984). "Practical Reasoning, Commitment, and Rational Action." *American Philosophical Quarterly* 21: 55–68. [Audi]

Robinson, Jenefer (1983). "Emotion, Judgment, and Desire." *The Journal of Philosophy* 80: 731–741. [Marks] [Taylor]

Rorty, Amélie Oksenberg (1980). "Where Does The Akratic Break Take Place?" *The Australasian Journal of Philosophy* 58: 333–346. [Stocker]

Rorty, Amélie Oksenberg (1983). "Akratic Believers." *American Philosophical Quarterly* 20: 175–183. [Stocker]

Russell, Bertrand (1921). *The Analysis of Mind.* London: George Allen & Unwin. [de Sousa]

Ryle, Gilbert (1949). *The Concept of Mind.* London: Hutchinson. [Green]

Ryle, Gilbert (1964). "Perception." In *Dilemmas.* Cambridge: Cambridge University Press. [de Sousa]

Santas, Gerasimos (1966). "Plato's Protagoras and Explanations of Weakness." *The Philosophical Review* 75: 3–33. [Stocker]

Sartre, Jean Paul (1962). *Sketch for a Theory of the Emotions,* translated by Philip Mairet. London: Methuen (originally published, 1939). [Green]

Saunders, Ruth (1983). "Quine and Davidson on the Reference of Theoretical Terms and Constraints on Psychology." *Philosophical Studies* 44: 121–139.

Schick, Frederic (1982). "Under Which Descriptions?" In Amartya Sen & Bernard Williams (Eds.), *Utilitarianism and Beyond.* Cambridge: Cambridge University Press.

Schiffer, Stephen (1976). "A Paradox of Desire." *American Philosophical Quarterly* 13: 195–203. [Davis] [de Sousa] [Marks]

Searle, John R. (1966). "Assertions and Aberrations." In Bernard Williams & Alan Montefiore (Eds.), *British Analytical Philosophy.* London:

Routledge & Kegan Paul. [Taylor]

Searle, John R. (1983). *Intentionality.* Cambridge: Cambridge University Press. [Marks]

Selby-Bigge, L. A. (Ed.) (1897). *British Moralists,* 2 vols. Oxford: Clarendon Press.

Sellars, W. (1963). "Imperatives, Intentions, and the Logic of 'Ought'." In Hector-Neri Castañeda & George Nakhnikian (Eds.), *Morality and the Language of Conduct.* Detroit: Wayne State University Press. [Davis]

Shaffer, Jerome A. (1978). "Sexual Desire." *The Journal of Philosophy* 75: 175–189.

Shaffer, Jerome A. (1983). "An Assessment of Emotion." *American Philosophical Quarterly* 20: 161–173. [Baier] [Marks] [Taylor]

Sher, George (1983). "Our Preferences, Ourselves." *Philosophy and Public Affairs* 12: 34–50.

Silver, Mitchell H. (1980). *Self-Concept and Self-Interest: A Study of Thomas Nagel's "The Possibility of Altruism."* Ph.D. dissertation, University of Connecticut. Ann Arbor: University Microfilms No. 8103238. [Marks]

Smythe, Thomas (1972). "Unconscious Desires and the Meaning of 'Desire'." *The Monist* 56: 413–425.

Snare, F. (1972). "Wants and Reasons." *Personalist* 53: 395–407. [Davis]

Solomon, Robert C. (1976). *The Passions: The Myth and Nature of Human Emotion.* Garden City, NY: Anchor Press/Doubleday. [Green] [Marks] [Taylor]

Spinoza, Benedict de (1949). *Ethics,* edited by J. Gutmann and translated by W. H. White & A. H. Stirling. New York: Hafner Press (originally published, 1677). [Baier] [Staude] [Taylor]

Stalnaker, Robert C. (1984). *Inquiry.* Cambridge, MA: MIT Press. [Stampe]

Stampe, Dennis W. (1975). "Show and Tell." In B. Freed, A. Marras, & P. Maynard (Eds.), *Forms of Representation: Proceedings of the 1972 Philosophy Colloquium of the University of Western Ontario.* Amsterdam: North-Holland Publishing Co. [Stampe]

Stampe, Dennis W. (1977). "Toward a Causal Account of Linguistic Representation." *Midwest Studies in Philosophy* 2: 42–63. Reprinted in Peter A. French, Theodore E. Uehling, Jr., & Howard K. Wettstein (Eds.), *Contemporary Perspectives in the Philosophy of Language.* Midwest Studies in Philosophy, vol. 2. Minneapolis: University of Minnesota Press, 1979. [Stampe]

Stampe, Dennis W. (1978). "Desire and Necessity." Paper presented to the Wisconsin Philosophical Association. [Stampe]

Stampe, Dennis W. (Forthcoming-a). "The Authority of Desire." [Stampe]

Stampe, Dennis W. (Forthcoming-b). "Need." [Stampe]

Stampe, Dennis W. (Forthcoming-c). "Verification and a Causal Account of Meaning." *Synthese.* [Stampe]

Staude, Mitchell (1979). *Desiring: An Analysis of One Concept of Wanting.* Ph.D. dissertation, University of Maryland. Ann Arbor: University Microfilms No. 8012663. [Marks] [Staude]

Staude, Mitchell (1982). "Want-Explanations and the Widest Sense of 'Wanting'." Paper presented at the Eastern Division Meeting of the

American Philosophical Association, Baltimore, December 27-30. [Marks] [Staude]

Stich, Stephen P. (1983). *From Folk Psychology to Cognitive Science: The Case Against Belief.* Cambridge, MA: MIT Press.

Stocker, Michael (1976). "The Schizophrenia of Modern Ethical Theories." *The Journal of Philosophy* 73: 453-466. [Stocker]

Stocker, Michael (1979). "Desiring the Bad: An Essay in Moral Psychology." *The Journal of Philosophy* 76: 738-753. [Davis] [Stocker]

Stocker, Michael (1981). "Values and Purposes." *The Journal of Philosophy* 78: 747-765. [Stocker]

Stocker, Michael (1983a). "Affectivity and Self-Concern: The Assumed Psychology in Aristotle's Ethics." *Pacific Philosophical Quarterly* 64: 211-229. [Stocker]

Stocker, Michael (1983b). "Psychic Feelings: Their Importance and Irreducibility." *The Australasian Journal of Philosophy* 61: 5-26. [Marks] [Stocker]

Stocker, Michael (1984). "Some Structures for Akrasia." *History of Philosophy Quarterly* 1: 267-280. [Stocker]

Taylor, C. C. W. (1963). "Pleasure." *Analysis* 23: supplement, 2-19. [Taylor]

Taylor, C. C. W. (1980). "Plato, Hare and Davidson on Akrasia." *Mind* 89: 499-518.

Taylor, Charles (1964). *The Explanation of Behaviour.* London: Routledge & Kegan Paul.

Taylor, Charles (1977). "Human Agency." In T. Mischel (Ed.), *The Self: Philosophical and Psychological Issues.* Oxford: Basil Blackwell. [Stocker]

Taylor, Richard (1964). "Voluntarism." In Paul Edwards (Ed.), *The Encyclopedia of Philosophy,* vol. 8. New York: Collier Macmillan. [Staude]

Taylor, Richard (1966). *Action and Purpose.* Englewood Cliffs, NJ: Prentice-Hall.

Taylor, Richard (1970). *Good and Evil: A New Direction.* New York: Macmillan. [Staude]

Thalberg, Irving (1978). "Hierarchical Analyses of Unfree Action." *Canadian Journal of Philosophy* 8: 211-226. [Green]

Thalberg, Irving (1984). "Analytical Action Theory: Breakthroughs and Deadlocks." Paper presented at the National Endowment for the Humanities Institute on Human Action, University of Nebraska—Lincoln. [Green]

Thalberg, Irving (1986). "Questions About Motivational Strength." In Ernest LePore & Brian McLaughlin (Eds.), *Actions and Events.* Oxford: Oxford University Press. [Audi]

Tinbergen, N. (1969). *The Study of Instinct.* Oxford: Oxford University Press. [de Sousa]

Troyer, John (1981). "Rationality and Maximization." In E. Morscher & R. Stranzinger (Eds.), *Ethics: Foundations, Problems, and Applications.* Vienna: Verlag Hölder-Pichler-Tempsky.

Vendler, Zeno (1967). "Verbs and Times." In *Linguistics in Philosophy.* Ithaca, NY: Cornell University Press. [de Sousa]

Visvader, John (1980). "Reply to Wayne Alt's 'There Is No Paradox of Desire in Buddhism'." *Philosophy East and West* 30: 64–65.

von Wright, Georg Henrik (1963). *The Varieties of Goodness*. London: Routledge & Kegan Paul. [Davis]

von Wright, Georg Henrik (1971). *Explanation and Understanding*. Ithaca, NY: Cornell University Press. [Davis]

Warner, R. (1980). "Enjoyment." *The Philosophical Review* 89. [Gordon] [Taylor]

Watson, Gary (1975). "Free Agency." *The Journal of Philosophy* 72: 205–220. [Davis] [Green]

Watson, Gary (Ed.) (1982). *Free Will*. Oxford: Oxford University Press.

Weirich, Paul (1984). "Interpersonal Utility in Principles of Social Choice." *Erkenntnis* 21: 295–317.

Wheeler III, Samuel C. (1982). "Comments on Staude." Paper presented at the Eastern Division Meeting of the American Philosophical Association, Baltimore, December 27–30. [Marks]

White, Alan R. (1958). "The Language of Motives." *Mind* 67: 258–263.

Wiggins, David (1970). "Freedom, Knowledge, Belief and Causality." In Godfrey Vesey (Ed.), *Knowledge and Necessity*. London: Methuen. [Green]

Wiggins, David (1978–79). "Weakness of Will, Commensurability, and the Objects of Deliberation and Desire." *Proceedings of the Aristotelian Society* n.s. 79: 251–277. [Stocker]

Williams, Bernard (1973). "Deciding to Believe." In *Problems of the Self*. Cambridge: Cambridge University Press. [Green]

Williams, Bernard (1981). *Moral Luck*. Cambridge: Cambridge University Press.

Wittgenstein, Ludwig (1958). *Philosophical Investigations* (2nd ed.). Oxford: Basil Blackwell. [de Sousa]

Wolf, Susan (1982). "Moral Saints." *The Journal of Philosophy* 79: 419–439. [Stocker]

Woodfield, Andrew (1982). "Desire, Intentional Content and Teleological Explanation." *Proceedings of the Aristotelian Society* n.s. 82: 69–88.

Wren, Thomas E. (1982). "Social Learning Theory and Morality." *Ethics* 92: 409–424.

Young, Thomas K. (1983). *The Role of Wants in the Nature and Justification of Practical Reasoning, with Special Reference to Richard Brandt's Theory of Rationality*. Ph.D. dissertation, Southern Illinois University, Carbondale. Ann Arbor: University Microfilms No. DA8311038.

Zimmerman, David (1981). "Hierarchical Motivation and Freedom of the Will." *Pacific Philosophical Quarterly* 62: 354–368.

INDEX